HUNTING

AROUND THE

WORLD

Thirteen-year-old Jack at fishing camp with the first gun he ever owned, a lever-action Model 39a Marlin .22 rifle. All the boys had brought their rifles in case there was time to do some squirrel hunting.

HUNTING
AROUND THE
WORLD

Fair Chase Pursuits from Backcountry
Wilderness to the Scottish Highlands

JACK WARD THOMAS

FOREWORD BY
Robert Model

A BOONE AND CROCKETT CLUB PUBLICATION
Missoula, Montana | 2015

Hunting Around the World

Fair Chase Pursuits from Backcountry
Wilderness to the Scottish Highlands
By Jack Ward Thomas

Library of Congress Catalog Card Number: 2015940102
Paperback ISBN: 978-1-940860-18-3
Hardcover ISBN: 978-1-940860-22-0
e-ISBN: 978-1-940860-19-0
Published July 2015

Published in the United States of America by the
Boone and Crockett Club
250 Station Drive, Missoula, Montana 59801
Phone (406) 542-1888
Fax (406) 542-0784
Toll-Free (888) 840-4868 (book orders only)
www.boone-crockett.org

Printed in the U.S.A.

This book is dedicated to

Robert "Bob" Model

*a dedicated conservationist who was
my host, mentor, and companion on
my hunting and shooting adventures in
Scotland, Spain, England, and many
places in the United States.*

CONTENTS

Jack with Bob Model (far right), *their stalker, and a downed stag after a successful hunt in Scotland, 1997.*

FOREWORD

I am humbled and grateful to have been asked to write the foreword for this wonderful book by Jack Ward Thomas. Jack is a great personal friend. He has also been a hero in the complex world of wildlife and natural resource management. He has the rare gift to synthesize the complex, while at the same time understanding what needs to take place in the future and how best to protect the many uses of America's natural resources. This in itself is a daunting task. Jack Ward Thomas is the person that the American people who love and enjoy our wildlife and its habitats can thank for understanding the important connectivity between the early hunter-explorer-naturalist and what became the science of wildlife and natural resource management.

Jack's long career started in Texas with the Texas Parks and Wildlife Department. He transitioned to the Forest Service, first as a biologist and researcher, then culminating his long and distinguished career as the chief. He is the bridge from what was to what is. He set the standard for wildlife and natural resource management of today. This will benefit the hunter-conservationist in the decades to come.

The Boone and Crockett Club is fortunate that Jack served as its Boone and Crockett Professor of Wildlife Conservation at the University of Montana. Jack took students who were focused on biology and resource management and taught them policy and how to implement that policy. This was a departure in science and forestry education.

x

Science and ethics, coupled with understanding good policy and how to best implement that policy, is the foundation of responsible management. We have complicated and contradictory land laws, which have been an impediment to common-sense management. Jack's grasp of these complicated issues has given us a roadmap of how best to fix these important issues that are the foundation for better management, which is essential to the future.

The Boone and Crockett Club had Theodore Roosevelt and George Bird Grinnell in the early days. Aldo Leopold, Durward Allen, and Olaus Murie were the next generation following our early founders of the conservation movement in this country. Jack is the leader of this generation of our heroes in conservation. He has an important place in history. Those of us who have had the privilege of working with him know that if we follow his leadership, we have the opportunity to make ensuing generations equally as important as those who came before. His work has touched many and will continue to do so. Jack has earned his place in history as one of America's great conservation leaders.

Please join me in enjoying the pages that follow. This collection of marvelous stories represents the ideals and examples of ethical and responsible hunting that all sportsmen should emulate. It is also a wonderful primer for our young people, who we hope will carry on this wonderful heritage as they enjoy our vast outdoors.

Robert Model
CODY, WYOMING

Robert Model is a past president of the Boone and Crockett Club (2003-2005) and in his capacity as B&C Chairman he spends countless hours working on conservation policy efforts in Washington, D.C.

PREFACE

I have been a dedicated hunter since I was ten years old. Growing up in Handley, Texas, a small unincorporated town seven miles down the road from Fort Worth toward Dallas, I spent much time—and wanted more—on my grandfather's farm near Handley, hunting and trapping cottontail, jack and swamp rabbits, fox and gray squirrels, bobwhite quail, opossums, raccoons, foxes, and even skunks. When I was as young as seven, I trailed after my Uncle Henry as he hunted and ran trap lines to provide a steady supply of meat for our extended family's table and furs to be traded for ammunition and traps during World War II.

As there were no public lands within 150 miles of Handley, my boyhood hunting and fishing was carried out on private lands, where permission from landowners was required and was increasingly difficult to attain "free for nothing." As a result permission might well involve the payment of a fee, which I couldn't pay. I begged permission to hunt small game and was known to do some fancy sneaking around upon occasions when such permission was not forthcoming. I became quite skilled at "sneaking" and never got caught or, what's more likely, my grandfather's neighbors simply winked at my transgressions. Looking back, I am not proud of that.

My interest in wildlife led me to pursue a degree in wildlife management at what is now Texas A&M University. I graduated in 1957 and obtained gainful employment—if one considers $285 per month "gainful"—with the Texas Game, Fish, and Oyster Commission (which evolved into the Texas Parks and Wildlife Department. Herein, I refer to both as the Texas Game Department (TGD). For the next ten years (1957-1966), I worked in the Edwards Plateau and Central Mineral Basin doing game management and research related primarily to white-tailed deer and wild turkeys. Every year during that period, I hunted white-tailed deer, mule deer, antelope, bobwhite and blue quail, plus wild turkeys at the invitation of various landowners. I didn't have the money to pay the fees, and they knew it.

In late 1966, I joined a newly established U.S. Forest Service (USFS) Research Work Unit at West Virginia University in Morgantown. It was on the Monongahela National Forest in West Virginia that I became intimately acquainted with national forests—public lands where I could hunt and fish without paying a fee or even asking permission. I thought that was pretty close to what heaven must be like. Nearly 50 years later I maintain that view.

In the 1970s, as the head of a USFS research unit in La Grande, Oregon, I met Will H. "Bill" Brown, the acknowledged "old mountain man" of the region. I suspect he may have bestowed that title on himself. In any case, he earned, deserved, and relished the title. Bill had been in the first class of wildlife biologists who graduated from Oregon State University in the late 1930s. His first professional wildlife job was with the Oregon Department of Fish and Wildlife trapping nuisance beavers. He eventually became the agency's regional director for northeast Oregon. He was a hunter and fisher *par excellence* whose hunting interests ranged from big game (elk, white-tailed deer, mule deer, bighorn sheep, and antelope) to game birds (quail, pheasants, chukars, and ruffed and blue grouse). He was as well known for his fine, well-trained bird dogs as for his thoroughbred horses. More than a half century ago, he introduced me to horse packing and elk hunting in the high lonesome of the Wallowa Mountains and the Eagle Cap Wilderness in eastern Oregon and the Bob Marshall Wilderness in Montana. Of all of the fellow pilgrims with whom I have traveled the wilderness in North America—and elsewhere around the globe—I cherish most the memories shared with Bill Brown.

On the last day of 1996, my thirty-year career in the USFS came to an end. On the first day of 1997, I began a new career as the endowed Boone and Crockett Club Professor of Wildlife Conservation in the College of Forestry and Conservation at the University of Montana in Missoula. I continued in that role until my final retirement, in terms of drawing a paycheck, on the last day of 2007 at the age of seventy-two—an even fifty years since I started my professional career as a wildlife biologist in Texas.

When I became USFS Chief in 1993, I was invited to become a Professional Member of the Boone and Crockett Club, the oldest extant organization in North America dedicated to the conservation of wildlife and hunting ethics. The membership of the Boone and Crockett Club overlaps considerably with that of the National Forest Foundation, a group of dedicated citizens that supports Forest Service Programs by raising funds for special projects and providing political support for the agency. Several members of these two groups were kind enough to invite me into their homes and include me in social events, especially memorable were those having to do with hunting and shooting. These new friends and professional associates provided me with entrée into hunting and shooting experiences that I had only heard of and read about.

Thus, over my long professional career, I was privileged to hunt in all of the regions and nearly all the states of the United States (excluding Hawaii) and in Canada, South America, Scotland, England, and Spain. I have taken more than a few big game animals that would could be classified as "trophies" by any measure. Yet only one of those trophies has ever been displayed in my home.

Why only one? First, in truth, my memories are my trophies, which some of my friends say reflects my basic cheapskate personality. Second, I was well into middle age before I could afford a taxidermist. Third, the two lovely, gentle ladies who have been my wives were intolerant of, as my first wife Margaret so delicately put it, "dead animal parts hanging on the walls in my house."

Margaret hunted with me only once. On her first and only hunt, she killed two whitetails with two shots and announced that the experience had satisfied her curiosity—and demonstrated to us both that she could and would do it. She never hunted again, though occasionally she would accompany me on hunting trips. She never objected to my hunting and encouraged our sons, Britt and Greg, to hunt. She must have cooked and helped consume a ton or so of wild game over the wonderful years that we shared. She never once complained about the butchering of wild game in the garage or on her kitchen counter (although she often left the house while it was going on).

Having been so lucky in love on the first try, after Margaret's passing, in 1993, I fell in love again—to my great surprise—with a lovely lady that I worked with in Washington. I convinced her to marry me and come with me to Montana when we both retired from the USFS. Kathy was a self-proclaimed city girl—she called herself "subway girl"—and was totally unacquainted with hunting or even much "outdoorsy" stuff. But, I believe, she came into this world feet first, yearning for adventure. As a result, she has accompanied me on hunting trips—even on caribou hunts in Alaska where we were delivered to our hunting camps by bush pilots landing on ridgelines or in lakes out on the tundra.

My fifty year career in conservation work brought me into close contact with a number of dedicated hunter-conservationists whose social and financial status was considerably more upscale than mine. They very generously invited me to participate in shooting and hunting experiences that I had only read about. As a professional game and hunting manager for the first ten years of my career, those experiences were something of a continuing education.

What wonderful and satisfying memories I have of my past hunts! Some of those memories are set down in this book, carefully selected to demonstrate the fun, foibles, and risks associated with my long career as a both wildlife biologist and as a hunter. At the same time, it was my intent to memorialize an era, places, and circumstances that are now fading into the past. It is my hope that the memories recounted herein might stimulate others to care—perhaps deeply—about hunting, about wildlife and wildlife habitats, and about the welfare and appropriate management of our public lands.

HUNTING

AROUND THE

WORLD

Splitting wood at Coyote Springs Camp, October 1986.

CHAPTER 1

WHISKEY JACKS TO BREAKFAST

The last ten days had been marked by beautiful fall weather with clear, warm days and cool, even crisp nights. The fall colors of the deciduous trees and shrubs were at their peak. Because of work assignments imposed on me from above in the USFS hierarchy, I had been unable to get away for even a couple of days of mule deer hunting. Sometimes one must comply with direct orders from superiors—and sometimes, not.

Due to that imposed deprivation by my superiors, my hunting fever had been on the rise—a precipitous rise—for the last two weeks. Then Bill Brown walked into my office at the USFS's Range and Wildlife Habitat Laboratory in La Grande, Oregon, and insisted that we get into the backcountry before the snow flew. Likely it was now or never for a hunt this year. He had it on good authority that both blue and ruffed grouse were plentiful and "distressingly tame" from lack of hunting in the Noregaard area north of La Grande. And, besides, our horses and bird dog were deemed sorely in need of exercise. Having already made one bad decision, now sorely regretted, to skip mule deer hunting season, it did not take us long to avoid making two such serious mistakes in one fall—first things first.

OCTOBER 10, 1986

We left La Grande after a late breakfast—late only because it took some time to gather, saddle, and load the horses and pick up some groceries. By midday, the horses were unloaded at the trailhead and quickly packed, and we were on our way. By midafternoon, we had set up our camp on the Noregaard Tract, lands which belonged to the Boise-Cascade Corporation, the primary woods product company in the Blue Mountains. The company most generously allowed public access to the area for hunting and recreation.

That was neighborly, generous, and a stroke of public relations genius—i.e., it was simply good business. However, while the area was open to hunting, it was closed to vehicular traffic and hunters had to travel the area via foot or horseback. As we owned some really good mountain horses, we considered that a marvelous idea! The terrain, relatively gentle for the Blue Mountains, had been selectively logged—with some small clear-cuts thrown in—over the previous thirty-five years. As a result, there was a network of both actively maintained and abandoned logging roads and spurs. By closing off access to vehicles during hunting seasons, the company's managers had created a superior hunting experience to go along with improved habitat for mule deer, elk, and grouse.

Boise-Cascade Corporation had done a good job, whether intentionally or not, of combining commercial forestry with creating and maintaining wildlife habitats and providing a superior hunting experience. Its management—and the welcoming of hunters—created good will for the company while protecting the very expensive logging roads from damage by hunters' vehicles during the snow and rain common in October and November. It was a "win-win" for company stockholders and the general public. And Bill and I were happy to say so publicly.

We camped at Coyote Springs. And, sure enough, as night fell, the namesake coyotes were yipping and howling nearby. We sat around a warming fire listening to coyote music and wondering what the various intonations meant. The night was crystal clear and crisp-cold with the frosted meadows standing out in the moonlight.

Perhaps the coyotes were simply "howling at the moon." So, I thought, might I—if I were a coyote! Just before crawling into our sleeping bags, Bill and I, perhaps encouraged by one too many nightcaps, joined the coyotes with our personalized versions of howling at the moon. It was a sad performance compared with the coyote music. But it was, I thought, a good effort. I wondered what the coyotes thought.

OCTOBER 11, 1986

I was awakened just at daylight by Bill leaving the tent. I surmised that his seventy-two-year-old kidneys had dictated a quick charge, in his unlaced boots, into the frosty world that lay outside. But when I heard the slide work on his twelve-gauge pump shotgun, I knew that he was on his way to the spring to see if the blue grouse that had strolled past us last night as we filled our water bags were still inclined to be so impertinent.

I lay warm and comfortable in my feathered cocoon with only my nose sticking out. I wondered if butterflies were as reluctant to depart their cocoons as I was this frosty morning. But the thought of how good the coffee would smell and taste led me to shuffle around with my sleeping bag until my head instead of my feet was closest to the sheepherder's stove. It didn't take long for me to build a fire using the pitch and kindling carefully set aside last night for that purpose. In a few minutes the fire was roaring.

When the water boiled, it was time to spoon in the coffee crystals. Instant coffee is neither as romantic nor aesthetic nor nearly as tasty as ground coffee—but it takes up less room on a packhorse, and was handy for making one or two cups of coffee at a time. There are things to be said for technology.

When the tent was toasty warm, I emerged from my sleeping bag and dressed in relative comfort and started to prepare breakfast. The smell of coffee and frying bacon must have traveled a goodly distance as I could hear Bill on his way back to the tent, at a double-time shuffle. The grouse had not pushed their luck and Bill's game bag was empty. There had been compensation for his efforts that were made evident as he eagerly told me about the nice mule deer buck he had encountered—up close and personal—providing another snapshot for his well-stocked photo album of memories.

Just after full sunup, we saddled two horses and rode out of camp with the intent of securing an adequate supply of grouse for supper. Ruffed or blue grouse? It made us no never mind. The grouse of both species, though in different habitats, were plentiful. It was quickly obvious that the grouse had "done went to school" since Bill hunted here two weeks earlier. They had ceased sauntering down the trail ahead of the horses and flying up into a tree to perch and watch folks pass by. Now they flew when we were still fifty yards or so away. Or if they were perched in a tree, they dove out and hit the ground running, commonly keeping a tree between "thee and me."

I must have dismounted ten times, dragged my shotgun from the scabbard, handed my lead rope to Bill, and advanced toward what I intended to be a grouse or two for supper, only to be flummoxed. And, by noon, the score was? Jack and Bill zero, grouse some two-dozen clean escapes. We rationalized that the dumb or unlucky grouse had already been converted into somebody else's supper. The ones that remained alive and fully functional were not inclined to share their brethren's fate.

We arrived back in camp just at sundown. Bill reckoned that we had ridden some fifteen to twenty miles up, down, and around logging roads. My mare, Summer, and I had gotten in a lot of training relative to her standing rock-solid as I mounted and walked her forward. Then I stopped, dismounted, dropped the reins to the ground, and pulled my shotgun out of its scabbard. I walked away ten to twenty yards, fired, walked back, put the gun back in the scabbard, gathered up the reins, and remounted. She soon caught on to the game and took the operation more and more as a matter of routine.

So, all in all, we considered this a really good day. After all, when grouse are scarce, time can be productively devoted to horse training. We agreed that our supper of Hamburger Helper was not, by any stretch of the imagination, equal to a bait of grouse and dumplings. But we also agreed that even though supper wasn't grouse, it was good chow anyway—especially after a celebratory drink or two of good sour mash whiskey.

And, for sure, the company—man, horses, and spotted dog— would have been hard to beat. For me, preparing study plans, measuring vegetation plots, counting deer and elk and/or their droppings, alternately smiling and yelling at my computer, and pecking out research reports seemed far away and perhaps, at the moment, even a bit trivial. Perspective can be a great constraint on the ego and a provider of measures of relative importance.

OCTOBER 12, 1986

We were awake at daylight but in no hurry to either exercise the horses and the dog or even pester the grouse. Gray jays (locally called "camp robbers") had been checking out the camp every couple of hours or so for the past two days. Bill insisted that the birds should be called "whiskey jacks." His father, an early supervisor for the old Oregon State Department of Forestry, had told young Bill that the whiskey jacks were the souls of dead timber cruisers. That seemed an appropriate description, as the birds did seem eerily ghostlike as they moved silently through the trees. They alone among the forest birds seemed to be attracted to humans in the woods, especially humans eating lunch. Upon invitation, they would occasionally share that lunch, provided their portion was proffered at an appropriately discreet distance. That distance depended, we suspected, on just how hungry the individual whiskey jack was. Our morning was dedicated to good talk around the fire and occasionally tossing a treat to the whiskey jacks and the chipmunks.

The three whiskey jacks that joined us for breakfast seemed to have brought along a guest, perhaps a first cousin—a Canada jay. The jay was more aggressive than the whiskey jacks were toward one another but much more reluctant to approach the food we set out. The jay waited until the whiskey jacks took the risk of getting close enough to us to snatch a morsel or two. Then, once a whiskey jack with food in its beak was some twenty yards from our fire, the jay would "bomb" the whiskey jack, sometimes forcing it to drop the morsel in question. The chipmunks attracted by the bait scattered every time a winged creature—no matter the species—flew in. We suspected that they were convinced that nothing good—or even harmless—ever arrived on silent wings. Likely those chipmunks that were not true believers, sooner or later, became lunch for owls or hawks.

After a short siesta following lunch, our rapidly weakening hunter's code of honor summoned us to at least give the impression of pursuing the wily grouse. The grouse were no less wild than yesterday, but we had developed the good sense not to dismount, draw our shotguns from their scabbards, and pursue them through the trees. As a result, we rode dutifully for five hours with our shotguns secure in their scabbards. The day was glorious as we rode along the breaks into the Grande Ronde and Wallowa Rivers. It was interesting to travel the country that I had so often looked up at from my rubber raft while floating the Grande Ronde River. Far off to the southwest we could make out Mount Emily perched at the edge of the Grande Ronde Valley knowing that our homes lay just below. At that moment, our hometown of La Grande seemed to be part of another world—a world much farther away than the thirty miles indicated on the map.

We arrived in camp just at dusk. The Canada jay—which had now become "our jay"—was waiting and seemed to scold us for our lack of attention to his needs. We obliged his demands with some bread scraps and bits of cheese. He still couldn't bring himself to risk coming closer to us.

About a half hour later, the whiskey jacks arrived like gray ghosts sliding soundlessly through the dark white fir stand and descended on the bounty. The jay, in turn, stole from one and then the other whiskey jacks when they were far enough from our presence to give them a feeling of safety. It seemed odd that the jay was afraid of us and would not venture near, while the whiskey jacks seemed unafraid but surrendered easily to the jay's intimidation. I guessed that we—men and birds alike—were simply afraid of different things and willing to take measured risks to gain our various ends.

OCTOBER 13, 1986

Last night Bill had tied all the horses to a picket line stretched between two ponderosa pines. Ordinarily he tied some horses and left others loose to graze. The supply of pelleted hay that we had packed into camp made it unnecessary for the horses to graze during the night. Oddly, I missed the sound of the horses' bells and had to remind myself that they were tied on the picket line and had not wandered off.

The whiskey jacks were outside the tent at daylight sorting through last night's dishes. The clanging of the pots and pans, as they were bumped off the log that served as a drainboard, was our alarm clock. The whiskey jacks responded to the clatter of the dishes with their trademark ratcheting call, which I interpreted as their demand for an easy breakfast. I suspected that the whiskey jacks were quickly training us to provide for their needs. Maybe we and the whiskey jacks had unintentionally negotiated an equitable deal. We paid with food, and they graced us with their presence and antics. They liked our food and we enjoyed their company. That seemed, to me, more than fair to both parties.

As we were in no hurry to get back to town, we dragged everything out—getting up and dressing, fixing breakfast, washing dishes, packing up, and saddling and packing the horses. We rode out of camp just before noon. As we followed an old logging spur to where our trucks waited, we could hear loggers and logging machinery busily making trees into logs. Boise-Cascade Corporation usually did what Bill and I considered a pretty fair job of forest management.

Their cutting prescriptions were, reasonably enough, based primarily on what made their stockholders the most money—today and for the foreseeable future. Harvested trees were chosen for what was needed at the mill at the time. Roads were built to the minimum necessary standards, desired species of trees were carefully spared, and cull trees were girdled and left standing, and provided nest sites for wood peckers and other cavity-nesting birds.

All in all, the company's pragmatic management seemed to yield an outcome for wildlife that was as good as or better than much of what the USFS prescribed. The difference, I thought, came from the roads that were already in place—i.e., there was no necessity for an individual logging show to pay for high-priced roads. That flexibility as to the location and extent of timber removal made a considerable difference.

The old stumps that were mixed in with trees of various ages and sizes attested to many decades of single-tree selection harvesting—and some clear-cutting in patches of less than five acres or so followed by planting to ponderosa pine. The current cutting practices seemed to be what foresters call "group selection" in one- to five-acre patches with residual noncommercial trees left standing—"pragmatic forestry" at its best.

We were a couple of hundred yards from the horse trucks when we finally came upon a seemingly uneducated ruffed grouse that exhibited no fear as it strolled off to the side of the road and began to strut. I thought to myself, "So now supper shows up? Where was a tame grouse when we needed one?" I had a sweet yellow onion, a green pepper, a can of chicken broth, and a box of rice packed away in the panniers just waiting for such a bird.

But now, damn it, we were on our way home and those fixings would have to wait to be used at another time. I exercised my godlike power of life and death over the strutting grouse—and this time came down on the side of life.

I did not detect that the grouse recognized my generous gift or that it was at all grateful. Here was a case of the right bird in the right place—at the wrong time. We arrived at the trucks just after noon, tossed the packs and panniers in the bed of my pickup, loaded the horses in the horse truck and trailer, and headed for home.

CHAPTER 2

NOT WILDERNESS—BUT REALLY CLOSE

Bill and I journeyed to a property located just west of Pendleton, Oregon, owned by the Oregon Department of Fish and Wildlife. Our purpose was to try the pheasant hunting and provide Bill's new bird dog with a training experience in a new and different habitat.

NOVEMBER 10, 1986

Our hunt took us along a small stream with a series of small dams and lakes. Ring-necked pheasants were common in the cattails around the edges of the lakes. They usually "flushed wild"—i.e., out of the range of our shotguns. Clearly, this wasn't these pheasants' "first rodeo," and they most certainly did not consider our presence benign.

We also flushed a number of mallards, widgeons, teal, and Canada geese from the myriad small ponds and creeks encountered along the way that took wing— reluctantly, it seemed—with loud vocal protests. They commonly circled and, sometimes, flew back directly over our heads. It was their very good fortune that neither of us possessed a Federal duck stamp. But the birds didn't know that. We raised our guns, led the birds, and fired phantom shots as they passed overhead—Bang! Bang! Bang! In my mind's eye, I was an awesome wing shot and didn't believe that I ever missed—not even a single shot!

Though enjoyable, the fantasy was a poor substitute for the real thing. We guessed that these seemingly naive waterfowl had very recently ridden the late-fall winds down from the north and had yet to discover the danger associated with flying low and slow over men with shotguns. As we had seen other hunters putting up blinds and setting out decoys, we suspected that the innocence of such new arrivals would be short-lived.

Soon Bill's pointer was trailing a pheasant down a long, narrow cover along an old fence line. We could tell from the dog's actions that a pheasant (or several) were running ahead of him. Bill signaled that he would train the dog and that I should hurry ahead to the end of the cover. I reached that point less than a minute or so before Bill and the dog arrived. I could see from the movements of the cattails that a pheasant was moving just ahead of the dog with Bill close behind. I called to Bill to be ready and he stopped. Now we were both ready, with guns up and feet carefully braced, leaving no chance for a slip or a false step. The pheasant came to the end of the cover with the dog close behind. With no option left, it flew straight up out of the reeds. The bird was so close that the sun glinted off the feathers and it was clear that the bird was a cock—therefore legal game. There was no need for me to hurry my shot. The cock rose almost straight up and leveled out to sail away. Bill fired methodically (it was his turn to shoot first)—once, twice, and then again, with no discernible result. The cock swerved and came directly over my head. There was plenty of time to think. I computed that the cock was sailing left and down. I adjusted accordingly and fired. I was so certain of my shot that, when the bird did not fold up in the air and drop to the ground, I simply stood there with my mouth hanging open.

How could both of us, well better than average shot gunners (at least in our humble opinions), have missed an easy shot four times? I thought I knew the answer. It had happened to me before—and more than once. We had simply had too much time to think. When I shoot fast, without thinking, instincts take over and misses are relatively rare. Given too much time to think and compute, a miss becomes ever more likely. There are some things that should be done instinctively, without thinking, and shooting fast-flying birds with a shotgun is one. Detailed analysis does not always yield better results. The acid test, of course, is to sense when to think and when to let instincts take over. The unscathed pheasant landed in the cattails along another fencerow several hundred yards ahead. We marked him down, and I set out at a trot to get into position for another shot. I stationed myself at the edge of the reeds to wait for Bill and the dog and luckily stumbled onto the cock. Once again, he flushed almost straight up catching me totally by surprise. But this time my reaction was instant and instinctive and the cock folded into lifelessness—and fell into the lake!

The dog, being a short-haired pointer, refused to play water dog and plopped down on his fanny at the water's edge. He looked alternately at the floating pheasant and at me. Maybe in this case, a little preliminary thinking would have been in order. Think too much and I miss. Think too little and the bird ends up in the lake. At this juncture, there was probably some great philosophical point to be garnered from the experience, but if so, it escaped me.

Wading after pheasants in November was not only bizarre but absolutely certain to be damned uncomfortable! I took off my boots and socks, my wool pants, and my long johns and did my duty, bare ass to the wind. The dog, sitting on his butt at water's edge, seemed to enjoy the show. After I got dressed, we hunted back along the ravine but on the opposite side, back toward where we had started. We emerged on a road that "just didn't seem right." But because there was only one road that showed on our map, provided by our Oregon Department of Fish and Wildlife buddies, we assumed it was the road on which we had left my truck. We walked a mile or so down the road as it became evermore glaringly obvious that we had made a really bad surmise. So we did a "to the rear march" and walked back to where we had started. Then we walked a mile or so in the other direction until it became clear that we were still not on the right track.

We were becoming more than a bit frustrated, embarrassed, and tired. We saw the critical landmarks. We were on the road. We had a map. In spite of all that, we were indisputably, flat-assed lost. We considered ourselves to be two pretty good mountain men, but it was useless to dispute that fact! We knew where we were, of course. Therefore, it seemed fair to us to say that it was the truck that was lost. We slogged back down the road a mile or so past where we had turned back before and came to a hub of six roads. It was getting along toward dark, we were tired, and we were now presented with a new opportunity to really screw up—magnifying our embarrassment in the process. We were beginning to contemplate gathering up enough wood for a fire, roasting a couple of pheasants, and settling in for the night.

At this most opportune of moments, a pickup truck with decals on the door proclaiming "OREGON DEPARTMENT OF FISH & WILDLIFE" pulled up. Bill did not want to admit, or even indicate, that we were lost. So he asked, with a perfectly straight face, "Have you seen a brown Ford pickup truck? It's lost."

The driver, trying to hide a smile, announced that he had not seen our pickup, so it must still be lost. He didn't laugh. Looking Bill in the face, he likely didn't dare. Laughing would come later. We spread out our map on the hood of his truck. We pointed to where we stood, then to where we believed the truck to be, and where we had been.

Light finally dawned—the road on which we were standing was not on the map! That was the second lesson to be learned from this fiasco. Things are not always as the map says. Pilgrims who have blind faith in such "sure" things need to think twice. Several times in the course of this ongoing screw-up we had mutually agreed that "the truck is right over there"—but according to the map, that just couldn't be. Had we followed our instincts instead of relying on the map, we could have saved ourselves six miles of walking, not counting the embarrassment involved with "losing" our truck.

The biologist, who worked for Bill, delivered us to our no longer lost truck. He didn't snicker or even smile. But we suspected, down deep, that we wouldn't hear the end of this for a while!

For me, one of the attributes of such hunting is that they give me time to wander about all alone and ponder things—sometimes quite odd things—without interference or distraction. For example, on this particular trip, I was troubled by an argument that I had earlier in the week with a colleague about a modified approach to a timber sale that would cost some immediate dollar profit but retain some semblance of good elk habitat. The forester—a colleague and a friend—in a very professional manner ended up calling me an "iconoclastic, anachro-nistic son-of-a-bitch." Strangely, I wasn't insulted, not being too sure of what I was being accused of, though the glowing redness of my colleague's face gave me a clue that no compliment was intended.

I had a chance to refresh my memory as to what those four-bit words meant. Sure enough, Webster's dictionary says that an iconoclast is "one who attacks cherished beliefs as shams" and an anachronism as "anything incongruous in point of time with its sur-roundings." Once I thought about it, I decided that was the nicest thing the fellow ever said to me. Besides, I had to admit his observa-tion, in this case anyway, was right on the money. Of course, I would rather be pleased with the truth than upset by it.

The statement was perhaps not only an accurate description of me but also of my vocation as a wildlife biologist. After all, my profes-sion's underpinning science of ecology has been called the "subversive science." Ecologists do seem to be increasingly in the way of the abject subservience to the icons of cost/benefit ratios, profit maximization, and efficiency. I thought it was no wonder that the academic field of economics was referred to as "the dismal science."

Ecologists do seem to dwell on many values that are not mea-surable in ciphers—certainly not dollars and cents—and likely never will be. If that was being iconoclast, I relished the title—both for me and for my profession. But in accepting that description, ecologists must recognize that, to most folks, "iconoclastic" is an epithet. Per-versity, I thought, brings its own rewards, good and bad.

Was I being anachronistic? Without doubt. That word contained a kernel of truth. Most wildlife biologists are in love with the remnant wild things—animals, plants, ecosystems, and places—that still ex-ist and mourn those that have passed away. This applies both to na-ture and to a vanishing way of life. Some, maybe most, of us feel our anachronism in our bones and know that, down deep, our chances of preserving wild things—and an appreciation for wild things and plac-es—seem destined to become increasingly small over the very long run.

Yet in the final analysis it is the only game in town for those who, in their anachronistic hearts and souls, care deeply about such things. The way is hard, with many defeats and fewer victories—and absolutely no victories that are final. Dropouts and burnouts among professionals are common. But there are many in our profession who stay the course and finish stronger and wiser than when they began.

Most wildlife biologists might well ascribe to a passage in T. K. Whipple's *Study Out the Land* that I had memorized in my youth: "All America lies at the end of the wilderness road, and our past is not a dead past, but still lives in us. Our forefathers had civilization inside themselves, the wild outside. We live in the civilization they created, but within us the wilderness still lingers. What they dreamed, we live, and what they lived, we dream."

Was such a comment iconoclastic? That seemed likely. Anachronistic? Maybe.

CHAPTER 3

CHASING MULE DEER BUCKS IN THE EAGLE CAP WILDERNESS

At long last was mule deer hunting season, and Bill and I headed for the Eagle Cap Wilderness. As there was just the two of us, we traveled in style with four packhorses—a veritable plethora of horseflesh and supplies.

OCTOBER 4, 1988

Bill and I traveled up the old sheep driveway from the trailhead to our often used hunting camp on Middle Catherine Creek. The day was hot, dry, and beautiful—much more like late summer than early fall. The summer has been inordinately hot and dry leading us to anticipate that grazing for the horses around the campsite we had in mind might well be depleted. Just in case, the two extra packhorses were each carrying 200 pounds of alfalfa pellets. Once that feed was exhausted, the horses would be available to pack out the two bucks we intended to harvest to add to our winter larders.

The old sheep driveway was bedded by volcanic ash that had been churned up repeatedly over the years by the hooves of bands of sheep on the way to and from their high mountain pastures. The clouds of dust raised by the horses' hooves hung in the hot, still air and clogged the nostrils of man and beast. Only the lead horse and rider—which was Bill, to my momentary envy—was spared the worst of the dust. The following horses periodically blew explosively through their nostrils to expel dust and mucus. The blue bandana tied over my nose and mouth was better than nothing—but not by much. My squinted, reddening eyes watered profusely.

At the Eagle Cap Wilderness boundary we encountered hand-lettered signs nailed to trees informing us that the trail over Burger Butte and down Elk Creek to the Minam River was in the process of being reconstructed and that periodic dynamite blasts should be expected. As it was Saturday and we had heard neither dynamite blasts nor chainsaw music, we assumed that the trail builders were taking a break to "pursue the wily buck," along with the rest of the folks apt to be in the backcountry on this special day.

We left the main trail and descended, via a secondary route, to the Middle Fork of the Minam River where we turned and followed the Minam River Trail upstream. Bill was riding along about half asleep when his horse turned off the trail at just the right place to take us to a "hidden meadow"—known to us as our "Middle Fork Camp." I was impressed, one more time, that a horse could remember a turnoff to a familiar campsite after not being there for several years—and maybe only once before. But the horses did remember, no matter whether we arrived in midafternoon or in the pitch-black of midnight. With time, I learned to rely on their memories and night vision. Bill, of course, had that figured out long before. He just kept it to himself.

More than once, I had returned in the dark to a horse that had been tied all day. I fumbled with cold-stiffened fingers to put on the bridle and tighten the cinch. I put my rifle in the scabbard hanging under the stirrup and stepped up in the saddle, sat there in the blackness, took a deep breath, and gave the horse its head. I sat tight in the saddle, with the reins hanging loose, and with my head bowed to keep the brim of my hat between my face and the possibility of encountering a tree limb. And sure enough, without fail, my horse delivered me to camp. I wasn't arrogant enough to think the horse much cared about me one way or the other, but camp was where the other horses were, along with grazing grounds and/or alfalfa pellets and access to water. And, the horse would be relieved of its burden.

I looked upon such a journey as involving two acts of faith. The first was my faith that my horse would stay on the trail and deliver me to camp. The horse had faith that, upon arrival at camp, she would be shed of me and the saddle and accoutrements, have a drink of cold water, and be provided with a belly full of pelleted alfalfa. It was a deal beneficial to both horse and rider. My favorite mare, Summer, came to a stop where she had been tied the night before. It was a beautiful campsite with perfectly level ground for the tent, tall spruce trees to shelter the camp and the horses from wind, wood in plentiful supply, good pasture, and with running, crystal-clear water only thirty yards away. Bill had arrived in camp an hour or so earlier and had coffee boiling on the sheepherder stove and a bottle of rum open and ready to provide a "touch" of medicinal seasoning. Life seemed very good indeed.

OCTOBER 5, 1988

We left camp on foot an hour before first light. Our intent was to reach the divide between the Catherine Creek and Minam River drainages by first light. It was in the scrubby pines just at timberline where we believed that the big mule deer spend their days this time of year. We parted company as we left camp and took separate paths toward the ridge. The uphill climb was tough, hot, slow work. By the time I reached the ridge, I had shed my coat, heavy wool shirt, and woolen cap and tied them to my hunting pack. Only my long johns covered my upper body. Steam rose from my head and upper body in the cold, still air.

As the sun peeked over the horizon, the tips of the highest surrounding peaks—Burger Butte and China Cap—were suddenly swathed in new light. I settled into a place in the rocks where I could see a half circle of open ground with a radius of some 200 yards lying below me. With the cessation of the exertion of the climb, my body temperature began to drop, and quickly, abetted by the chill of the rocks and a freshening downslope breeze. Suddenly, all the clothes I could put on were not enough, but now they would have to do.

For an hour or so, I shivered in the off-and-on mists until the rising sun finally cleared the mountaintops. Now, the cold granite rocks reflected the sun to where I sat. My dark gray wool jacket absorbed the heat, and I gradually became warm, comfortable, and drowsy. Dozing in the sun can be one of the truly delicious moments of hunting on a brisk fall day. Most hunters won't admit, until they are older and less intense, to such weakness and lack of discipline. I would wager that most have enjoyed many such brief, stolen naps in the warm sunlight.

From time to time, I came fully awake, lifted my head, and checked out the slope lying below me through my field glasses looking for a big mule deer buck that was surely on the way to me. Finding none, I nodded off again. Then I was jarred awake by the sound of rolling rocks. My eyes popped wide open as all my senses sprang to life. Down below, some quarter mile away, two mule deer bucks were quartering up the slope toward the tree line—and straight toward me. They paused every now and then to look over their back trail. Finally, they were within 200 yards, but as they were moving through the trees, they did not present me with a shot I was willing to chance. I was in the prescribed sitting position for marksmen and locked into my rifle and its sling. I tracked the buck through my 4-power telescopic sight, waiting patiently for a clear shot. I slipped into the trancelike state my grandfather called "shooter's focus." I began the pertinent calculations—"doing the math"—including distance to target, wind, and anticipated trajectory of the bullet.

The waiting and the anticipation sharpened my senses to the point where things seemed to transition into slow motion while colors, sounds, and smells were seemingly magnified. Perhaps that was the predator in my nature clawing its way to the surface through the protective veneer laid down by civilization. Then, as if by magic, there was the big four-point buck, clearly visible between two trees, standing stock-still and facing me head-on. There were no impediments between the muzzle of my Winchester featherweight .30-06 and the buck. He seemed more puzzled, or maybe more curious, than alarmed. I was aware that he might become uneasy and bounce off down hill at any moment, mule deer style.

The Lord of the Hunt had done his part. Now it was time for me to shoot—and shoot straight. My focus was complete and intense. My third full, deep breath was slowly exhaled by half and held. Now the only discernible motion in my scope was the slight twitch of my heartbeat showing in the crosshairs. The trigger squeeze commenced. The roar of the discharge and the recoil came as a surprise—and somehow seemed an intrusion. I was not conscious of any recoil, which was actually quite pronounced from the "featherweight" rifle known for its recoil. The buck simply disappeared. But I knew the sight picture was perfect and the trigger squeeze was good. Surely, I thought, the buck was lying dead in his last tracks. Just then, I heard another shot from a mile or so away to the north, echoing back and forth across the canyon. I had no doubt that the bullet had struck its target, as the paired sound of the firing and the strike of the bullet into flesh was clearly discernible. It seemed safe for me to assume that Bill, too, had been successful.

Sure enough, "my buck"—he was indeed mine now—was lying exactly in the spot where he stood when I squeezed the trigger. He was big and beautiful, sleek and fat, with three points on one antler and four on the other. As I knelt down and touched him, old familiar jumbled feelings swept over me—sadness, elation, appreciation, and respect. I knew, as I had always known in such moments, that one of life's circles of life and death was complete. For that brief moment, we melded into one—the deer and I—and time seemed to stand still. As I dressed and skinned the buck, yellow jackets began to arrive on the scene. Soon there were, I surmised, at least twenty-five of the little carnivores on the carcass and the blood on the pine needles, with more arriving every minute. That made my job of field dressing the buck a bit more challenging. To my relief, the yellow jackets were too intent on the blood and flesh of the deer to pay any attention to me as I went about my work. The trick to not being stung was to avoid accidentally grabbing or squeezing one of the little critters or giving in to the urge to swat.

Once the deer was skinned and quartered, I placed the quarters in clean cotton sacks and hung them up to cool. I made as close to a beeline as I could for camp to procure the services of my saddle mare and a packhorse. I set aside the liver, heart, and neck in a cotton bag that I tied to my hunting pack. Whatever happened during the rest of the day, a "hunter's celebration" supper resided in that sack.

Coming down off the ridge, I ran across tracks that I recognized as Bill's headed downhill toward camp. Now I felt even more certain that it was he who had fired the shot that I heard strike home earlier. Otherwise, I had no doubt that the old hunter would have hung out in "buck country" at the tree line until after dark.

When I could make out the tent through the trees, there was smoke coming from the stovepipe and there was the smell of boiling coffee wafting in the upslope breeze. I gave out a "Hello" to the camp!" which solicited a reply—"Wah!"

When I arrived in camp, Bill stepped out of the tent and handed me a cup of coffee containing a shot of good bourbon—"just for the taste," he assured me. The coffee and the ample portion of "taste" were almost as good as the combination smelled.

We were both tired—looked it, felt it, and even admitted to it. In spite of that, after a bit of discussion, we deemed it best to get the two deer back to camp before dark. Though the chances were small, there was a risk of a black bear not yet in hibernation finding supper neatly prepared and hanging in cotton sacks. When I attempted to laugh away that concern, Bill told me of the bear tracks he had seen in the fresh early snow. That settled the debate.

We encountered no trouble working the horses right up to both deer. The quarters were quickly bundled into manty packs and lashed onto the horses, and we were on the trail and back in camp about "zero dark thirty." We were, by now, very tired—a good, successful hunter's tiredness. We attempted to prolong and preserve the moment with a few leisurely drinks before the traditional first supper after a kill—floured sliced liver and heart with ample dashes of salt and pepper, fried in very hot bacon grease, and then smothered in steamed onions. It tasted somewhere this side of very good.

OCTOBER 6, 1988

Our hunting done, we used the spare day earned by our early hunting successes to ride up the old Catherine Creek Trail to Burger Pass just for a look-see. This trail had originally been constructed following the traditional sheepherders' route and was pretty rough going. In spite of that, we arrived in the pass at midday and ate our lunch of summer sausage, rat cheese, and dried apricots.

As we gazed back down Trail Creek toward the Minam River, we used our binoculars to search out landmarks, old campsites, locations of past elk and deer kills and to remember other trips and old friends that had been our *compadres* on those sojourns. Off to the side of the trail we spotted a cache of some sort, covered with a cinched-down blue tarp. As we were deep in the Eagle Cap Wilderness, we were overwhelmed by curiosity. Inspection revealed the cache to contain cases of dynamite that had been deposited for use by the USFS crew constructing a new trail from Catherine Creek over Burger Butte and down Elk Creek to the juncture with the Minam River Trail.

We were lying on our backs in the sun, giving our lunches a chance to settle, when three hunters rode up from the direction of Elk Creek. After the usual exchange of pleasantries, one of the riders remarked, with some degree of aggravation in his voice as he nodded toward the cache, "It really gravels my ass for those big-shot elk hunters and their damned hired guides to pack in their stuff in and leave it for a month or so before elk season even starts. Yesterday we talked about emptying our rifles into that pile. Well, I may do it yet."

Bill suggested that it might be worth the man's time and effort to take a peek under the tarp before he shot things up. The big fellow grinned, walked over to the pile, and threw back the edge of the blue tarp. After standing dead quiet for a moment, he neatly replaced the tarp, walked to his horse, mounted, and rode away. He didn't smile or even wave good-bye. I thought he looked a bit peaked.

I had no idea of whether a bullet fired into a pile of dynamite would cause an explosion—I sure as hell didn't want to find out. Obviously the big fellow, with mouth to match, wasn't too keen to find out, either. As we rode back down the trail, it was apparent that there had been a lot of dynamite work already carried out in blasting out a trail through the rock outcrops. The trees that had been removed were cut with a crosscut saw rather than motorized equipment in order to preserve the "wilderness character." I was impressed with the logic: blast out the trail with dynamite but use crosscut saws to remove trees because chainsaws make too much noise. Oh well, we reasoned, at least it was quiet between dynamite blasts and decades between such trail reconstruction efforts. When we crossed the Eagle Cap Wilderness boundary, we could tell the rules of engagement between the trees and the trail builders had changed as the stumps now bore the telltale marks of chainsaws.

It seemed strange what lines on maps can produce. On this side of the line, you can do one thing and on that side, another—and vice versa. On this side of a line, language A is spoken, and on that side, language B. Step across this line or that line and you become a trespasser or an invader. Come to think about it, it seemed to me that more people had been killed arguing over lines on maps than any other reason I could think of. I suspected that the number of lines per unit of area on a map was directly correlated with the intensity of human activity and regulation. The "blank spots" on today's maps do not mean that the mapmakers did not know what was there—it just means that there were, as yet, fewer or no lines—and no need, just yet, for any.

We crossed back over the line that delineated the boundary of the Eagle Cap Wilderness. Today, one side of the line looked like the other. But, I thought, that was but a temporary state of affairs. Farther down the mountain, logging roads were being extended, year by year, closer and closer to where we stood. Some year soon, the boundaries of the clear-cutting units would be delineated along the edge of the Wilderness boundary.

When that day comes—it will come and soon—the stage will be set for the test of national will relative to the continued conservation of such wild places. A period of economic stress or of war, of which nations seem to produce an endless supply, will inevitably come. Or will a period of severe recession engender an increasing cacophony of voices demanding changes in those lines to allow more logging or mining or roads or some other form of economic exploitation? Or maybe states and even county governments will claim authority to manage (i.e. "exploit") federal lands. I asked Bill, "What then?"

He mused, "Well, that will be a test for the next generation. At least we will have given them their chance to choose. That may well be our greatest legacy—choices. Then it will be all up to them. Time will tell." Sure enough, I thought, no decision is forever. Well, I mused, for the moment the decisions had been made and in those decisions lay a legacy to generations to come. Many of those decisions have already entailed "split the baby" decisions. Now generations to come, each in their turn, will have to make their decisions. That, I thought, was the best any generation could do—leave choices for those that follow. I pondered those questions as we rode back to camp in the fading light. Will succeeding generations of Americans treasure wildernesses, national parks, national wildlife refuges, and national forests? Will they treasure and sustain the elk, the deer, the bighorn sheep, and the other species so carefully brought back from the brink of extirpation—even extinction—by preceding generations? I didn't know, but, by God, they will have a choice. Whether they choose to recognize and maybe even thank the Bill Browns of the current era for that precious ability to choose really doesn't matter. Each generation must make their choices in their time in such matters—and many times. That is the blessing and the curse of living in democracy—We the People making choices.

We arrived at camp just at twilight. The tied-up horses and our mounts whinnied back and forth their chorus of greetings. I liked the sound and interpreted the exchange as saying, "Welcome home!" Or could it be more realistically interpreted as, "Where the hell have you guys been? Let us loose! And, by the way, right now would be good. We're hungry and thirsty." I expected that my second interpretation was closer to the truth than the first. But I liked the first interpretation better and decided to stick with it. I laughed to myself. Now I was thinking like a horse, or thought I was. No doubt Bill considered that an improvement—I sometimes think he likes horses better than people.

OCTOBER 7, 1988

We were up at dawn with every intention of making an early start for the trailhead. In spite of our best intentions, we dawdled. We were both aware that we really didn't want to leave, so we simply put off our departure. Why not? In midafternoon we finally saddled the horses, made up and loaded the packs, mounted up, and headed down the trail. We had allowed ourselves just enough time to get to the trailhead just before full dark. That seemed soon enough for this sojourn in the wilderness to end—really too soon for me.

CHAPTER 4

ELK HUNTING IN WILDERNESS—FOR ME, THE ULTIMATE HUNTING EXPERIENCE

Elk season has, at long last, come around. Bill Brown and I had invited Robert "Bob" Nelson (director of Fish and Wildlife for the USFS in the Washington, D.C., office) and Randy Fisher (director of the Oregon Department of Fish and Wildlife DF&W) to join us in our camp two miles below Minam Lake on the upper Minam River for elk season. Bill and I had already taken a cow elk apiece during an earlier special hunting season and we would serve as "outfitters and guides" for our two friends.

OCTOBER 24, 1988

Bill, Bob, and I left the trailhead at Two Pan campground on the Lostine River at noon with our camp outfit and two fifty-pound bags of pelleted horse feed. Our intention for this day was to set up camp. Tomorrow Bob would gather and chop a week's wood supply while Bill and I returned to the trailhead to pick up Randy, his gear, and four additional bags of alfalfa pellets. The fall weather was beautiful with warm sunshine and clear skies. There was, as yet, no snow on the ground.

Taking a calculated chance on the weather, we had established our camp high in the Wallowa Mountains. A sudden change in the weather at 7,400 feet would make things difficult for men and horses, and PDQ. Several times in the past, when hunting out of this camp, our party had managed to kill a bull elk or two or three. It was an admitted gamble with the weather—but a gamble that had a history of paying off. We recalled the old poker player's motto: "No guts, no blue chips."

The ride into camp was uneventful—if one can call a ride into the wilderness "uneventful." I spent most of my time watching Bob riding just in front of me. He was clearly back in his element. He had served for twenty-five-plus years as a wildlife biologist and a line officer for the USFS before becoming director of Fish and Wildlife in the Washington office. He had joined up with what USFS folks call "the outfit" in the day when there were only a handful of fish and wildlife biologists in the entire agency. His career had spanned the agency's period of evolution toward a more balanced program stretching far beyond timber and range management and concerns over watersheds to include more emphasis on fish and wildlife and recreation.

Bob had been a critical force in the ongoing rise of fish and wildlife biologists to positions of increasing influence in the agency. A person would never know the significance of the efforts of this self-effacing man or the degree of his accomplishments or influence by simply talking to him. On other hand, he didn't have to extol his achievements; they spoke for themselves—as they should—and were well known and appreciated by his professional colleagues in both federal and state conservation agencies.

Over the past thirty years, many of the USFS's pioneering fisheries and wildlife biologists had purposefully avoided being promoted into administrative positions, choosing to remain in field positions close to the wildlife and wild places that they cherished. Bob, on the other hand, understood early on in his career that the real fight for wildlife would be decided largely in bureaucratic budgetary and policy development processes. The agency now employed a bevy of good field biologists with more demand on their services than they could ever satisfy. The need for their specialized services was great—and increasing by leaps and bounds. At the same time experienced, skilled, skookum fish and wildlife professionals were scarce, and the leadership that Bob provided was sorely needed—and more and more appreciated. Bob was the kind of man that General Omar Bradley must have had in mind when he observed, "It is amazing how much a man can achieve when he doesn't care who gets the credit." In my opinion, and that of many fish and wildlife professionals, Bob Nelson was the quietest, most self-effacing, and surely the most effective Director of Fish and Wildlife in USFS history. Likely, he will never receive the credit that is his due. But he knows and his compatriots know. I suspect that's enough for Bob.

This trip was one way that Bill and I could demonstrate that we knew and appreciated what he had done, was doing, and would do. But Bob had paid a dear price for what he cared about most. That price was "moving to town" as promotions and opportunities came his way, first to the Forest Service regional office in San Francisco and then to Washington, D.C. That equated to, on a day-to-day basis, separation from the wild places and wild things that were his underlying motivation for service. Now his day-to-day world was made up of commuting, government-ugly offices, airplanes, motels, and endless meetings. His reward lay in the knowing that the wild places and wild things were better off for his caring and his service. Most important among his achievements, Bob had sought out, sponsored, trained, and positioned a cadre of younger fisheries and wildlife biologists so that they, over time, could and would have a chance to influence USFS management for the next two or three decades and maybe longer. His work and influence would surely outlast him— and he knew it.

The horses were well conditioned from a summer of work in the backcountry, and they climbed steadily toward our intended campsite without exhibiting any need to stop and rest. We topped out at Minam Lake in midafternoon, having covered ten miles in three hours while climbing 2,500 feet in the process. The view was spectacular, as we were surrounded by granite peaks. It was a view that made me feel small, insignificant, and humble. It was the feeling that I think the author of the Book of Job must have felt when he described the Creator asking Job, "Where wast thou when I laid the foundations of the earth? Declare if thou hast understanding. Who hath laid the measures thereof, if thou knowest? Or who hath stretched the line upon it? Whereupon are the foundations thereof fastened? Or who laid the cornerstone thereof; when the morning stars sang together, and all the sons of God sang for joy?"

For me, these mountains were that foundation. I loved this high country. As always, it gave me the impression of being simultaneously new and ancient, clean and fresh, and yet so simple and so complex. The mountains were thrust up from the bowels of the earth and then eroded over eons by alternating exposure to bitter cold and blazing sun, by water that froze and thawed and then ran rapidly down toward the sea carrying traces of the decaying rock. The soils forming from these rocks were still primitive, yet well on their way to being the ever-finer particles of soil that they would become—maybe a hundred thousand or a million years hence.

The world encountered at such high elevations is not yet rich in favorable weather, nutrient-rich soil, or flat ground that holds both soil and water in place and produces abundant plant life. Those riches lay in the newer world down below in the foothills, valleys, and plains. The riches of that newer world attract and support *Homo sapiens* in ever-increasing numbers. And, oddly, down below where the soil is rich and the topography more gentle is where deer and elk, if tolerated by man, are the most plentiful and the most productive.

We do not hunt in the wilderness because the deer and elk are more plentiful here. We hunt here because it is our land, belonging to all the people, and we need no one's permission and we pay no "trespass fees." And, better yet, this special category of land—wilderness—is without roads, so hunting in such circumstances demands special knowledge and skills and hardiness.

Wilderness is a special category of land to be visited and enjoyed and appreciated by a special subset of *Homo sapiens*. I have come to believe that many who are curious about "beginnings"—theirs and our nation's—return to this younger world in the course of their search for answers. Do they search here for the sources of life and perhaps to gain perspectives on "life" in the process? Perhaps they visit such places to ponder and reach their own conclusions. Such mountains are indeed, to me, the pillars of the earth. A visit to such wild places simultaneously facilitates dreaming and living for a time in what has been, what is, and what may be for us and our children—even our children's children.

When we arrived at our campsite, there was just enough daylight left to facilitate setting up tents and stoves and caring for the horses. Our previous year's wood supply remained just where we had hidden it, sparing us from having to gather and prepare wood for cooking and heating the tent. We hurried to take care of the horses, get a fire started, and get camp set up before darkness rendered those tasks more difficult.

As we watched the sunshine fade on the mountain peaks, Bob said, "It's a very long way from Washington, D.C." Then, for just a moment, we stood still in the twilight and listened long and carefully to the silence. It was, indeed, a long way from Washington or even La Grande, Oregon—in more ways than one.

OCTOBER 25, 1988

Just at full light Bill and I saddled up and left camp on our way back to the trailhead to pick up Randy, his gear, and another 400 pounds of pelleted alfalfa for the horses. Bob stayed behind to gather and cut some more wood for the sheepherder stoves set up in the two tents. I don't think Bob minded staying behind, as he was a little stiff and sore from the ride in. Riding a swivel chair ten hours or more a day for months at a time did not harden one's ass for hour after hour and mile after mile in the saddle. We left one packhorse tied in camp that had banged up a fetlock sometime during the night. Bill judged her to be too crippled up—we hoped temporarily—to make the trip to the trailhead and return. Bill left instructions for Bob to stand the mare in the cold river for ten minutes every hour or so.

Once we were on the trail and lined out, the horses traveled steadily. As we climbed toward Minam Lake, we could hear swans calling as they circled overhead in the mist. When we reached the lake, we saw six swans were swimming and leaving their wakes on the mirror-like surface. The surrounding granite peaks were reflected on the huge mirror provided by the lake. Not a breath of air was stirring, and the only ripples on the lake trailed behind the swimming swans. It seemed a magic moment—so very still and so very quiet. We sat silently on our horses and watched the swans, each of us immersed in our own thoughts. The only sounds were the breathing of the horses and the creak of saddle leather when a rider or horse shifted position.

We crossed the summit and traveled downslope on the trail alongside the Lostine River and on downhill toward the trailhead. At the first crossing of the Lostine River, we paused to let the horses drink. From down the trail, we heard an approaching rider carrying on an intense and exuberant conversation with the jack mule he was riding. The mule was not outfitted with a bridle and bit. The rider exerted whatever control he perceived that he had over the mule by means of two strands of nylon parachute cord tied to the halter. It had obviously been a long time since the mule had benefited from a drink, as he lunged into the midst of our six horses—much to their consternation—to get to water and attempt to suck. The mule's rider, a small, roundish man with a heavy white beard who was probably in his mid-seventies, broke off his one-sided conversation with the mule and turned his attention to our outfit.

After looking us over, he asked—or maybe it was more of a comment—"Why don't you ever see any young fellers back here in the outback anymore? I don't ever seem to see much of anybody up here anymore but old, fat, white-headed, worn-out guys! And you damned sure don't see many folks with sense enough to ride mules. Mules got horses beat all hollow!"

Here was a fellow wilderness sojourner who had things all sorted out. Ignoring the implied insult about the horses, Bill drolly commented, while keeping a wary eye on our horses, "That's a nice jack mule you're riding there, old-timer. Don't see many riding mules this day and time."

"Got a better one at home. Only three or four years old, though. I don't want to ruin him by starting him out too early. Besides, this here mule is only seventeen. I figure that he's got twenty more years in him. By then I'll be ninety-five and most likely won't need no mule no more."

That said, he flailed at the mule's flanks with his heels, only one of which was adorned with a nubbin spur, and the two-foot-long willow stick in his right hand whacked the mule's ass lightly as he started on up the trail. Once underway, he resumed his heart-to-heart conversation with the mule. That one-sided conversation was still on-going when he disappeared from our view and then from earshot. Now, I thought to myself, that's a man having a good time. I couldn't say that about the mule.

When we arrived at the trailhead, there were four different out-fits engaged in packing up their stock and getting ready to move out up the trails toward the high country. As we had an hour or so be-fore Randy's expected arrival, we tied our horses to our horse trailer and watched the show. In my humble opinion, it beat any television show going.

So much of this kind of backcountry elk hunting resembled a loosely choreographed play involving carefully contrived costumes, cultivated language suitable to the event, and specific physical be-haviors. The standard dress of the actors was made up of a broad-brimmed felt hat, preferably more than a little bit battered and stained with grease, dirt, and sweat; a wool shirt, likely checkered; a black silk kerchief tied around the neck; denim pants, blue or black; battered lace-up packer's boots; red or, maybe, green or black suspenders; a sheath knife (some big enough and wicked-looking enough to fight grizzly bears); a week's stubble of beard; and buck-skin leather gloves shoved in a back pocket. A certain rolling, walk-ing gait seemed *de rigueur*—the stoved-up, stiffened gait of an old cowboy. I couldn't figure how so many old stoved-up cowboys or mountain men could show in up in one place at one time.

It was pure theater and, I supposed, an intentional retreat from the present and back into an earlier time. For the next ten days or so, we actors in our wilderness play would be free to reestablish contact with a still-primitive world, freed from many of the constraints of our "real lives." We could take chances, test ourselves, recoup some of what our forebears knew, and exhibit and depend upon archaic but cherished skills that no longer have a place down below in the cities and towns. We and our fellow escapees were free—at least for a pre-cious little while—to become what, deep in our core, part of what we perceived ourselves to be.

As I watched my fellow pilgrims and part-time actors at the trailhead, it was obvious that old traditions were being played out on a stage that could have been—and maybe was—preserved partially for just such purposes. We players at the wilderness hunting game recognized one another and what we were doing. Yet we did not laugh. Instead, the brief conversations involved the standard comments about horses, equipment, and destinations. Some actors had a "chaw" of tobacco in their cheeks. There was a lot of spitting and scratching going on. Occasionally, a pint of good cheer would be extracted from a saddlebag and passed around.

The fancy trucks, horse trailers, and trailer houses in the parking lot stood out in stark contrast to the horses and mules. The saddles and packs had barely changed, except for the materials used in their construction, in well over a century—likely two or more centuries. When the riders put a foot in a stirrup and stepped up to mount, gathered the lead ropes of the packhorses, and headed out up the trail for the high country, time seemed to run backward in its course. Those who don't understand that phenomenon lack a complete understanding and appreciation of what elk hunting—especially elk hunting in the wilderness—is all about.

At the appointed hour of rendezvous, high noon, Randy drove into the parking lot. Just shy of an hour later, after a lunch break, his gear and several hundred pounds of pelleted alfalfa were secured on the packhorses. We—ourselves in full costume—mounted up, lined out, and headed back up the trail toward camp. The swans still graced the mirror-like surface of Minam Lake when we passed. Our new friend, now formally christened by Bill as "Don Quixote," met us, just shy of the summit, coming back down the trail on his mule. As near as we could discern, his conversation with his jack mule seemed likely to have continued unabated since our last encounter. I was tempted to ask him as to the whereabouts and health of Sancho Panza but stifled the urge, fearing that either he wouldn't understand my humor or, worse yet, understand and take umbrage. After all, he carried an old-time single-action Colt revolver in a shoulder holster under his left arm.

We could make out smoke rising from our camp when we were still a full mile away. When we go closer, we could tell that the smoke was rising from the stovepipe, an almost sure sign that there was hot coffee waiting on the stove. A cup of hot coffee with a generous dash of good cheer would be most welcome after our twenty-five-mile ride. Anticipation had filled my thoughts during that last mile of the long ride. As the magic of the wilderness settled over us, our minds turned more and more toward simple things—hot coffee, a shot or two of bourbon, a warm tent, and a hot meal. Our world was shrinking down to the here and now. What could be better than that?

OCTOBER 26, 1988

Bill and I were up and dressed well before dawn to heat up the cook tent, feed the hunters, fix their lunches, and put them on their way to their hunting grounds before the first hint of light reached the bottom of the canyon. When we stepped out of the tent, our world was still awash in moonlight so bright that it rendered all but the brightest of the stars invisible. The granite outcrops on the mountains surrounding our camp gleamed almost as white as snow in the moonlight. Heavy frost had arrived during the night, and the moonlight glistened off the ice crystals that coated the elk sedge in the meadow.

The periodic clanging of the bells on the horses loosed to graze directed my eyes toward the sound. The horses were clearly visible in the moonlight, some a couple of hundred yards above camp. The fog from their breathing hung briefly in the air—translucent in the bright moonlight. I looked up. The Big Dipper had made a half turn around the North Star since bedtime last night. It seemed a magic moment until my reverie was broken by Bob and Randy arriving at the cook tent ready for coffee and already planning their hunts for the day.

After several cups of steaming hot coffee and a hearty breakfast of fried eggs, bacon, and pancakes, they prepared their lunch and slipped on their hunting packs, slung their rifles over their shoulders, and quietly left, a full hour before first light. They intended to gain some significant elevation before the coming of day brought legal permission to slay their quarry. As Bill and I weren't hunting, we enthusiastically played our roles of camp tenders, packers, horse wranglers, hunting guides, and cooks. Those amalgamated roles allowed us to luxuriate off and on in the warm tent over additional cups of coffee and watch through the tent flap as the sun gradually stole the night from the moon.

By midmorning, the sunlight was pouring directly into the valley and the temperature had risen thirty degrees in about an hour. The coming of the new day was glorious—and unbelievably warm and bright for so late in October. I spent much of the rest of the day walking through the high meadows, glassing the mountain slopes for mule deer—maybe an elk, philosophizing on paper (writing in my journal), reading, and catching little catnaps as I lay flat on my back basking in the warmth of the sun. It seemed such a privilege to just be alive—especially right here and right now. Bill and I spent the entire day "just piddling," talking of many things, past, present, and future, and just sitting silently being one with the wilderness.

When the sun dropped behind the mountain across the valley—seemingly a bit more slowly than it had risen over the opposite mountain only six hours earlier—it was time for me to start the stew for supper. We anticipated that our hunters would arrive in camp an hour or so after full dark, thirsty, hungry, tired, and quiet if they had not killed an elk. Or, if one or both had been successful, they would be thirsty, hungry, tired, exuberant, and full of hunter's talk and regaling us with blow-by-blow descriptions of their feats. There would be elk quarters hanging somewhere up on the mountain, to be fetched into camp tomorrow.

Unfortunately, tired and quiet was the appropriate mood tonight. Yet both hunters talked in animated tones of the glorious day, where they had journeyed, and what they had seen and heard. They didn't speak of what they felt—talking about feelings would not be within the wilderness hunter's code. But Bill and I knew—and they knew—about feelings. After a few drinks, a bellyful of hot beef stew replete with dumplings, and a final cup of coffee laced with good cheer, they headed off to their tent so as to be rested and ready to go again two hours before sunup.

Bill and I sat near the stove and savored one last cup of coffee with just a dab of rum for taste. Then we too sought out the warmth of our down sleeping bags. As I waited for sleep to come, I listened to the sounds: horse bells, an owl, the popping of the cooling sheepherder stove, Bob's soft snoring from the other tent, and a rock rolling down from the slope above. That rolling rock gave my imagination license to visualize a big bull elk—surely a six-pointer—carefully picking his way across the high slope in the moonlight and, in the process, dislodging the rock, starting it on its centuries-long journey to the sea. All of them were good sounds, visions, and dreams. Such would do to sleep on.

OCTOBER 27, 1988

The night seemed very short when the aggravating squeal of the battery-powered alarm clock insisted that it was time for the cook—that being me—to rise and shine. The kindling, matches, and wood for the morning fire had been carefully arranged last night to facilitate my ability to start the fire with only my head and shoulders out of my sleeping bag. The fire was quickly laid and a match touched to the tinder. I shut the door to stove, latched it, and slid open the draft hole. As the chimney began to draw, it was time to squirm back down into my sleeping bag to wait for the stove to perform its magic.

Soon enough the fire was blazing. The stove made a "chugging" sound as it exhausted air up the stove pipe faster than it could come in through the draft hole. I popped my head out of my sleeping bag and saw the stovepipe and the surrounding part of the stove glowing red in the darkness—a simultaneously dangerous and pleasant thing. The tent quickly became delightfully warm.

Adjustments to the damper in the stovepipe and the draft hole at the front of the stove calmed the roar and ardor of the fire. It was a luxury to be able to get dressed in a warm place when the outside temperature was well below freezing. I could hear the hunters stirring in their tent, cursing gently as they struggled to dress quickly in the cold so they could crawl outside and likely answer the insistent call of nature. The effort of getting their feet into their cold-stiffened leather boots could be imagined from the sound of grunts and the stamping of feet.

They were guided to the cook tent by the light of the Coleman lantern shining through the walls of the green nylon tent—and no doubt by the smell of frying bacon and boiling coffee. The hunters, obviously stiff from their unaccustomed exertions of the last few days, grunted with discomfort as they lowered themselves to sit—squat might be a better term—on the low-slung camp stools. Soon the warmth from the stove and the coffee, eggs, bacon, and biscuits they put in their bellies readied them for their hike up to Frazier Pass and the high mountain lake on the other side.

They set out on their journey in full darkness with the intent of being halfway to the pass by daybreak. Their headlamps seem to dance together as Bill and I watched them work their way cross-country to the trail. As I watched the lights disappear from view, it came to me that I was chilled—shivering cold. I laughed at finding myself standing in the frigid morning cold, clad only in my long johns and camp moccasins sans socks.

As Bill and I sat hunched over the stove nursing just one more cup of coffee, we concluded that packing, guiding, and cooking for enthusiastic hunters might be almost as satisfying as hunting. It was certainly more comfortable on such a morning as this. I spent the morning doing camp chores, tending horses, and listening to Bill recount "mountain man" stories from his time working as a fire lookout for the Oregon Department of Forestry the 1930s in southwestern Oregon. Though I had heard the stories before, they were good stories, and it pleasured him to tell them—and have me listen. Obviously, he had told the same stories many times before because he told them exactly the same way every time.

Shortly before noon, Randy ambled back into camp without having seen an elk and convinced that "if there were any elk here, we've moved them out." About that time, I saw Bob walking across the flat with a big grin on his face. Blood was obvious on his wool hunting pants. After studying Bob through his binoculars, Bill allowed that "he has either killed an elk or cut his own throat." Upon Bob's arrival in camp, he reported that he had killed a four-point bull just below Frazier Lake. The elk was gutted, skinned out, quartered, and hanging. Bill and I saddled horses while Bob had some fresh coffee—with a touch of the spirits—while regaling Randy with a blow-by-blow account of just how the heroic deed was masterfully accomplished.

We were able to ride our horses right up to Bob's elk. That meant, after we prepared the manty packs, we could load the quarters directly onto the packhorses—no backpacking required. Another hunter had fired a shot at this same bull and had come close to dropping the animal. The bullet had cut a groove on the inside of the right antler only two inches above the skull. In this case, one hunter's bad luck was another hunter's good fortune.

Randy, now thoroughly convinced that we "had not moved the elk out" after all, left us on foot to hunt up past Frazier Lake over the ridge and then back down to the Minam River. He planned to be back at camp shortly after dark. The three of us made short work of loading the horses. The packing of each of three packhorses was deemed worthy of a "salute" from the brandy flask, which had been "discovered" deep in one of Bill's saddle bags—no doubt inadvertently left there by mistake at the end of some earlier trip.

We were halfway back to Frazier Pass as the sun began to slide behind the peaks to the west. Darkness was settling in as we rode through the pass and began the descent toward our camp on the Minam River. The horses moved surely and swiftly in the dark; they knew exactly where they were headed and just how to get there, knowing that a dinner of pelleted alfalfa would be forthcoming upon arrival. Then, just shy of an hour later, we could see the green glow from the Coleman lantern in the cook tent and smoke rising from the stovepipe. Randy, moving on foot in a race with darkness, had beaten us back to camp. The night's gourmet fare featured thinly sliced elk liver and heart rolled in egg and flour, fast-fried in bacon grease, and smothered in sweet onions. Nothing ever tasted better to me than that first traditional "celebratory meal" of heart and liver in an elk camp. This most wondrous tasty treat may have had more to do with the spirit of the moment, just maybe including the spirits imbibed, and the traditions involved than with genuine gastronomic delight. It seemed so very good that there was a spontaneous and unanimous demand to "save the leftovers for tomorrow's sandwiches." But, as usual, the leftovers were unlikely to find their way into the sandwiches for tomorrow's lunch. In the cold dark morning, baloney, cheese, and mayo would seem a better and easier choice. Tradition!

Then, the dishes done, the hunters eyes began to droop, and they excused themselves to respond to the persistent tug and call of their sleeping bags. Bill and I, loath to end such a wonderful day, sat a while longer near the stove. There was no talking, only the staring into the fire through the open door of the sheepherder stove and the thinking of private thoughts.

OCTOBER 28, 1988

Now there were three camp tenders to service our one hunter still in hot pursuit of the wily elk. That seemed about the right ratio to the camp tenders. But the enthusiasm of our sole remaining hunter was noticeably—and rapidly—waning. Yet perhaps as a matter of sheer pride, he was away from camp just after daybreak. I spent most of the day outside doing my camp chores, listening to Bob and Bill discuss just how the USFS ought to be managing the national forests. It was a most excellent way for me to attend school—not that I didn't have my own opinions. I found myself wishing for a video camera. An edited tape of their discussion would beat any seminar or lecture on the subject I had ever heard in too many years on university campuses. The two old farts knew their business—after all, they had "been there and done that" and for a lot of years. "Winning some and losing some" was an unbeatable educational forum.

In the late afternoon—just after the sun went over the yardarm—there was a seeming fusillade of shots from the camp a half mile or so downriver from ours. The shots came too close together to count, but they were many, from several different rifles, and seemed to be aimed in the direction of our camp.

We later learned that Randy had spooked a spike bull that had unwittingly tried to make its getaway through a camp of five hunters. All the hunters in that camp had given up hunting two days ago and were sitting on stools around the campfire when the elk trotted up to pay a visit. The last Randy saw of them, the five "hunters" were standing around the dead spike bull, arguing vigorously about whose bullet, out of the dozen or so fired and the half dozen that struck home, had actually delivered the death blow.

During supper, Randy announced that he had enjoyed about all the elk hunting he cared anything about for this year. He reckoned that tomorrow would be a good day for us to head for the barn. Bob, whose elk was quartered and hanging up to chill, concurred. So we made plans to get an early start the next morning. After breakfast, Bob and Randy would take off on foot for the trailhead. Bill and I would pack up Bob and Randy's gear, along with Bob's elk, and meet them there. Then they would depart for Portland, and Bill and I would ride back to camp, spend the night, and pack out the rest of the camp the next day.

OCTOBER 29, 1988

After a hearty breakfast of fried eggs, Canadian bacon, pancakes, and boiled coffee, Randy and Bob struck out on foot for the trailhead, about an hour after first light, carrying their hunting packs and rifles. They left their personal gear, which was bundled into manty packs. Bill and I followed some two hours later with each of us leading two packhorses laden with their packs, camp gear, and Bob's elk.

The swans were still on Minam Lake to be admired as we passed. The presence of the swans buoyed my spirits. As long as they were on the lake, I could pretend that the coming of the dark, gray winter was not really inevitable. Of course, winter would come, as it always did, but as the years went by, the cold gray of winter seemed to come earlier and stay longer.

We traveled the thirteen miles to the trailhead at Two Pan without taking a break. The horses were "lean and mean" at the end of the nine-month packing season and they knew the trail by heart. I suspected that they were weary of being tied up and eating alfalfa pellets, had had enough of elk hunting, and were ready to go home for their winter break where the living was easy. I wondered if they knew that, having done their duty for the last nine months, they were due a three-month vacation, complete with nights in the shelter of the barn, ice-free water in the trough, and good alfalfa hay twice a day. What more could there be for a horse? To my mind, they had most surely earned their upcoming vacation.

Bob and Randy were waiting at the trailhead when we arrived. The horses were quickly relieved of their packs, the manty packs unrolled, and Bob and Randy's gear transferred to Randy's van. After a quick good-bye, Bill and I headed back up the trail. The weather was turning colder and the sky darkening. By the time we reached Minam Lake, the blackening sky was spitting snow. The swans had apparently departed for warmer climes, and ice was forming along the edges of the lake. Winter had come to the high country.

As we headed down into the Minam River canyon, it came to me that there would be no light in the tent and no smoke coming from the chimney when we arrived. Our friends were gone. It was a lonely thought that quickly passed. The horses moved along quietly and efficiently with little interaction. After all, camp lay ahead, and that meant freedom from the weight they carried and the saddles and harness they wore as well as a well-earned ration of pelleted alfalfa. What else was there—for men or horses? It would be a quiet camp this night.

OCTOBER 30, 1988

Bill and I were ready to move out for the trailhead two hours after first light. The hunt was over and we had neither inclination nor reason to linger any longer. When we reached Minam Lake, heavy wet snow was falling and accumulating rapidly. We dismounted to check the horses' rigging and packs and to put on rain slickers over our wool coats. The wind was sharp and seemed even colder than yesterday. Our departure, it turned out, was perfectly timed.

I looked over the lake with my binoculars, hoping that, some-how for some reason, the swans might still be there. No such luck. The swans had gone south. Ice extended farther from the edges out into the lake than when we passed by yesterday. The trail seemed longer as the inner glow from the hunt and the inherent camaraderie faded. We rode along without incident and without talking as the horses, like well-conditioned, foolproof pieces of machinery, steadily made their way. We paused at the juncture of the Minam River and Copper Creek trails to check the horses' rigging and packs. All was well. We remounted and resumed our journey.

Then, with no warning, Bill's mare, Manita, exploded sideways from a white rock that, inexplicably, must have appeared to her as something large and white and somehow terrible. The initial lunge left Bill half out of the saddle causing him to lose one stirrup. The pack-horses bolted ahead on his left side, wrapping the lead rope around his waist in the process. Then all four horses bolted in somewhat different directions. Bill came loose from his saddle, landed face first in the meadow, turned two flips end over end, and came to rest lying face down—and lay dead still. It seemed to me that the "dead" part was a distinct possibility. Strangely enough, it popped into my mind that if Bill were indeed dead, this would be the way he would have wanted death to come—quick and clean and on a hunt in the wilderness.

After I settled my horse down—along the two packhorses I had in tow—I rode over to where he lay motionless. I dismounted, tied my saddle horse and lead packhorse, and knelt down beside him. I asked, in what I hoped was a calm voice, if he could hear me. He nodded, "yes." Fearing that he had broken his neck, I asked if he could move his feet. He moved his feet. I told him not to move any more.

I caught and tied his horses. By that time, Bill was sitting up, trying to get both eyes pointed the same direction at the same time. We sorted through things; one bone and one joint at a time. We con-cluded: first, he was alive; second, there was nothing obviously bro-ken—cracked maybe and certainly bruised, but not broken.

I helped him, against his protests, to his feet. I grabbed him by his belt and walked him around. He said he could ride but made the concession of letting me place his foot in the stirrup and boost him up onto his horse. I gathered up the four packhorses, tied them into a four-horse string, and led them rest of the way to the truck. Bill let Manita have her head, and she followed along behind the pack string with Bill sitting straight up in the saddle, holding on to the saddle horn with both hands, while trying to keep his head in the middle.

By the time we reached the trailhead, Bill had recuperated to the point that he was convinced that he could drive his horse truck the three hours to La Grande. When I protested, he reminded me, in as stern a voice as he could muster, that he was the senior offi-cer present and was therefore in command until he relinquished said command. Clearly, I was to understand that he was in charge and if he desired my advice, he would surely ask for it.

Though he had "assumed command," we had to stop twice for me to clear the gunk out his eyes. When he landed face first in the overgrazed meadow, he managed to get a goodly amount of horse shit in his eyes, which had—very quickly—developed evidence of serious infection in the form of pus. Within an hour, I was periodically wiping pus out of his severely inflamed eyes. The man was seventy-five years old! He may well have been the toughest SOB I had ever known—in both mind and body—maybe not too smart sometimes but whet-leather tough.

When we arrived at the trailhead, he acceded to my unpacking the horses, transferring the gear into my pickup, loading the horses in the trailer, and getting things ready for departure. After I flushed his eyes out with the hydrogen peroxide stashed in the big first aid kit in the gear box of my pickup, he declared himself fit to drive the horse truck to his place in La Grande. I made him promise to stop at two designated places alongside the road so that I could flush out his eyes. He kept his word and we got to his place with no problems, save for the very slow pace.

It would be at least three or four months before we would once again be able to head for the high lonesome of the wilderness. But now we had stories—wonderful stories—to tell in front of the fireplace.

Minam River, Eagle Cap Wilderness, 1985.

CHAPTER 5

GETTING THERE FIRST AND STAKING A CLAIM—EVEN WILDERNESS CAN GET CROWDED

My last week at the USFS's Range and Wildlife Laboratory in La Grande had passed slowly. My body was on duty, but my mind and heart were already deep in the Eagle Cap Wilderness. Finally, the day before the opening of elk season arrived, along with the first heavy snow of the year. By late afternoon, snow was accumulating rapidly in the Grande Ronde Valley and surely even faster in the high Wallowas.

OCTOBER 16, 1989

Bill and I had packed in and set up our elk camp in the upper Minam River drainage. We were a week ahead of the opening of elk season, but we wanted to "stake out ownership" of our favorite elk camp and not have to waste any time searching out a suitable camp when we came back with hunting on our minds.

There was only a skiff of snow, and the trip in went without a hitch. After we had the tents up for cooking and sleeping, we spent the rest of the day gathering and chopping wood to length for the Sims stove. All the canned goods, liquor, lantern fuel, bedrolls, tools, tarps, two quarts of 150-proof Jamaican rum in aluminum bottles, and other camp paraphernalia were stored in a two-person, nylon pop tent. Before we left camp, we dropped the main tent over all the gear to prevent any chance of the tent collapsing if there was heavy snow before we returned in a week for hunting season. The pop tent was left erected, tucked under the drooping canopy of a very large white fir to keep it from collapsing under a heavy snowfall. We rode out the next morning, trailing three empty packhorses, and enjoyed an uneventful ride to the trailhead.

OCTOBER 24, 1989

Well before first light we had the horses saddled and loaded into Bill's thirty-year-old Chevy horse truck and my horse trailer behind my three-quarter-ton, four-wheel-drive Ford pickup. Then things started to go wrong. An inside tire on the dually setup on Bill's truck was going flat. We unloaded the horses, jacked up the truck, and got the tire off, and headed to Les Schwab's tire store. We had to wait an hour for the store to open and another half hour for the repair.

Now we were already two hours behind schedule. We climbed out of the Grande Ronde Valley on a road headed for the Eagle Cap Wilderness in the Wallowa-Whitman National Forest. The road, with switchback after switchback, led high into the Wallowa Mountains. Soon we encountered increasing snow depths, which made it necessary to chain up the rear tires on Bill's horse truck. That done, we were now three hours behind schedule.

I was convinced that with my Ford pickup with four-wheel drive and a mega engine, I could get through the pass and to the USFS campground at the ridgetop without the aid of chains. Halfway up, we came upon a pickup truck pulling a horse trailer that had jackknifed and was blocking the road. Once I came to a stop, I could not regain traction. There was no option but to chain up all four wheels. That done, we were four and a half hours behind schedule.

We discussed chaining up the wheels on the horse trailer to make sure the it would track behind the truck with no danger of sliding off the road into the borrow ditch. But we figured it wasn't far to the top and decided we could make it. Then I came to another pickup and horse trailer that was stuck half on and half off the road. When I came to a stop, the horse trailer slid sideways into the borrow ditch. Yet another bad decision.

First, we worked with the guys in the truck that was off the road ahead of us. When we got them back on the road and headed downhill, we turned back to our problem.

We unloaded the horses, which was not easy and really quite dangerous, as the horse trailer was tilted at least thirty degrees. However, once the horses were unloaded, I could pull the horse trailer back up onto the road without difficulty. Clearly we needed to chain up the tires on the trailer. Once that was accomplished, we reloaded the horses and proceeded on our journey.

Now we were nearly seven hours behind schedule, and it was after two o'clock in the afternoon. We had planned to be encamped by this time and toasting our toes by the fire. The going the rest of the way to the trailhead was slow, tricky, and more than a tad hazardous. Once there, we unloaded and saddled the horses. The packhorses were loaded with pelleted horse feed, sleeping bags, and our personal gear. Finally, we were ready to get on the trail nine hours behind schedule and we had not eaten for ten hours. The snow was coming down soft and heavy—and piling up fast. The trail was easy to follow, as the horse traffic into the wilderness had been ongoing all day. We made steady progress, stopping only once to tighten cinches and britchens and adjust packs.

Bill was riding in the lead with his chin on his chest so that his hat brim would more or less keep the heavy blowing snow out of his face when his gelding, Keno, suddenly left the main trail and headed for camp, picking his way through a decadent stand of mature lodgepole pines. Many of the pines, which had succumbed to attack by mountain pine beetles, lay jackstrawed on the ground and made the going difficult. When we came to the Minam River, the horses broke through the ice lining the banks to reach our campsite on the other bank.

Neither Bill nor I could see much in the blowing snow, but Bill's horse Keno knew exactly where he was and came to a stop in front of the tent we had left collapsed a week earlier. We dropped the manty packs off the horses, tied them on a picket line, and considered our next move. We scraped the half foot of snow off the flattened tent, fitted the ridgepole and tent poles together, and raised the tent.

Bill said he would unsaddle the horses and take them to water and give them their well-earned rations of alfalfa pellets. I was assigned the task of getting the tent set up, building a fire in the Sims stove, and fetching water. Thirty or so minutes later Bill arrived back at the tent after tending to the horses. There was no fire in the stove, no buckets filled with water, and no mixed drink of rum and Tang waiting—and no Jack.

He called out for me and got no response. He called again and set out to look for me. He spotted my headlamp about fifty yards from camp. I was told later that I was picking up wood, very slowly and deliberately, and adding it to the bundle cradled in my left arm. He could see that I was dropping as much wood as I was picking up. Clearly there was something wrong.

Bill asked, "Are you okay?" I didn't respond and kept on picking up and dropping small sticks of wood. He asked again, "Jack, are you okay? I didn't answer and kept on picking up and dropping wood. He stepped directly in front of me and asked again, louder this time, "Jack, are you okay?"

I tried to focus on his face and told him I felt really funny—shaky and weak and quite sweaty. There was clearly something seriously wrong with me.

Bill took me by the arm and guided me the seventy or so yards to the tent. It had been more than sixteen hours since we had eaten. I sat down in the floor of the tent with the wood I had gathered still cradled in my left arm. Bill fired up the Coleman lantern and got a fire going in the stove. He asked, "Do you have any idea what's wrong with you? Do you hurt?"

I thought deeply about his question. I told him that I thought maybe that I was dehydrated. I was definitely very cold, and at the same time very sweaty, and having a hard time focusing. Bill figured that I needed to warm up, drink some water, and get a shot of energy. The fire roaring in the Sims stove was warming up the tent—and fast. Bill went to the river and came back with two buckets of water—one he put on the stove to heat. He figured that a hot Tang, loaded with sugar and rum, might well cure whatever ailed me.

He went to the supply tent to get one of the aluminum canisters of rum and a container of Tang. It was then that he discovered the back of the supply tent had been ripped open. I heard could hear him cursing and saying that we had been raided by a bear—a "Gawd-damned bear"—as he so gently put it.

He came back holding the mutilated container with the remnants of the Tang supply. He figured that there was enough left for a few drinks. Then he delivered the really bad news: the bear had bitten a hole in one of the one aluminum bottles that contained the rum supply. The bear's bite had punched one hole in the bottle and, evidently not relishing the taste, had dropped the bottle. It had landed in the chuck box with the hole upward, the only possible position that prevented the contents from completely draining out. The Lord of the Hunt must have smiled, as the bear shifted its attention to chewing on the aluminum cook kit and spared the other container of rum.

At that point it became apparent that the marauding bear had bitten into a pressurized can of gun oil, which, we guessed, must have resulted in a small explosion of gun oil into the bear's mouth. That probably discouraged the bear from biting into the tin cans of food supply, but the bursting of the oil container must have set off a temper tantrum. Canned goods and cooking utensils were scattered about, and the bear had exited the supply tent by ripping a back door through the tent's rear wall. We had been deprived of our full supply of medicinal rum, nearly all of our Tang supply, and our supply of gun oil.

Bill fixed me a cocktail of brandy and Tang (which was mostly sugar). One was good and two was better. It was the right "medicine," as I began to feel much better and the brain fog dissipated. I cooked us a supper of pork chops, mashed potatoes, and gravy.

In reconstructing things, I concluded that my symptoms indicated that I had suffered from a combination of dehydration and significant hypoglycemia (low blood sugar). That backcountry diagnosis told me I needed to see a doctor when we got home. I suspected type 2 diabetes, from which both my father and grandfather had suffered. I was pretty sure that my diagnosis was correct, though I thought surely there were easier and less dangerous ways for me to get the message. Now I needed to decide if my "sinking spell" was serious enough for me to give up our hunt and get myself back to town. In the course of that deliberation we ate supper and had a couple of more Tangs. That combination seemed to cure what ailed me, and there was no further discussion of heading for home.

OCTOBER 25, 1989

Still a little shaky on my pins, I spent the day watching the snowslide above camp in case a bull elk might wander by. That didn't work out. As I returned to camp, an hour or so after the sun dropped below the canyon wall, I saw lantern light emanating from an old surplus Army squad tent in a lodgepole thicket across the Minam River from our camp. I decided to see if anybody was home and, in the process, maybe bum a cup of coffee. When I got within fifty yards, I "helloed" the camp, and a fellow pilgrim threw back the tent flap and invited me in. He handed me a tin cup of coffee before I even asked.

My host was a volunteer with the USFS, and was, therefore, something of a brother in service. A hunting party that had camped nearby during an earlier hunting season had killed two elk and wanted to lighten their load for the trip home. So they had left my new friend their leftover tucker, which included three full quarts of exceptionally cheap bourbon. And, praise be to the gods, our new friend identified himself as a recovering alcoholic and said he would be pleased if I removed the temptation. He also offered whatever of the left-behind supplies I needed or wanted. I was able to replenish or replace the items our friendly bear had eaten or trashed—flour, sugar, and, believe it or not, a quart jar of Tang. I loaded my booty into an empty burlap feed sack and extended my hand in thanks and invited our fellow wilderness sojourner to supper. I headed for the river crossing.

Bill was in camp, and there were a couple of horses saddled and tied nearby. When I whistled, Bill came out of the tent, mounted up, and rode across the river, towing my saddle horse to give me a ride. He didn't ask me what was in my poke, which I had tied to my McClellan saddle. I didn't offer an explanation.

After we unsaddled and brushed the horses, we went to the tent. I dropped my burlap poke in the middle of the floor and poured myself a cup of coffee. Bill kept eying my poke but refused to ask me what was inside. Game on! Bill kept looking at the bag, and I pretended not to notice. Finally Bill asked, "I see you have something in that bag."

"Yep," I nodded.

"Something you found?"

"Yep," I nodded.

"It looks heavy."

A couple of minutes of silence passed. Bill broke down. "Damn it, what you got in the poke?"

I carefully dumped out the contents, including the three quarts of cheap bourbon.

Bill's eyes got even larger as he sorted through the contents. "Where in hell did you get all of this stuff, especially the whiskey?" I started out to spin a yarn about walking back out to the trailhead or maybe robbing a fellow traveler at gunpoint. Then I decided that the truth was implausible and entertaining enough and require no embellishment. I put the additions to our grocery supply away and prepared us a couple of drinks of Tang and exceedingly cheap bourbon. Bill smacked his lips. After a second round, we formulated a hypothesis that the intrinsic quality of liquor increases in a positive correlation with the distance to a licensed purveyor of spirits.

As the chill left my bones and chicken-fried steak sizzled on the Sims stove, I conjured up the "Hallelujah Chorus" from memory. I was almost ready to forgive the bear its trespasses. Sleep came quickly and easily. Hallelujah! Somehow, I just knew we had an appointment with a couple of cow elk upon the mountain on the morrow. Hallelujah! After all, all good things come to those who wait. Hallelujah!

OCTOBER 26, 1989

We were awake before dawn and quickly dressed. Bill crawled out of the tent without a jacket and with his boots unlaced to answer nature's call and immediately went from a crawl to flat on his belly. Crawling backward into the tent, he whispered that there was a cow elk and a calf grazing in the meadow across the river less than 200 yards away. Then he belly-crawled to where our rifles, in their scabbards, were leaning against a tree and covered by a manty tarp. Carefully, carefully he slid his 9mm old German Army Mauser out from under the tarp. He eased the rifle out of the scabbard, slowly and quietly worked the bolt to seat a round in the chamber, worked his left arm into the sling, and assumed a picture-perfect prone position. In short order, he fired, and the cow humped up and dropped stone dead. The calf, seemingly confused, ran into the trees and then came back for another look before disappearing for good.

When we checked out the cow, it was obvious that Bill had made a perfect heart shot and there was no need to attempt to bleed her out. We went back to the tent, started a fire in the stove, and made coffee, soon followed by a celebratory breakfast. After the dishes were washed and put away, we dressed out, skinned, and quartered the cow where she lay. The quarters, neck, liver, and the intact part of the heart were put in cotton meat sacks and pulled up into a big ponderosa pine tree.

Bill's hunt was over while mine was just beginning. I made myself a lunch, gathered up my gear and my Winchester .30-06 featherweight rifle, and started my climb up from the river to the timberline. Elk sign was plentiful, though I encountered no elk during my slow climb, punctuated by numerous stops to look and listen—and to catch my breath.

I spent most of the day moving slowly along the scattered trees at or near the timberline. By noon I had encountered two bulls—one spike and one small branch antlered bull—that would have been almost certain kills. But this trip they were off-limits as I (fortunately?) had a cow tag. At midafternoon it was time to start working my way back toward camp. In the process I encountered two magnificent mule deer bucks that had delayed their departure from the high lonesome down to their winter range. I watched them for a while through my rifle scope and took several imaginary shots. My aim was impeccable. The bucks didn't seem to notice.

It was time to head for camp. I hit the Minam River trail with maybe twenty minutes of shooting time left. It was that magic time that many elk and deer hunters call the "witching hour." Given the horse traffic along the Minam River Trail, I really didn't expect to encounter any elk on the rest of the way to camp. I was wrong and heard elk coming down the trail before I saw them. I stepped behind a huge ponderosa pine beside the trail, braced against the tree, and aimed down the trail. Less than a minute later, and not more than fifty yards away, six elk appeared, walking single file with a big cow in the lead. For some reason, the lead cow stopped and threw up her head to look and listen. I aimed just under her chin and squeezed off a round. She collapsed like a puppet with the strings cut.

As it was less than three-quarters of a mile to camp and I was feeling a bit shaky, I decided to go for help before taking on the chore of dressing out and quartering the cow. When I got to camp, Bill had already saddled up four horses—two saddle horses and two pack-horses—based on the probability that the single shot had been mine. I took time for a cup of coffee laced with a shot of brandy and ate some summer sausage and crackers and a Baby Ruth candy bar before heading back up the trail to where my cow elk was awaiting attention.

Two hunters working on gutting, skinning, quartering, and bundling the meat into manty packs made that effort much safer, easier, and quicker than working alone. We had been very lucky. In only two days of hunting, we had our winter's meat supply in hand. As it was plenty cold enough to keep the elk carcasses from spoiling and the weather was good, we could pack up and head out tomorrow; it would take two trips to the trailhead to get our gear and the two elk to the trucks. Or, as nobody expected us home soon and we had plenty of supplies, we could choose to stay over another three or four days and simply enjoy the wilderness.

After we got to camp, hung up the elk quarters, and took care of the horses, we had a long evening of washing up, cooking, eating, cleaning up, and telling hunting stories—today's and yesterday's. Supper was fried elk liver and heart, potatoes and gravy, sliced onions, and biscuits, with coffee laced with brandy—before, during, and after. The Lord of the Hunt had indeed been kind to us this year: we had both killed nice mule deer bucks during the deer season and now two fat cow elk. We were appreciative.

OCTOBER 27, 1989

During breakfast we discussed our options. We concluded that it would be wise to pack out the elk today using both saddle horses and packhorses to do the job—we would pack all the horses with elk quarters, lead them out to the trailhead, and ride back. We were on the trail by midmorning on foot and taking our time. We "tailed" our packed saddle horses on the uphill portions of the trail—i.e., we held onto the horses' tails and let them pull us along, which served to "flatten out" the steep inclines. The saddle horses had been trained to this maneuver and responded to voice commands in the process.

We had no problems getting to the trailhead and hanging the elk in my horse trailer. We were joined by a couple of old-timers; they were tending camp for their sons, who had hunted out from the trailhead on foot. They kindly invited us over to their camp trailer to warm up and partake of some hot coffee with a whiskey chaser. It "went down real good," as our hosts put it.

We left our elk hanging in the horse trailer, mounted up, and headed back to camp, arriving just as the sun dipped below the mountain. The pressure was off. Our wood supply was in and covered. There was clean, clear water less than thirty yards away. There was plenty of pelleted feed for the horses. We had way more than enough to eat in camp and plenty of time to cook. The coffee and very cheap bourbon supply was bountiful. And there were stories to tell—and there was time to just stare into the fire and remember.

OCTOBER 28, 1989

We spent the day riding deeper and deeper into the core of the Eagle Cap Wilderness and then back to camp. We encountered six different outfits along the trail as they headed out for the trailhead. Some were packing elk. Most were not. We met one party of six young men on foot backpacking the boned-out meat from two cow elk that they had harvested. I thought I could remember what it was to be that young and that strong. We stopped and visited with each set of pilgrims and traded stories of triumph and disappointment. These men did not seem like strangers but rather fellow travelers engaged in an escape, however brief, from reality—or just maybe it was an escape to reality.

Was this reality, and what lay down below "where the people is" the escape from reality? By late afternoon, more and more clouds were scudding across darkening skies. There was both increasing cold and the likelihood of snow blowing in on the wind. When we got to camp, we concluded that tomorrow was as good time as any to head for home. We had two elk hanging in my horse trailer at the trailhead and a couple of days of riding the high lonesome to our credit. We concluded it was time to "git while the gittin's good."

OCTOBER 29, 1989

The winds blew all night with an increasing howling vengeance that threatened the tent more than once. We heard a couple of trees crash to the ground over the course of the night. At first light the snow was blowing sideways. It was, as Bill put it, indeed "time to get our happy asses down the hill." We ate a cold breakfast of *charqui* and leftover biscuits—and wrapped up a couple of biscuits apiece to put in our saddlebags for emergency rations.

The wind and the occasional racket of a tree crashing to the ground during the long night had made both us and the horses nervous, but the saddling and packing went without a serious hitch. We scattered what remained of the alfalfa cubes as a parting gift to the deer and elk and set out for the trailhead.

The horses seemed to know that their work for this year would soon be over and from now to spring it would easy living on hay with the barn to shelter them from the weather. It was not necessary to stop to give the horses a breather on the way out. They knew we were headed for the barn, and clearly wanted to get there.

CHAPTER 6

"DID YOU SEE ANYTHING?"—YES, NOTHING AND EVERYTHING

ill Brown and I had lost the services of our two top pack-horses for several weeks due to wire cuts. That left us to do some fancy figuring on how to provide for the two USFS guests we had invited for a backcountry deer hunt in the Eagle Cap Wilderness. Our final solution was that Bill and I would pack the tents, our possibles, groceries, and other camp gear to our selected campsite the day before our guests arrived. We would set up the tents, store the gear inside, gather firewood, and ride back out to the trailhead. The next day we would return with our guests, John Butruille, regional forester for the USFS Pacific Northwest Region, and Lamar Beasley, director of the Southern Forest Experiment Station. Our camp, at the juncture of the Minam River and Frazier Pass trails, was four hours by horse from the trailhead at Two Pan on the Lostine River. That distance was short enough to allow us to make an easy round trip from camp to the trailhead in one day. Therefore, we could outfit their hunt even while being short a couple of horses.

SEPTEMBER 27, 1990

We were enjoying Indian summer at its best. The day was bright, clear, and warm with just enough wind to whisper seductively from the spruce thickets. When we arrived at our campsite, it was obvious that no one had camped here since Bill and I hunted elk out of the camp two years ago. The pile of wood—all cut to stove length—remained just as we had left it. Water was running in a narrow incised channel only fifty feet away.

With the water so close and with a wood supply already in hand, it didn't take long to set up camp and take care of the horses. There was very little conversation while we watched the shadows play on the granite peaks that loomed above camp as the sun went down.

We noted several saplings that were the worse for wear as the result of uncontested combat with a rutting bull elk—or was it a mule deer buck? From nearby, we could hear a bull—maybe the one that had damaged the trees—squealing and grunting in the gloaming. It was good to know that there was at the very least one bull elk within hunting distance of camp.

This is my fifty-sixth birthday. Just being here with my good friend Bill is gift enough!

SEPTEMBER 28, 1990

Off and on during the night, we heard a bull elk squeal—whether in lust or in protest of our preemption of his courting grounds, we didn't know. Sometime in the very early morning and after the moon set, the call of nature coaxed me outside the tent. The display of stars in the crystal-clear sky—without the lights of civilization to interfere—was indeed awesome. An elk, maybe the elk, squealed from very nearby. I convinced myself that I could see him against the spruce thicket slightly uphill from camp—but then again, maybe not.

It really didn't matter. He was out there somewhere in the starlight, and it made for a very special moment. I stood stock-still and looked and listened until the cold drove me back into the tent. My breath was smoking in the cold.

On our ride from camp to pick up John and Lamar at the trailhead, we met several horse outfits and a dozen hardy young men on foot with backpacks and rifles on the way to their hunting grounds. They were young and strong and testing themselves. I wondered if they knew how lucky they were to be so able, young, and eager and to have such a place as this in which to be all of that. I wondered, would they take the time and trouble to hold on to what they would experience today for their sons and daughters—and their offspring? Would they even think of such matters? While I had my doubts, I hoped so. We arrived at the trailhead at noon, and our guests drove up just shy of a half hour later.

We switched the saddles on two of the horses—McClellan cavalry saddles from the early 1900s replaced the pack saddles. They could be both ridden and packed. The four of us had an easy ride back to camp and arrived with ample daylight remaining to enjoy the evening. And we most certainly did just that. As the stew simmered on the sheepherder stove, we sipped coffee and relived our salad days when we were all more eager and simple souls—new to the conservation game—and convinced that we knew what was right and that we could change things for the better. Now, after a collective 150 years or so of experience in conservation work, we had learned a few lessons and were a bit more humble. This was a convening of old scarred warriors, each with "war stories" to tell involving small victories and sore losses—along with great experiences and adventures. We were kindred spirits. The old veteran's talk was warm and comfortable and came easily.

Sitting on campstools around the campfire, we talked late into the night until heads began to nod. We were all eager for our sleeping bags, but no one wanted to be the first to break the spell. Then, as if responding to some silent signal, we all rose, more or less simultaneously, and went to our tents.

SEPTEMBER 29, 1990

Twice during the night, I awakened just enough to hear elk close by. I imagined that it was the bull that had done battle with the young spruce. In my mind's eye I could just barely make him out in the meadow, bathed in the moonlight and studying our camp and the intruders into his wilderness therein. Then sleep came and I dreamed no more.

The next thing I heard was the steam-train-like huffing coming from the sheepherder stove as it demanded more air for the hot fire than the vent hole in the door could provide. The base of stovepipe glowed dull red, and Bill was sitting up, fully clothed, and tugging on his boots.

I pulled my sleeping bag up over my head and waited for the heat from the stove to fill the tent. It was a delicious moment. From far up the valley wall there came one last squeal from the bull that was growing ever bigger and—in my mind—more bountifully supplied with antlers.

Breakfast was quickly prepared—and just as quickly consumed. We were eager to be away on our individual hunts. We talked last night, as old hunters do, of how just getting away from the world down below and the experience of the hunt was really everything. The hunting—and certainly the killing—was secondary. We lied. The hunt was indeed of the essence, but the kill was important too. But why? I no longer cared to examine the question too closely, having done so too many times in the past without reaching a final resolution. There was probably no one answer that fit all hunters. Hunting—with success in mind—was simply part of who and what I am. Or perhaps it was but part of some age-old ritual passed down through generations that I do not pretend to understand. For whatever reason, hunting is part of me—an important part. That was enough for me. I thought that sometimes I spent too much time questioning and reexamining things. Some things should simply be accepted and experienced for what they are. But didn't some philosopher say that "the unexamined life is not worth living"?

Today I saw a snowshoe hare sitting tight in its hiding place, and I eased closer and closer until I could have reached out touched it with the barrel of my rifle. Its coat was a mottled mix of its grayish summer coat and the emerging snow-white coat of winter. But at the moment the emerging white fur was highly and most inconveniently conspicuous. This seemed a most excellent place to eat my lunch. Two gray jays suddenly appeared to share my repast. Three pine squirrels ran the length of a log that I was leaning against; obviously more intent on procreation than on whatever danger I might pose.

Twice, very early in the day, I heard geese honking as they passed overhead on their way to warmer climes. As I squatted down to fill my canteen from the Minam River, a water shrew came out to see what was going on. I followed the tracks of some elk cows and calves for a while. Twice I could hear them moving ahead of me through the trees but never saw them. They talked cow-calf talk as they moved. With the sun at my back, I could see the sunlight glistening off the dribbles of their urine on the vegetation that they left behind—perhaps a mechanism to keep their social groups intact?

I slept briefly in the sun and then woke to build a small fire so I could warm myself. I encountered a marten track in the trail and a cougar track by a spring. The wind whispered to me from the spruces along the ridge. I found a wallow where a bull elk, perhaps the one of my musings, had rubbed and thrashed a nearby sapling. Once I thought I could smell a bear, but wasn't sure.

On the trail back to camp, I met a young hunter. We stood in the trail and passed the time of day. He said that these days he hailed from California but reluctantly admitted that he didn't like it much because there were too many "gooks," "greasers," "niggers," "chinks," and "rednecks"—in addition to being too crowded and too expensive. I could only imagine what he thought of me as I responded to his comments in an exaggerated Texas drawl. He seemed to be a spiritually bankrupt man very unsure of his own worth.

He did not speak at all of what he had seen and felt and smelled and heard today. He said that he "hadn't seen anything"—by which, I supposed, he meant a buck deer. When he asked if I had seen anything, I told him of some of the things that I had seen: sunrise, mist rising from the river, wind stirring in the trees, fish rising in the river, and various other things seen and felt and smelled. He looked at me as if he had encountered a very weird old man with white hair and stubble and a strange accent. That, I supposed, was reasonable enough to surmise.

The poor man, I thought. He had no idea what hunting—especially hunting in the wilderness—should be all about. He brought his everyday problems—and his hatreds, perceptions, and prejudices—with him into the wilderness. He just couldn't let them go, not even in this place for this brief moment. He had eyes but did not see. He had a soul but did not feel. He had a brain but did not comprehend. But he was very young and strong and there was time for him to learn. I wished him luck as we parted, both in terms of the hunt and in terms of life.

As the day faded into twilight, the members of our party wandered into camp, one by one, from various directions. As hunters do, without speaking we casually checked out one another for blood on hands or clothes. There was none—not a speck in the whole bunch. But each hunter—each seeker—was animated and alive in the moment. Each told of the things seen, smelled, and felt. Obviously, each had found at least some of what he had sought in this place. Each had hunted and in his own way for his own reasons. For real hunters, there is so much more to the hunt than bringing an animal to bag, though each of us would have killed, and without hesitation, given the opportunity and the appropriate circumstances. The important thing was not the killing—or the lack thereof. That importance was, simply enough, being in the moment. And, after all, tomorrow was another day, and out there somewhere, waiting, was the buck—and the moment—that we each sought.

SEPTEMBER 30, 1990

It was still dark when we picked up our hunting packs and rifles and left the tent, having enjoyed a breakfast of ham and pancakes and sufficient coffee. The stars seemed to crackle in electrical intensity in the clear, cold, still sky. It was dead still, and the smoke from the stovepipe went straight up. The crunch of the frosty vegetation underfoot seemed quite loud as I walked across the meadow, carrying my hunting pack and rifle, to intersect the trail that would lead me up over Frazier Pass and into the West Eagle Creek drainage.

Upon reaching Frazier Pass, I intended to contour around the mountain just at tree line to Pup Lake arriving just before sunrise. There I would await the mule deer buck that somehow I knew was on the way to meet me.

The trail was steep and created more to sheepherder standards—the shortest distance between two points being a straight line—than to the specifications in the USFS manual about appropriate grade. When dawn glowed orange in the eastern sky, I was nearing the pass. Early on, I had shed my woolen jacket and tied it onto my pack. My wool and cotton shirts were unbuttoned to my waist to vent heat. When I stopped to catch my breath, which was more and more frequent as the elevation increased and the slope steepened, steam rose from my bald head and open shirt front. My breath formed clouds of vapor as I exhaled from the bottom of my lungs—it felt good. At each stop to catch my breath and ease the burning in my thighs, I rested for only for a moment, as I knew the sun was coming. And I was in a hurry to keep an appointment that I somehow felt was imminent with a four-point mule deer buck in the meadow below Pup Lake. It would not do for me to be late.

But when I arrived at the lake about a half hour after first light, the buck was not there. Had I missed my appointment? I was disappointed. Yet all was not lost. There were elk there in the deer's stead, a five-point bull, three cows, and two calves. Though there was sunlight shining bright on the mountainside, the meadow was still in deep shadow and the ground cover was heavy with frost. The elks' breaths smoked and hung briefly in the cold, still air.

The mental games commenced—"doing the math." I computed the distance to the bull elk at somewhere around 300 yards. I could lie down on my belly, snap down the bipod on my rifle, compute the point of aim, and squeeze off a shot. I felt that I could put him down. But I also knew that doing so was far from a sure thing—the distance was too great and I might just wound the magnificent animal. So, for me, taking the shot would be unacceptable or even unethical. I sat down and pulled my binoculars out of my jacket. There was, after all, more than one kind of trophy.

Sometimes trophies of memory are the most significant of all. This was such a moment. I sat down cross-legged and watched the bull through my binoculars. Some time passed, I had no idea how much, before I realized that I was uncomfortably cold and getting colder as the body heat generated during my climb and sequestered inside my shirts turned to a slowly, chilling damp. If I moved to button my shirts, shuck my pack, and retrieve and don my wool coat, the elk would almost surely see me and the magic moment would end. There would be time for such things—including a warming fire— when the magic moment came to its inevitable end.

Then, from far away down the Minam Canyon, came the re-verberating echoes of a rifle shot and then another and another and another and another—five shots in all. The sounds, which rolled up the canyon and ricocheted back and forth between the walls, were too closely spaced to be those of an experienced rifleman. There was inadequate time between the shots to allow for well-considered, care-fully aimed, deliberately squeezed-off shots. From the absence of a "whomp" sound of a large-caliber bullet striking a big animal, I con-cluded that all the bullets had missed their target.

The elk I was watching raised their heads at the far-off sound of the gunfire and resumed picking their way across the meadow, grazing here and there en route. When they disappeared into the trees bringing the magic moment to an end, I became aware that I was shivering and my teeth were chattering. It was time to button my shirts, don my heavy jacket, and get a warming fire started. Soon I sat under overhanging spruce boughs hunkered over with a small fire and waited for the sun to ascend well above the mountain's rim. With the rising sun, a slight breeze moved the smoke column as the sun heated the granite walls that loomed above. The breeze produced ripples on Pup Lake.

Often a magic moment comes just at daylight when the world of wildlife suddenly comes most fully alive. The creatures of the night can still be heard and seen and the creatures of the day are com-ing fully awake. Birds' songs are heard—from how far depending on the volume of their songs and the vegetation and the topography. Up close, there is a flutter here, a scurry there, a rustle over there. For a perceptive hunter this is the moment of maximum awareness. I never felt more intensely alive and aware when hunting than just at daylight—and, again, just at dusk. Was this moment of enhanced awareness—what my grandfather called the "magic witching hour"— what I sought even more than the deer or elk that I pursued? Yes, I thought, yes!

I shut my eyes and listened. I could hear the myriad wildlife sounds, the movement of air whispering through the trees, my own heart beating in my ears, and my breathing. I could feel the sun be-gin to warm my face while the cold ground still sapped heat from my body. At this moment it seemed possible to feel both small and insignificant and very large at the same time, as a part of a perceived, integrated whole that I could sense but not pretend to understand. Such magic moments must have evolved, I thought, from untold eons of struggle, of trial and error, and of constant change. And likely that goes on and on and on. It was but a split second in the scheme of things, but "we"—me and the wildlife—were here in the moment. That was something to be savored—that truly magic moment—even if not fully understood.

My hearing has been much diminished by the gradual onset of "olditis" and too much exposure to loud noises—aircraft engines, construction sounds, explosions, and far too much gunfire, among other things. The doctor had told me precisely how much my hearing had been affected. Yet as I sat here in this time and place with my eyes shut and listening with my being, it seemed that I could hear everything! It didn't matter if that were true—the feeling was everything. Perhaps the way we perceive our individual world is like that. Over time, what we lose from our natural world is so gradual that we do not perceive what is happening, neither seeing nor feeling the gradual loss.

Each new generation starts anew with a given situation—a starting point—not really knowing from personal experience what went before. Surely, many of those fortunate enough to have known the flights of the passenger pigeons or the moving masses of buffalo on the Great Plains missed them when they were gone. Perhaps even their children missed them when they watched the faces and heard the voices and tales of those who had actually witnessed those events and creatures. But, given time, "the missing" disappeared from current consciousness.

There were those who knew firsthand that the earth had been diminished by the extinction of the passenger pigeon and the reduction of the buffalo to a remnant few that survive at the pleasure of man. But to know and to feel are very different things. But, unlike my hearing, the situation for wildlife and what it represents can be improved. The ecosystems—the parts and pieces that still exist—can be sustained and even restored to some extent.

I belong to a profession that has had much success in restoring wildlife, admittedly accompanied by many failures. In the beginning it was essential to convince enough people that such things were important before progress could be made in saving wild places and wild things.

Again, I felt content, at least for this brief moment. It was in such moments of contentment that have made it possible to endure the sieges of discontent that have come along with too many losses and failures. It is these moments beside the still waters in the high wilderness that, indeed, restoreth my soul. I remained in this beautiful place until just past midday on the off chance that a big buck would appear in the meadow.

By noon, the sunlight coming from a perfectly clear sky and reflecting off the white granite rocks warmed my nook in the rocks and rendering me irresistibly sleepy. As I dozed off, an insect awakened by the warming sunlight from the immobility imposed by the cold of night buzzed about my head. It was likely that this was its last flight before tonight's frost would end its life. But for this moment, we—the insect and I—each enjoyed the warmth of the sun and our beings in our own ways.

As the sun moved across the sky, I found myself in deep shadow; the mountain looming above me had come between the sun and my hiding/resting place in the rocks. I was awakened by the sudden cold. The insects had descended from flight, perhaps for their last time. It was time to fish out my lunch sack buried deep in my hunting pack and build a small fire to heat water in a tin cup for tea. My lunch—cold biscuits, bacon, and a thick slice of onion with hot tea to moisten its passage—seemed a banquet. There was no one present to object to the smell of onions on my breath save my insect friend now sitting immobilized on a rock; it didn't seem to mind. The hours passed quickly.

A family of red-tailed hawks—two adults and two young of the year—twisted and turned above the meadow. Off to the south I heard an elk squealing. Very late in the day, some Canada geese passed over, talking their goose talk on their way south. Though I couldn't locate them in the darkening sky, I visualized their vee formation.

It was past time to strike out for camp. It would be best, I thought, to have my feet on Frazier Trail before full darkness arrived. Darkness and my arrival on Frazier Trail came simultaneously—and none too soon. The soles of my feet were hot and my ankles trembling from contouring around the very steep mountainside. Now that I was on the trail, it should be comparatively easy going to camp. When I was a half mile above camp, I could hear voices and laughter from down below disturbing the stillness. Soon I saw the nylon tent glowing bright green and white from the light of the Coleman lantern within.

John and Lamar were already in camp as Bill and I arrived at essentially the same time from different directions. Each of us told his individual story in words that said, one way or another, "I didn't see a legal deer, but I had a great day." What we really meant was that we all saw a hundred things, smelled smells, heard sounds, felt the sun and wind, and were alone and able to think—and, by the way, we didn't see any deer that we could legally shoot. And, we concluded, all things considered, it had been a very good day. Why do we more mature hunters so seldom say what we really mean? Maybe such was not necessary between *compadres* as it was simply understood. Such feelings could only be cheapened by words.

OCTOBER 1, 1990

Winter, tardy though it was, had arrived during the night. Near midnight, intermittent winds began to whip the tents. When the call of nature obliged me to briefly exit the tent, I noted the mares' tails skittering across the face of the moon. When I treated myself to a drink of water, there was ice on the water in the bucket. Winter comes early and stays long above 7,000 feet. After I snuggled back into my sleeping bag, I zipped the bag up to the top and tied the hood over my head and around my face. Sleep came along with the sound of sleet rattling against the plastic tent fly.

Day arrived cold and gray. The grasses and trees glistened with ice crystals. Yesterday was, almost certainly, the last day for my insect friend that had buzzed around me as I slept in the sun yesterday. It seemed strange that I would think about that.

Today's world, high in the Eagle Cap Wilderness, was much different from yesterday's. The woods were quieter. Had the birds left for warmer environs? Certainly not all: the gray jays joined me for lunch. Now the woods increasingly belonged to them and a few other stalwarts. But very soon they too would have to give in to the reality that winter had come and move down slope and, maybe, south.

A large owl brushed past my head on my way back to camp. Its flight was silent, as the special feather arrangement unique to owls dampened the sounds of its flight. I felt, more than heard, the owls' passage in the gloaming. Death must come to an owl's prey like that—silent, sudden, and very final.

When I arrived my fellow hunters were already in camp. Smoke was pluming from the stovepipe. Hot coffee was welcome, as was the warmth of the tent. The evening passed pleasantly. Conversation soon turned to old times and old friends. The professional natural resource management fraternity is really quite small. And old pros have many of the same friends and colleagues—and adversaries—in common. We talked of those friends and lifted a few toasts—to remembered hunts, victories, defeats, good times and bad, and to *compadres* gone on to their final rewards. Finally, lifting his cup in salute, Bill said, "To absent friends." To which John replied, "To friends who are never absent." I wished I had thought of that—I would remember.

OCTOBER 2, 1990

We were going out today—back to the "real world." As soon as their personal gear was packed and breakfast was finished, John and Lamar struck out on foot for the trailhead, carrying their hunting packs and rifles—just in case they had to fight off an unexpected molestation by a big mule deer buck somewhere along the trail.

Two and a half hours later, Bill and I had made up the manty packs and lashed them onto the Decker pack saddles, snapped on the panniers, loaded the top packs, tied down the covering manties, saddled our riding horses, and were ready to move out for the trailhead. We figured the temperature to be somewhere around zero, maybe less. We had on all the clothes we had brought with us and wished for more—at least I did. When we crossed over the pass at Minam Lake, it was snowing and the ground was lightly powdered. As we moved on over the top and started down toward the Lostine River, the temperature warmed quickly, which coupled with the increasing loss of elevation making the world a warmer and more hospitable place.

We were going home—and the horses knew it. Walkers and riders arrived at the Two Pan Campground within minutes of one another. Within a half hour, everything was loaded into the trucks, and we all departed for La Grande after agreeing to meet in Wallowa at the Eagle's Nest Cafe for lunch. The Eagle's Nest was noted for its cuisine—pretty much the only cuisine in town.

As we sipped some pretty stiff, very hot, very much anticipated coffee at the cafe, I spied a newspaper that had been abandoned on the lunch counter. The bold headline of the *Portland Oregonian* proclaimed, "Thomas Plan Wins." I studied John Butruille's face as he read the story. As the USFS's regional forester for the Pacific Northwest, he was on the hot seat to carry out the decision. I didn't think the "split the baby" decision described in the newspaper would stand up to court challenge—and I surmised that he thought the same. Clearly it was simply a ploy to "kick the can down the road" until after the upcoming presidential election. You have to love politics and politicians.

But, in the meantime, John would have to live every day with a decision that had been taken out of his most competent hands by the administration. However, in my opinion, he was the right person in the right place at the right time. If I had to pick the person to be regional forester in the Pacific Northwest at this moment, I would pick John Butruille. And, best of all, he wants to be exactly where he is.

Our hunt—for both deer and tranquility in the calm of the wilderness—was at an end. But maybe as a result of our wilderness interlude, we were a bit better prepared for the challenges ahead than we were before we headed into the Eagle Cap Wilderness.

CHAPTER 7

DESPACIO, DESPACIO—A MODEL FOR HUNTING (AND LIVING)

In the midst of taking two weeks of vacation time, I was on my way to Bill Brown's place to load up our horses and gear for an elk hunt in the Eagle Cap Wilderness when I dropped by my office at the Range and Wildlife Habitat Research Laboratory in La Grande to take a look at my mail. There were notes on my desk indicating that I had six calls from the media and a dozen or more from various members of Congress. I turned around and walked out of the office—I was on vacation, after all. This was my first break from work in nearly six weeks, which had consisted mostly of twelve-hour workdays. Significantly, there were only five days left in the elk-hunting season. After a tense but brief internalized debate, an escape to the wilderness for what remained of the hunting season emerged as the absolutely correct thing to do in order to preserve both sanity and long-term effectiveness.

OCTOBER 5, 1991

Bill and I got a late start and wouldn't get to our campsite until well after dark. When I arrived at Bill's house, he had everything loaded—including the horses in his horse truck and my horse trailer. We hooked the trailer onto my pickup and were off.

It had been a dry and unusually warm fall with daytime temperatures hitting the mid-eighties in La Grande. By the time we arrived at the trailhead and unloaded and packed the horses, there was a decided nip in the air. We set out up the trail toward Burger Pass with a six-horse string—two saddle horses and four packhorses. Bill, as usual, was riding in the lead. We were shy one horse. With my permission, Bill had given away Meg's twenty-year-old mare, "Old Kitty," to a young girl who had a love affair with horses. Kitty was still willing, but she wasn't as big and stout as the other horses and now struggled to keep up with the string, even when carrying only a light pack. She had a value of a few hundred dollars for slaughter. But she had served me, and especially Meg, for nearly fifteen years, and she had several more years left in her for a youngster who needed a horse with a gentle disposition.

The bottom line was that if Bill and I both killed an elk, we would be one packhorse short coming out. That meant that we would pack my mare, after converting my McClellan saddle for use as a pack saddle, and I would have to hump it out to the trailhead on foot. I chuckled when I told myself that this was a very good reason to be very careful not to slay more than one elk—if any at all.

The string traveled easy and fast with their packs riding steady. When we crossed Burger Pass, the wind was blowing a gale and the air was filled with dust. The trail was literally powder-dry, and the volcanic ash soil stirred up by the horses' hooves was whipped by the wind into swirls of dust making for most unpleasant traveling conditions. From time to time, we heard a tree crash to the ground. It did not set my mind at ease to look up and see the trees swaying wildly in the wind; a couple of times I saw the top of a tree snap off and get tossed aside by the wind. The wind seemed to increase incrementally as we climbed steadily toward the timberline.

In spite of the wind and an occasional tree down across the trail, we reached our campsite just below the timberline about an hour after full dark. Erecting the tent proved to be an exercise requiring patience and determination. Several times in the process we debated simply crawling into our sleeping bags, wrapping up in the tent, and waiting for daylight. In the meantime, we could only hope that the snow predicted for tonight would hold off until midmorning tomorrow. That seemed less and less likely as the night wore on.

After more than an hour of frustrating struggle, we got the tent up and adequately staked down to withstand the wind gusts. The night was pitch black, and our headlamps proved indispensable as we struggled with the chores at hand. With the tent up and the Sims stove in place, I gathered wood and Bill wrangled the horses. By the time Bill was finished with the horses, I had a fire going in the stove and coffee brewing. Once Bill was in the tent and everything was "buttoned up," the fire roaring in the stove and the hot coffee combined to work their magic. We felt warm and more or less secure. Those feelings persisted in spite of the unsettling wind gusts that threatened to lift the tent off its stakes.

The T-bone steaks were still frozen when they went on the griddle to thaw. By the time the steaks were ready, I realized I was simply too bushed to eat, after too many consecutive nights of inadequate sleep and too many days of stress. Keeping my wits about me and my temper under control had been exhausting. I sat down and pulled off my boots, stretched out on my sleeping pad, pulled my sleeping bag over me, and went to sleep while Bill was still eating—both his steak and some of mine.

It was an uneasy night as the wind alternatively died down to near stillness and then—from time to time—roared back to vigorous life. With each blast of wind the tent shuddered and the plastic fly stretched over the top snapped and popped. Over and over, we wondered if the next wind blast would bring the tent down. By morning, the wind had died down, and by some miracle the tent was still standing—if just barely. The tent was a sad sight, but it had done its job. The first chore of the new day was to put things right as far as our tent and camp went.

I fried up some bacon and eggs, toasted bread on the stove top, made coffee, and prepared our lunches while Bill tended the horses. We were ready, willing, and eager to pursue the wily elk a half hour before daybreak. We departed camp on foot in opposite directions in search of a fat cow elk—maybe two. By mutual agreement, any cows taken were to be killed near camp so that it would be easy to get to them with a packhorse. At least that was the admonition we each gave the other. We both knew better.

It was just common sense that, as Bill put it, "you kill elk where you hunt." In other words, if you don't hunt in excessively rugged places from which it is difficult to retrieve an elk, you won't have to face that problem. There was wisdom in that simple observation. But a few days into the hunting season, the elk seem to have that all figured out and head for the places where they are least likely to encounter the number one threat to their lives—a human predator with a rifle.

Just after dawn, I heard coyotes singing their songs back and forth across the Minam River, which lay some 1,500 feet below camp. I worked my way along the slope toward Granite Creek until I found what looked to be a perfect stand on the edge of a spruce thicket overlooking a large opening. The wind picked up, bringing a chill with it that marked the end of Indian summer. I untied my wool hunting coat from my hunting pack, snuggled in, and built a warming fire. The fire felt good. I crouched close.

The upslope breeze carried the smoke into the spruce stand behind me. As I became increasingly warm and comfortable, I began to nod and then doze until the sound of a twig snapping brought me wide awake. Whatever broke that twig was behind me and very close at hand. I turned slowly and carefully while bringing my .30-06 Winchester featherweight slowly to my shoulder.

Not seventy-five yards away stood a six-by-six bull elk that seemed to have been trailing the wood smoke from my warming fire. He had his head up and his nose into the wind. He was alone. I concentrated on him as he came on steadily and slowly toward me. It seemed odd that he couldn't smell me. Maybe, I thought, the wood smoke was masking my odor. Or maybe he had never scented a man before and did not yet associate the human smell with danger.

I was cursing fate as the cow tag in my wallet precluded me from dropping him where he stood. But maybe this was the better experience. I had killed more than several elk in my life, but I had never seen anything quite like this. The bull stopped every few steps and looked and listened. I had my rifle aimed at him now with the crosshairs of the 4-power scope centered right on his nose.

He was simply magnificent in his relatively new winter coat. His antlers were perfectly symmetrical with dark shafts and polished ivory tips. Now he was not more than fifty yards away. He was, by far, the most magnificent bull elk I had ever had in my sights. The wind shifted slightly, and I could smell him—a musky smell of urine and crushed spruce needles. He was maleness, wildness, and mystery, all mixed into one. He was, I thought, the essence of this place—his place. Was I the intruder? Or did I, of an equally ancient predator line, belong here as much as he?

Then as I studied him, he became aware of my presence, seemingly by sorting out my smell from that of the wood smoke. I could see his preorbital glands flare wide open just before he spun away and dived into the cover of the spruces. I heard him for the next ten minutes as he climbed out over the ridge toward New Deal Lake. He wasn't sneaking or pussyfooting—he was just "getting gone" and taking no time to look back. The "god of all elk" was on his side this day, as manifested by the cow elk tag in my pocket—literally through the luck of the draw.

Now that I had no claim on the bull, I found myself wishing him a long life. I hoped he would remember that trailing wood smoke might again lead him to a hunter, maybe one not encumbered by possession of a cow tag. I hoped we would meet again on the slopes on another day in another year. He was, to me, the essence of this place and all places like it. My day, even my entire hunt, was now fully satisfied, no matter what happened for the rest of the trip.

I suddenly felt chilled. My warming fire had burned down to coals and ashes. I stirred them in an effort to rekindle the flames. The sun suddenly broke through the clouds and flooded me with the warmth of direct sunlight. The wind had died down to a whisper. I was intensely aware of this being a very special moment on a very special day.

After taking a half hour to enjoy the full sun and the warmth it brought while I ate my Spam and sweet onion sandwich, I extinguished the fire and moved out slowly and carefully along the slope at a hunter's walk. The walk my grandfather taught me, so long ago now, was defined at its core by never getting out of breath and never overheating. A hunter out of breath when the time comes to shoot will face highly magnified chances for a miss—or a wounded animal. And a hunter who is hot and sweaty on a very cold day will, when he stops, become chilled. Over a quarter century earlier, I had received the same advice from a Mexican ranch hand in South Texas when he guided me in pursuit of trophy white-tailed deer and Rio Grande turkeys. He repeated to me over and over, "*despacio, despacio*—slowly, slowly." It was good advice—for hunting and for life. I found that is much more to see and learn when one moves *despacio*.

I moved slowly, carefully, and quietly—*muy despacio*. An elk had bedded here under this spruce—and not so long ago. There was a urine spot in the snow, and the spot was rich with elk smell. And, just here, a hawk had killed and eaten a young blue grouse. The remains of the grouse were obvious, and there was a feather in the mix that I guessed had come from a goshawk. A chipmunk, not yet in hibernation, watched from a nearby perch soaking up the sun's rays. A coyote had paid a visit and left tracks in the soft ash soil. I could see the wind move like waves here and there in the trees in the vast drainage that stretched out below. The wind made a sound that reminded me of an old steam-powered locomotive "chuffing." The sound built up and then died down to a whimper, only to rise up and die down over and over.

Chipmunks ran here and there, and some sat on the tops of granite boulders. Were they just admiring the scenery or were they claiming their territories? I could tell that their behavior, whatever it meant, was likely a very dangerous pastime. Owl pellets that I had found under a tree at the edge of the open space were replete with the remains of what I judged to be chipmunks.

Life is filled with risks, and there was something to be said for both a good view and a secure territory. Gray jays moved silently, as was their wont, through the spruces—I thought of gray shadows or maybe gray ghosts. I wondered what I might be able to see if I could move so silently and so freely.

Many of the more mature spruce trees were afflicted with bark beetles. Some were already dead, and many more were dying. The ground was almost free of vegetation under the spruces, but I could see bits of charcoal here and there and an occasional charred stump—legacies of a stand that occupied this same site maybe a hundred or more years ago and had been destroyed by a stand-replacement fire. The ground, which was now too bare to carry a wildfire, would, in a year or two or three, be so littered with dead wood from the carcasses of these insect-infested trees as to be able to sustain a stand-replacement fire for the first time in many decades.

From the scars on some of the trees I could tell that lightening strikes were common at this elevation when fierce thunderstorms boil up in mid- and late summer. Sooner or later, one of those strikes would hit the lower edge of the old stand and ignite a fire. That fire would sweep upslope, feeding on the carcasses of the dead trees that made up the old stand and, in the process, make way for a new stand. It would leave behind charcoal for another hunter—maybe a century or so hence—to ponder while moving through the area—perhaps *despacio*.

Moving *despacio* with the senses attuned to one's surroundings is conducive, at least to some, to thinking on things beyond the doings of mice and men. Moving *despacio* with senses attuned helps put things in perspective. I thought that the circumstances of being deep in the wilderness and moving *despacio* accentuated that possibility. But now, it was getting dark, and I realized that I didn't know exactly where camp was, though I had a general idea.

As is always wise when such a conclusion has been reached, I sat down to think through things. My calculations told me that I was above camp. Had I come far enough around the slope to be directly above camp? Or had I come too far? Or maybe not far enough? When in doubt in such circumstances, the better part of good wisdom is to take time to ponder the situation, study the lay of the land, and come up with a plan. In the midst of my careful considerations, the wind shifted and the solution to my problem was at hand. I heard horse bells from a half mile or so directly downslope. The sounds of those bells on the horses grazing near camp would guide me home.

When I walked into the meadow that contained our camp and saw the horses, I made out the tent in the deepening twilight. I knew Bill was already there, as I could see smoke vigorously rising from the stovepipe. When the horses that had been loosed to graze saw me across the meadow, they came running in full expectation that I was carrying cubes of compacted alfalfa hay in my pocket for their benefit. Fulfilling their hopes and rewarding their confidence, I gave each pony a cube or two and headed for camp with the horses following close behind.

When I saw Bill step out of the tent, I hollered my greeting just to let him know I was home, "Got any blood on you?"

The answer came back: "No blood on me. How about you? Any blood on you?"

Before I got to camp, I had removed the live round from the chamber of my rifle and closed the bolt on the empty chamber. When I arrived at the tent, I leaned my rifle against a tree and shucked my hunting pack, Bill asked, "Did you see anything? I didn't."

I said that I didn't see anything—meaning that I had not seen a cow elk that was legal game. He knew and I knew that we were both lying. After all, Bill also moves through the woods *despacio*. We had both seen plenty of things—wonderful things!

OCTOBER 6, 1991

We were up about an hour before daylight. Bill fed and watered the horses while I fixed our lunches, cooked breakfast, and washed the dishes after we finished eating. As I was getting my hunting gear together, I sensed that Bill had something on his mind and wanted to talk. I didn't refuse when he suggested, "One more cup of coffee for the road?"

He stared into the fire and reminisced about all the years he had camped in this spot with a wide variety of companions, with emphasis on his first wife Blanche and young son Harvey. He told me about the big bull elk and the trophy mule deer he had killed hunting out of this camp over more than three decades. His uninterrupted monologue went on for nearly two hours. He wound up by announcing that this was his last elk hunt. He wanted me to remember how to find this special camp—"his" camp—and understand that I was free to camp here and call it mine. Then he laughed, noting that I was most likely the only other person who could even find this special place.

Then, while scratching in the dirt with a stick for a few minutes, he broke the silence and looked up at me and asked if I would do him the honor of spreading his cremated ashes here after his death. He pointed to the open slope just above camp and told me, "Spread them right up there where they will go to growing fat deer and elk." He smiled. I could tell that the idea—rather the vision—pleased him. I assured him that I would be pleased to do as he asked and would consider it an honor and a privilege. Then it came to me that he had spent more and more time on our most recent journeys into the wilderness talking about his "last big trout" or his "last elk hunt" or his "last time" to visit this place or that.

Some years back, in 1982, fellow wildlife biologist Dale Toweill and I had compiled and edited a widely acclaimed, prize-winning book titled *The Elk of North America—Ecology and Management*, published by the Wildlife Management Institute, which became known as "the elk bible." We dedicated the book to Bill Brown and gave him the first copy off the press. Bill's dedication to wildlife, particularly elk, symbolized the efforts of the first generation of wildlife biologists who devoted their lives to establishing scientifically-based wildlife management and improving wildlife resources. Bill seemed to treasure that book—maybe above all his other possessions except his horses and bird dogs. Now he said he wanted me to have that copy back to leave to one of my sons. Bill was seriously thinking about dying and was getting the really important things settled.

The spell was broken when we looked up and saw two camp does that had first shown up the previous evening. They seemed more curious than cautious. When I emerged from the tent, shouldered my hunting pack and rifle, and headed up the mountain, they ran away a few yards, stopped, and looked back before heading over the ridge. A half hour later, I reached a spot from where I could look back down on camp. Through my binoculars I could see Bill sitting on a campstool in the sun, tossing salted peanuts to where the two camp does would surely find them.

OCTOBER 7, 1991

Bill and I left camp, in opposite directions, just before full daylight for our last day of hunting on this trip. Bill commented as we parted company—just in case I had not heard him yesterday—that this was

Jack after a long hard day of elk hunting, Eagle Cap Wilderness, 1991.

his last elk hunt. If so, it was a perfect day for a last hunt. The day was filled from start to finish with stillness and warm sunlight emanating from a cloudless sky.

Late in the afternoon, I had taken a stand fifty yards above a well-used elk trail. About an hour later, two cow elk came walking steadily down the trail looking neither left nor right. I could hear them coming for at least a quarter mile and see them for fifty yards. I shot the trailing cow—right behind the elbow of her front leg— through the heart. She was, I believed, dead before she hit the ground. There was no need to hurry down and sever the arteries and veins in her neck to bleed her out; the almost certain heart shot had taken care of that. All creatures die. Maybe, in a sense, her death was a "good death." For her, up to the second the bullet tore through her heart, this had been just one more day like any other. She was alive and un-concerned one minute and dead the next.

Now the hard work began. I skinned her out, removed every-thing from the body cavity, cut off the head and legs, and cut the car-cass into quarters. The parts were put into cotton bags that I retrieved from my hunting pack. Using parachute cord, I hoisted the bags high off the ground to cool. I took the heart and liver with me as I headed for camp to get a couple of pack horses.

I arrived in camp an hour after sunset, built a fire in the sheepherder stove, and had coffee brewing when Bill showed up. I greeted him with a cup of coffee "sweetened" with a double dash of rum. After an initial deep swallow, he noted the cleaned-up liver and heart hanging from a tree branch to cool out and took a seat to listen to my story—which he really didn't have to coax out of me. That was only fair, as I would play that listener role willingly if the situation were reversed—which it often had been over the years we hunted together.

Then it was time for Bill to describe what he had proclaimed was his last day of elk hunting. A few hours earlier he had been sitting at the edge of a spruce thicket, having built a warming fire that would also serve to heat some water for tea. Just as he finished his tea, he looked up to see a five-point bull elk a bit more than a quarter mile away, seemingly trailing the smoke toward where he was seated. He watched the bull through his binoculars for several minutes. Then the bull detected him and spun around and disappeared into the trees.

Bill was in storytelling mode now. "He was so close that, through my binoculars, I could see his eyes pop wide open when he saw me. Then he did an immediate 180-degree turn and disappeared into the trees without ever looking back." He continued, "That's not too sorry a way to end up my elk-hunting career. I think I will always remember that bull when I think of this place—and my last elk hunt. By God, that elk is this place. Or maybe this place is that elk." After a very long pause, during which he stared steadily into the fire, he broke the silence by saying, "Well, the Lord of the Hunt gave me one last elk."

Looking away so that he would not see the tears in my eyes, I agreed with a nod. I did not trust that my voice would not crack if I were to speak. I noted that he had raised his glasses, turned his head away, and rubbed away a tear or two. There was no reason for his embarrassment. But that was old soldier Bill's code—never display any visible emotion. So we simply sat and stared into the fire for an hour or so, saying little and listening to the wind in the trees and the occasional stirring of the horses. We stepped outside the tent and looked up at the open sky awash with stars. There was no talking. Giving in to the chill, we ducked back into the tent, undressed, and crawled into our sleeping bags and pulled manty tarps over us. Light flickered through the stove's damper hole. Sleep came quickly.

OCTOBER 8, 1991

After we retrieved the cow that I had shot, dressed, and left hanging the day before, we broke camp and were on the trail toward home less than two hours after full light. The trip out to the trailhead was a pleasure afforded by a perfect blending of good horses that stood calmly for being saddled and packed, beautiful weather, a clean dry trail, horses that loaded into the truck and trailer without a hitch, trucks that started, and dry roads home. And we had an elk for winter meat. I wondered if this would be, indeed, Bill's last elk hunt. Maybe, but maybe not. Time would tell. Whatever happened, he would have enough elk in his freezer to get him through the winter. First things first.

CHAPTER 8

YOU KILL ELK WHERE YOU HUNT

When I headed up the USFS research unit in La Grande, Oregon, foremost among my pleasures was the pursuit of the wily elk in the Eagle Cap Wilderness of the Wallowa-Whitman National Forest in northeastern Oregon. My hunting partner, Bill Brown, had a passion for the welfare of Rocky Mountain elk and the pursuit thereof.

For Bill, elk personified the spirit of wilderness. For Bill, there was no sound sweeter than the bugling of a bull elk on a cold crisp morning or the mewling of cows and calves signaling to one another as they grazed in a high mountain meadow in early fall. For Bill, no challenge and no achievement in big game hunting exceeded the successful pursuit of huge-antlered bull elk. Of all the trophy bulls he killed in over forty years of hunting the high lonesome, he kept the antlers of only one, taken in the Minam River drainage in the Eagle Cap Wilderness in 1958. It was displayed in a place of honor in his living room.

When I asked why he had preserved only one trophy out of so many, he replied, "One bragging bull is enough for a lifetime." That bull, still registered in the Boone and Crockett Club's records book, was certainly "bull enough" by any standard.

Now that trophy hangs in my den—my sole inheritance from Bill—who passed over the great divide in 2012. Bill prided himself as a most excellent big game hunter who well deserved such a title, even as a very old man. He often confided to me, in our talks around the many campfires we shared over several decades, that he wanted to be the oldest hunter in the Pacific Northwest who still pursued and killed big bull elk in the high lonesome. He just may have achieved that ambition; if not, he was damned close. It kept him going long after old cherished *compadres* hung up their saddles and took to their rocking chairs to stare into a fireplace and conjure up the old days and big bulls from the flames.

OCTOBER 1993

Predators establish territories that they protect against others of their own kind. This evolved behavior enhances the chances of success in taking prey, which in turn translates to survival and reproduction. Many accomplished elk hunters do the same, even though their physical survival is not at stake.

Bill and I protected our elk-hunting territories from other hunters by deflecting questions, making misleading statements, withholding information, and occasionally telling outright lies. Within our hunting territories—really, Bill's long-established hunting territories that he generously shared with me—we had an increased advantage over the elk and other hunters because he knew where bull elk were apt to be under various weather and seasonal conditions, disturbance by hunters, and habitat conditions. We could, and did, adjust our hunting efforts to fit changing circumstances.

Within one of our prime hunting territories in the high lonesome of the Eagle Cap Wilderness, I located what I called my "honey hole" for elk. It was a 200-acre or so stand of overmature lodgepole pines located just below the timberline. Steep, rocky slopes surrounded it on three sides. No horse trails led into the stand or along the adjacent ridgelines; the three upper sides were too steep and the other side was too logged in to encourage access. Foot travel was, to say the very least, exceedingly difficult. As a result, other hunters were damned scarce to nonexistent.

The lodgepole stand was what foresters call "decadent." The dominant trees were a smidge shy of a century old, and individual trees were succumbing, along with younger, smaller trees, tree by tree and in small clusters, to the vagaries of old age, mountain pine beetle infestation, and blowdown from the winds that whistled down the bare slopes. Dead trees lay like jackstraws on the ground. Some still-living old trees and many smaller, younger lodgepole pines poked up here and there in the maze. It was nearly impossible for a horse to traverse the area—and plenty tough enough for a man on foot.

Over the years, I discovered that elk often holed up in this stand in the midst of hunting season. First, no predator, including humans, could traverse the downed trees without difficulty or without making *beaucoup* noise in the process. Second, no hunters in their right minds would want to wrestle a dead elk out of what Bill called a "Gawd-aw-ful" tangle. Third, enough sunlight came through the broken canopy to encourage patches of the food plants that elk preferred.

One year, when my more common hunting spots had not paid off, I imprudently decided to give the "honey hole" a try. Late one evening, after I was through hunting for the day, I marked a path into the middle of the honey hole with plastic ribbons and picked a spot for a blind from which I could see a reasonable distance in all directions. I constructed a crude hunting blind and stashed some items inside: four manty tarps, pack ropes, butchering tools, a double-bitted axe, and a bow saw. Very early the next morning, I left camp with my saddle horse and one packhorse and rode by moonlight in spitting snow to within a half mile of the honey hole. After tying the horses, I used a small flashlight to follow, as quietly as possible, the ribbons through the tangle to my blind. I was snuggled in my tarps well before daylight and in a serious frame of mind to let the air out of a big bull elk.

Even an elk couldn't move through the honey hole without making occasional noise. I heard a thud now and then when an elk clipped a log with a foot as it jumped over, the crack of breaking branches, or the mewling sound of elk talk as they kept track of one another in the tangle. With my ears tuned and focused for early elk detection, I was able to grab snatches of half-sleep waiting for the sun to pop up over the ridge.

Just at dawn, as the sky began to glow red and orange, I heard elk moving. My eyes popped open, and I went into full-blown pred-ator mode. Which direction? How far? How many? What kind? I quietly threw back the tarps, rolled up onto my knees, and raised my head until my eyes were just above the logs. There was no air moving. Swirling breezes would soon come as the sun warmed the slopes.

I saw the antlers before I saw the bull's body. He was not a really big bull, but he would surely do for my purposes. I ducked down and waited and waited, tracking the bull's progress with my ears. I eased a round into the chamber of my Winchester .30-06 featherweight and cranked the magnification on my adjustable scope down to 2-power—if there was to be a shot, it would be up close and personal. Finally, I raised my head to peep over the logs.

The bull was standing sideways to me at less than forty yards, looking back over his shoulder. I had a clear shot. I would not have much time to aim before he moved or, worse yet, detected my presence. I ducked my head down and took deep breaths. I let out half of the last breath, popped up, and rested my rifle on the log in one continuous motion. He turned to look at me as I put the crosshairs in the middle of his chest and squeezed the trigger. I could hear the solid "thump" as the bullet went home. The young bull humped up, jumped one log, tripped over the second, went down in a heap—forever still.

Now the hard work began. I used my axe to clear an area around the bull large enough to accommodate field-dressing, skinning, quartering, and hanging the quarters, neck, and head. I was extremely careful with the razor-sharp axe and knives as I was cold and stiff, especially my hands, and a long way from help. I built a warming fire, took the thermos of strong black coffee out of my hunting pack, settled down against a log, and let the adrenaline seep away into the pine needles.

Once the carcass was skinned and quartered, the quarters went into muslin meat sacks and were hoisted up out of the reach of whatever predators might come up on the scene. I washed the heart and liver in snow, wrapped them in a cotton sack, and lashed the package, along with axe and bow saw, onto my pack frame. I rested frequently to avoid sweating and to assure that I did no damage to myself with the axes.

It was late afternoon before I followed the ribbons—and my tracks in the snow—back to the where the horses were tied. My saddle mare, Summer, and our pack mare, Casey, nickered greetings. The horses were clearly ready to head back to camp to join their buddies and be rewarded with their well-earned ration of grain. Knowing exactly where they were going and how to get there, the horses traveled steadily through the pitch blackness. From a half mile, I saw the green nylon sides and white top of the tent glowing in the darkness from the light of the Coleman lantern hanging from the ridgepole. It was a beautiful and most welcome sight. White smoke was rising vigorously from the stovepipe. A quarter mile out of camp, the horses began their "horse talk" with those tied in camp and kept it up until they were reunited.

Bill looked me over when I stepped into the tent. "Well, I can tell from all the blood that you must have blundered into some luck—unless, of course, you managed to cut your own throat. I suppose there is a dead bull smack dab in the middle of what you euphemistically term the 'honey hole?'" Sometimes he actually talked like that. Euphemistically? More than likely.

I nodded. "Thanks for the medicine." I dumped the elk's heart and liver in the snow to chill down. "I'm pretty sure you don't want any of the poor creature's heart and liver. Which I, the world's greatest camp cook present here at this time and place, intend to cook—rolled in canned milk, floured, and fried in bacon grease with onions—for our meager repast." Sometimes, in retaliation, I talked like that.

From time to time, Bill suffered from gout, an ailment sometimes aggravated by eating organ meat—especially when fried in bacon grease. However, on occasions such as this, Bill was willing to risk an attack of gout—even a small chance of death—for a bait of elk liver and heart cooked in what he called "mountain-man style." Circumstances that justified such risks were being in the high lonesome, having two "Tang cocktails" in the company of a treasured colleague, and celebrating the kill of a bull elk. Our celebration went on until near midnight, when the fire burned down, the woodpile was depleted, and we didn't want to hustle in more wood.

Bill was up before daylight and singing as he wrangled, fed, and saddled the horses. I cooked up a breakfast of leftover heart and liver with some fried eggs and made lunches with the leftovers. He showed no signs of gout—or a hangover. Sometimes, I mused, the Lord of the Hunt grants dispensations to faithful true believers.

Shortly after daylight, we were mounted and on our way, each leading a packhorse. We had a plan. Bill would begin clearing a path to allow the passage of the horses to where the elk quarters were hanging. I would go ahead on foot and bundle the quarters into four manty packs and lash together the head, neck, and hide. Then I would wrestle the packs, one at a time, as far as I could, back along the trail of ribbons, to meet up with Bill.

I crawled over, under, and around the downed trees to where I had left the elk quarters hanging—I reckoned about 200 yards into the maze. Using the tarps and ropes that I had stashed, I made up the elk quarters into four packs. That done, I tied one pack onto my pack board and struggled toward where Bill was alternately hacking and sawing. When I got within fifty yards or so, he shouted for me to drop the pack and go back for another. I left the first manty pack and started back to the scene of the crime, which was how I was beginning to think of my act of the day before.

The second manty pack seemed at least twenty pounds heavier than the first, and the distance had surely increased by at least a third. After a long blow, I went back for another pack. When I returned, Bill was sitting on a log, stripped down to his undershirt in the well-below-freezing temperature. He had his wool hat off, and steam rose from his head and upper body.

I dropped my pack and propped myself up with both hands on a waist-high log. Sweat dripped off the tip of my nose. I gasped, "Old man, I guess you're ready to quit?" Just maybe, I could goad him into taking responsibility for quitting for the day. The old bulldog took my comment as a challenge.

"I'll tell you what, sonny boy, you just go on back and get the last load. I will be sitting on my butt waiting right where you are now!"

I was near flat-dabbed bushed and ready to admit it. "Bill, I'm seriously pooped! It's plenty cold enough that we don't have to worry about the meat souring. How about we call it a day?"

I could detect the hint of a sneer. "Well, I guess that's up to you."

YOU KILL ELK WHERE YOU HUNT

Knowing a challenge when I heard one, I struggled to my feet, put on my pack board, and headed back for the last manty pack. He kept up his methodical chopping, and the sound of every stroke was a challenge. When, with almost no juice left, I finally dropped the last manty pack on the pile, Bill was still thirty yards away.

A half-dozen logs, several suspended chest high, separated Bill and the pile of elk meat—logs too big to cut out and impossible to go around. As we were whipped, we built a fire, ate some venison jerky, rehydrated, and braced ourselves with a couple of snorts of emergency brandy.

Double-teaming now, we wrestled the four packs over the intervening logs to a point to which Bill could lead the packhorses. I leaned back against a log and went to sleep in the midafternoon sun. I awakened when I heard a horse whinny from about ten yards away.

We basket-hitched the manty packs on the Decker pack saddles on the packhorses. The third packhorse carried the hide, neck, and head. We led the horses back the way that Bill had cleared. It wasn't pretty, but we were able to work the horses to the edge of the honey hole. The horses showed their stuff as sure-enough mountain horses. It was near pitch dark when we mounted and let Bill's gelding, Keno, lead us back to camp.

I was too pooped to cook. So we had Vienna sausages, rat cheese, and crackers for supper. Oddly, Bill ate the Vienna sausages without complaint. He usually tended to become hostile at the mere mention of Vienna sausages, claiming that during World War II, on the island of Attu in the Aleutian Island Campaign, he had eaten Vienna sausages three meals a day for three straight months. He had promised God that, if he survived, he would never ever again eat another Vienna sausage.

Bill had one day left to hunt. I cooked his breakfast, and he was off well before first light in earnest pursuit of the wily elk. When dawn broke, I tidied up the camp; lashed the elk quarters and head, neck, and hide onto three packhorses; saddled Summer; and led out for the trailhead, upon arrival I unwrapped the manties and hung the meat sacks in the horse trailer.

Just as I arrived back in camp and stepped down off my horse, I heard a shot and the whomp of a large-caliber bullet striking home. A few seconds later, I heard another shot and another whomp. In spite of the reverberating echoes, I guessed that the sound had originated a half mile or so above camp.

An hour later, I had elk stew cooking on the Sims stove when Bill walked into camp. He had just enough blood on him for me to know he had been successful—admittedly, he was a much neater butcher than I. "Well?" I inquired.

"I heart-shot a spike bull, then once more to make dead sure. He's quartered and hanging. It's a real easy place for us to pick him up early in the morning and pack him out to the trailhead—and be back in camp for an early supper." There was no contrast made between the site of his kill and mine in the "honey hole"—though it was certainly implied. I chose to ignore it.

The round trip to the trucks went without a hitch. Our last night in camp was a genuine pleasure. Two young "eating elk" were hanging in our horse trucks at the trailhead. We were still stiff and sore from our efforts to retrieve my elk. Just before bedtime, Bill remarked, "You know, partner, we damned near busted a gut retrieving an elk out of your so-called 'honey hole.' To tell the truth, I have enjoyed about all of that that I care to."

Poking at the fire in the stove, he continued, "My old daddy told me something that came to make a lot of sense over the years." There was a long, very pregnant pause. "You kill elk where you hunt."

"You kill elk where you hunt? Is that all?"

"That's it. You kill elk where you hunt." He blew out the candle, turned his back, and snuggled into his sleeping bag.

"You kill elk where you hunt." I repeated that observation over and over in my head as I waited for the sleep of the righteous. It came to make sense. That was my last hunt in the honey hole.

CHAPTER 9

RETREAT TO A TOUCHSTONE—RETURN TO THREE BUCK CAMP

Bill and I had two guests along on this trip to the Eagle Cap Wilderness—Robert "Bob" Nelson, Director of Fish and Wildlife for the USFS, and Dr. James "Jim" Applegate, professor of wildlife biology and department chair at Rutgers University. We were headed for what Bill and I called "Three Buck Camp" on the Minam River.

OCTOBER 14, 1994

Bill and I were on horseback, each leading a packhorse loaded with the camp gear, groceries, and libations. Bob and Jim followed on foot, carrying their rifles and hunting packs. Bill set a pace such that Bob and Jim could keep up with the horses on the flat and downhill stretches without straining. On the steep, uphill portions of the trail they "tailed" a trailing packhorse—i.e., they held on to the horse's tail and were towed along, making the steep trails easier to conquer. We had no trouble along the trail and stopped only once or twice to let Bob and Jim catch up. The frequent rest stops seemed to puzzle the horses.

It was snowing lightly when we rode into our campsite about an hour before sunset. Three Buck Camp was my favorite camp in the Eagle Cap Wilderness. Bill and I and a mixed bag of companions had occupied it many times over the previous decade when hunting for mule deer and elk. Open snowslide areas above the camp and a small open meadow at their termination provided abundant grazing for the horses, except for the few times when the snowdrifts were too deep during elk-hunting season.

When I was "just being" in quiet still moments, Three Buck Camp conjured up the essence of companions I had camped here with in the past. Memories included the deer and elk carcasses hanging from the meat pole tied high between two trees, ribald jokes, embellished "war stories," serious plans, trepidations, ambitions, regrets, and, most of all, warm feelings of camaraderie and shared experiences of a kind that were slowly disappearing into the past.

Without anyone saying so, all present seemed struck with that special feeing that can come with the first night in a wilderness camp. We had escaped from one world and entered into an almost parallel universe. For the next week we would dwell—and live intensely—in a very different and older world, far from towns and far beyond where the roads end. For the next week, it was likely that we would not encounter another human being outside of those making up our party.

Bill took care of the horses while Bob and Jim set up the tents and I gathered and cut wood, got a fire going, and prepared supper—a concoction referred to as "chili, cheese, and noodles." After a couple of celebratory drinks of Wild Turkey rye whiskey, it didn't seem half bad. After supper, Jim quickly washed and stored the pots and pans and dishes. We—especially the two hikers—were eager for our sleeping bags. Snow began falling softly and steadily. On such nights the malady that strikes older men and requires trips outside the tent to relieve pressure on the bladder serves a useful, even essential, function. It was the duty of anyone leaving the tent, however briefly, to slam the back of his hands against the tent roof to knock off rapidly accumulating snow and feed the fire in the stove. After lights-out I pondered the flickering light I could see through the damper in the door of the sheepherder stove and let my mind drift to pleasant memories. Worries and fears slipped away.

OCTOBER 15, 1994

Tomorrow is the opening of the elk-hunting season, so we have a whole day to work in and around camp to be ready to sustain ourselves and the horses for the duration of the trip. Bill and I rode the eighteen-mile round trip to and from the trailhead to pack in enough pelleted alfalfa to feed the horses for the rest of the trip. Bob and Jim spent the day gathering and cutting wood for the stoves and, snowfall permitting, an outdoor stand-around fire or two—hopefully in celebration of a kill. It was a division of labor amenable to all, as neither Bill nor I was enamored of gathering and cutting wood; Jim and Bob, having severe cases of tender ass as a result of riding swivel chairs for eleven months, had no desire to ride to the trailhead and back.

About a foot of snow had accumulated during the night but caused no problems for the horses on the journey to the trailhead. There had been no wind as the snow fell yesterday and last night. As a result, there were no significant snowdrifts across the trail for the horses to buck through.

We met only two other parties on the trail. The leader of the first party—a big burly, black-bearded fellow carrying a large-caliber, long-barreled revolver in a shoulder holster worn on the outside of his red-and-black-checkered mackinaw coat—informed us that his party intended to camp just below Minam Lake on the Lostine River. We were pleased to hear that, as it meant our two parties were not likely to encroach upon one another. The lead rider in the second outfit told Bill that his party intended to make camp just below the junction of the Minam River Trail and the trail up to Frazier Pass. That put their camp just about a half mile below ours. However, we noted that they were not packing horse feed and were banking on grazing their horses in the small meadow near their camp. As the snow was already more than a foot deep and still falling steadily, it seemed likely that they would be forced to camp farther down the Minam River where they would be more likely to find grazing for their horses and mules. In any case, our three parties wouldn't likely encroach upon one another. Bill and I concluded that Bob and Jim would have the upper Minam drainage all to themselves. As we crossed back over the ridge at Minam Lake, the snowfall intensified, reducing visibility to some fifty to a hundred yards.

The wind was just strong enough and the temperature low enough to plaster the heavy snow to our woolen clothing so that we soon appeared to be snowmen sitting astride horses. The body heat generated by the horses quickly melted away the snow that struck them. When we arrived in camp, a look at my watch told me that we had made the round trip—about eighteen miles—in just over five hours, which included a lunch stop and packing up the horses at the trailhead. That was good time, even in good weather. Our pack outfit might have been, as Bill put it, "a little over age in grade," but they were, I believed, still among the best of the horse outfits plying their trade in these mountains.

When Bill and I rode back into camp, we saw that Bob and Jim had completed their assigned tasks. There was more than ample stacked dry wood—a mixture of spruce and subalpine fir—all cut to length for the sheepherder stove and several stand-around fires if the snow ever stopped. The density of the growth rings on the chunks of firewood reflected the harshness of the conditions at the site as well as the short growing season at this elevation. The combination of those constraints produced very dense wood that burned hot and long in the stove. As the softly falling snow accumulated, it was increasingly likely that our gamble on the weather may have been a bad bet. Likely the elk would be moving downslope as colder temperatures and deepening snows caused them to expend ever more energy digging through the snow to find forage.

On the other hand, there were many fewer hunters up this high. We treasured our solitude almost as much as successfully stalking elk. Yet we retained hope that there was still a good chance we would encounter a band of elk that had delayed their inevitable downslope migration. I wondered if the elk, like us, cherished the high lonesome and gave up and moved down to the foothills with reluctance. Here in the high country they were truly free—no fences to jump, no roads to cross, no competition from livestock, and fewer predators, including those of the *Homo sapien* persuasion, out to do them harm. I realized that my thoughts were anthropomorphic and, as such, unbecoming to a professional wildlife biologist/scientist. I was quite knowingly indulging myself.

Far down the hill there was a lesser accumulation of snow, gentler terrain, better growing sites, and warmer temperatures, adding up to a better energy balance for the deer and elk—fewer calories out and more calories in. That, sooner or later, would inevitably compel the elk to capitulate to simple biological realities. Yet there were always a few elk that tarried longer just below the timberline than their fellows. Perhaps we would meet up with such an elk or two. I thought likely not, but just maybe? We would see.

My last waking moments on days such as this were such a pleasure. My companions were sound asleep. I could hear Bob and Jim snoring in their tent. The sheepherder stove popped as the fire died and the metal cooled. The fire in the stove flickered out, and then coals glowed in the darkness. Light from a candle provided just enough light for me to write in my journal. The wind was blowing in the firs behind the tent. I reflected on what had transpired this day—and what the brief respite from the "real world" meant to each member of our party. Such reflection made the experience whole and was fixed in my memory through the process of putting my feelings and thoughts down on paper. Then, with the coals dying in the stove, the intensifying cold came more quickly through the walls of the tent. It was time to put my journal aside, zip up my down sleeping bag around my face, and let sleep come. I was untroubled. I felt truly alive.

OCTOBER 16, 1994

We were well into our first day of hunting, and none of us had had an opportunity to kill an elk. My initial impression was that we had gambled on such a high-elevation hunt and lost. Late in the day I saw several elk far above me on the mountainside headed over the ridge, with the lower Minam River drainage on the other side. Outside of that one encounter, we had seen only one bit of evidence that any elk remained with us in the upper Minam River drainage.

During the night the wind howled down from the mountains all night long, keeping me awake wondering if the tent would continue to stand as each surge of wind threatened to take the tent down or topple a tree on a tent or a horse. It was a long night of worry with little sleep—and that sleep fitful.

The winds abated just before dawn. We were happy to be up, warmly dressed, and sitting around the stove eating breakfast and drinking stout coffee when first light told us that it was time to pursue our quarry.

One by one, we stood and slipped into our hunting packs, slung our rifles over our shoulders, and departed in our various selected directions.

Within a half mile of camp, Jim came across a spot where the winds had toppled four big snags festooned with lichens. Tracks showed that elk had fed heavily on that protein-rich food source during the night. He spent the day watching the spot, betting on the return of the elk. He bet wrong, but it seemed a good wager. None of us were successful.

Collectively, we saw the tracks of a cougar and a marten; encountered several magnificent mule deer bucks; slept in the sun on the south-facing slopes; huddled over small fires, soaking up the warmth of the sun stored in the dry wood and released by combustion; broke the ice and drank from trickling streams; watched clouds entangle themselves with mountain peaks; witnessed sunrises and sunsets; saw moonlight on the granite peaks; heard the wind roar and sigh and lie down altogether; ate well; told lies and jokes; remembered old times and old friends; rode fine horses; sipped good bourbon; heard coyotes howl; tramped miles through the snow; enjoyed both solitude and comradeship; and, in the process, helped re-create ourselves anew.

But I felt—and feared—that such days in places like this were coming to an end for me. My old football knee was badly swollen and getting worse. The pain was constant, even when dampened with pain pills and a medicinal touch or two of the spirits. By the end of the second day of hunting, though the spirit was willing, I simply could not travel more than a couple of miles through the now crusted snow. And even that travel involved frequent long stops for rest. The doctors had told me that there is nothing more they could do for my knee except a knee replacement.

But, I told myself, not just yet. And even when that time was upon me—and that day was surely coming—I promised myself that I would still be able to travel here, and a hundred other places like this, in mind and spirit. After all, I remembered so many such wonderful places: the Cross-Timbers and the Hill Country of Texas, the Ridge and Valley Province of the Appalachians, the woodlands of New England, the old growth forests, the mountains and the high desert of the Pacific Northwest, and the tundra in Alaska. I remembered them with clarity and in detail. I could, upon demand, remember and, to a degree, even relive my experiences there.

Those carefully cultivated memories were among my greatest treasures, more meaningful than my minuscule accumulation of stocks and bonds. I had, truth be known, invested much more in such experiences than in gaining wealth as defined by financial resources. And such was a good investment, in that I valued those experiences and the memories more than material things and even professional achievement. Today, in thinking over such matters, I found that I was not regretful of the accumulated consequences of my choices.

Some of my staff in Washington, and certainly my politically appointed overseers, chided me, albeit gently, for being gone from my post too frequently. While I conceded that they had a point, I commonly worked ten to twelve hours a day six or seven days a week. With such intensity of effort, I simply had to be able to escape, to retreat, to the wilderness from time to time to retain my sanity and vigor. I simply had to sustain contact "with the ground"— terrain, wildlife, and people—in order to know, understand, and rekindle my passion for wild things and the stewardship of the national forests. That passion, for me, had long ago evolved beyond the intellectual to become more and more visceral. And that was what kept me going.

The only way I could bear what I increasingly thought of as my temporary exile in Washington, enduring the eternal petty power struggles and fits of egos, was to know what we, the hardcore natural resources professionals, were working for and toward. A respite in the wilderness was one way that I knew. It was here in the wilderness that answers to mysteries and quandaries seemed to emerge with clarity out of a growing confusion of mind and soul.

OCTOBER 17, 1994

During the night I reluctantly crawled out of my sleeping bag, tugged on my insulated hunting boots, and stepped out of the tent. The sky was crystal clear, the night dead still, and the moon full. I walked through the crusted snow to the bottom edge of the opening created by past late-winter snowslides and looked up at the cleared slope. My breath created small clouds in the crisp air that dissipated quickly.

The clear, cold sky seemed to have sucked away the warmth of the earth, as the temperature had dropped significantly since sundown.

The world—this new/old world—was awash in moonglow, and the stars seemed to crackle in the sky. The granite peaks that loomed above camp were swathed in that magic moonlight that seemed to soften their ruggedness that was so glaringly obvious by day. A chorus of coyote music ensued from the upper basin—at least three animals yipped and howled. Those calls were answered by a similar chorus from another group of their kind on the opposite slope. Then for a brief magic moment, they sang together. Then it went quiet. I felt blessed to have been present at this most excellent of concerts in this wonderful amphitheater with the very best of lighting and acoustics. Though I knew the concert was not performed for my enjoyment, I chose to believe otherwise.

When the coyote chorale ceased their concert, I suddenly felt the cold and considered the state of my concert dress. My jacket was an old holey hooded sweatshirt. The hood covered my red wool balaclava stocking cap that had been pulled down over my face and ears—only my eyes and nose were left uncovered. My "trousers" were baggy, waffle-knit long johns. Bare feet were stuffed into unlaced wool-insulated hunting boots. My elegant wardrobe was set off by gray wool fingerless gloves.

The incongruity of the scene, my reverie, and my appearance tickled my funny bone, and I raised my arms toward the moon and laughed aloud in a spontaneous outbreak of pure joy. My laughter echoed back to me from the granite hillsides. It came to me that I had not felt so happy—and so relieved and glad to be alive—for the nearly two long years since Meg's passing.

The snow crunched underfoot as I walked back to the tent. I heard my companions—all three of them—snoring gently. I stuffed the sheepherder stove full of wood and closed the damper to slow the rate of burn, kicked off my boots, and wormed my way down into my sleeping bag. I was chilled, but warmed up quickly. I lay awake watching the fire flickering from the cracks around the door of the stove until it was time to get up, cook breakfast, and ready myself for another glorious day—likely one more day of futile hunting—futile, however, only in the sense of bagging an elk or not.

OCTOBER 18, 1994

We were all off in pursuit of what we jokingly called "the wily wapiti" just at dawn. To compensate for my sore and swollen knee that was increasingly constraining my travel speed in the crusted snow, I found a spot in the granite boulder field some half mile or so above camp. I knew that there the rising sun would afford some warmth and I could see a significant area of meadow and some varying distances into the open stands of old-growth fir trees.

By midmorning I had seen several mule deer, including a magnificent buck—which I found encouraging—but no elk. Seemingly, there was not a breath of air stirring. Warmed by the rising sun, I lay back, rested my head on my hunting pack, and dozed off. I dreamed a pleasant, uncoordinated, disconnected potpourri of dreams of things past—of my Meg and other hunts; the jungles of India and tigers and elephants and the foothills of the Hindu Kush; bird dogs and hunting bobwhite quail with my Big Dad in the Cross Timbers of Texas; big trout rising to perfectly cast flies; and fields of bluebonnets and Indian paintbrush in the Texas Hill Country. That mishmash of dreams produced an overall feeling of warmth and peace, a potpourri of good memories deliciously scrambled together and garnished with wildflowers.

At midday I dug into my hunting pack and feasted on dried cherries and apricots, jerky made from a mule deer buck killed last season down in the valley below, and drank cold river water from my old aluminum canteen I bought for a quarter from an army surplus store in Fort Worth when I was twelve years old. It was stamped "1942." In midafternoon I deemed it time to terminate my elk hunt and hobbled down the hill toward camp a mile or so down below. I met Bob on the way, and we walked back to camp together. Bill was waiting when we arrived. After we built a fire in the stove to make some coffee, Bill had Bob and me pose for pictures with the horses as he finished up the roll of film in his camera—a sure sign that he considered his hunt over.

Just then, from a mile or so up above camp, we heard a single shot. The sound bounced back and forth between the canyon's walls. We heard the bullet "thud" home. We heard no more shots and figured that an elk was down. Some two hours of daylight were remaining, and there was likely an elk to gut, skin out, quarter, pack into camp, and hang out to cool. Bob gathered our hunting packs and made sure we had skinning knives, ropes, axes, saws, and manty tarps. Bill and I saddled two packhorses. Within a half hour we were off, following Jim's tracks out of camp.

We had not gone far when I saw Jim, a quarter mile upslope and headed for camp; I looked him over through my binoculars. He knew I was watching him and waved. He was all smiles and held two thumbs up over his head. I waved back and gestured for him to sit down and wait. When we got to him with the two packhorses, he was still pumped up and obviously elated—one's first kill of an elk will do that. He seemed filled with that special feeling that comes to a real hunter after a hunt well executed and a one-shot kill cleanly made.

Jim led us to the elk—now his elk. Like all good hunting companions should, we listened attentively to the successful hunter's tale. He had remembered the elk that had been feeding on lichens on a downed snag. So, all else having failed, when young Dr. Applegate came across several old-growth spruce trees, festooned with lichens that had blown down in the windstorm of two nights ago, he put two and two together. Being a pretty fair wildlife biologist for a college professor, he knew that the lichens were rich in proteins and that their not being buried in the deepening snows had created a situation where he could quite legally "hunt over bait." From the plethora of elk tracks, he knew that elk were already taking advantage of their literal "windfall." He looked things over, took note of the wind, studied the tracks in the snow, and took a position downwind from the direction in which the elk had departed.

He fashioned a crude hunting blind and settled down to wait. After some three hours, he heard elk cautiously approaching through the trees. Jim picked out an adult cow and waited until she was within 100 yards—he knew his rifle scope was sighted dead-on at that distance. There was therefore no need to do the math; it was simply a matter of just holding the crosshairs on her heart and squeezing the trigger. He clearly identified the target, made sure the background was clear, saw nothing that would deflect the bullet, steadied his rifle over a log, took three deep breaths, let out half his last breath, and squeezed the trigger on his .30-06 Remington rifle. The cow simply dropped and did not move. To this point, the day for her had been just another day, a day like all other days. Now, for her, it was over—both the day and her life.

I saw where Jim had knelt down in the snow next to the cow, and I visualized him reaching out and touching her in respect, awe, and appreciation. How would I know that? I knew because I had done the same thing so many times in the past—whether for a rabbit, a squirrel, a turkey, a deer, or an elk. It was only appropriate to show respect for the prey and to take time to feel and understand what had occurred. The Spanish philosopher Ortega y Gasset observed that "true hunters" do not hunt in order to kill, but rather kill in order to have hunted. I knew that many would be puzzled by that insight and might even dispute Ortega's observation. I was not of that mind, and I was pretty sure Jim wasn't either.

The four of us made short work of caring for Jim's elk—his elk now. The hunting ritual was complete except for the communal partaking of the animal's flesh. That eternal circle would be completed tonight with a traditional supper of the elk's liver and heart, prepared in whatever manner the camp cook had inherited from a mentor. As I was the cook in this camp, I followed the traditional processes taught to me by my father and my Big Dad as they prepared the ritual first meal of liver and heart from white-tailed deer in Texas. I cut the heart and liver into cubes, added salt and pepper, rolled the pieces in canned milk and flour, and deep-fried the meat in hot bacon grease. The result was then smothered in chunks of sweet onions that had been marinated in butter. The pan was covered, and the steaming went on until the liver and heart were tender or the drinks ran out, whichever came first. When all three critical elements come to fruition at the same time, the result could justly be deemed *perfecto*! Such was the case this night. Ours was a happy camp.

The big game hunters' ritual was partly complete. The never-ending circle of life and death—of reunion with the earth—had been consummated and appropriately celebrated. We, collectively and individually, were content. These were circumstances and feelings that those who are not hunters would likely never experience

An elk hunt in the Eagle Cap Wilderness, 1994. Left to right: *Bill Brown, Jack, and Jim Applegate, professor of wildlife biology at Rutgers University. The photo was taken by Bob Nelson, director of Fish and Wildlife for the USFS.*

or understand. We four hunters squatting on campstools around a sheepherder stove in a tent pitched in a high mountain meadow in the Eagle Cap Wilderness, having just finished that ritual meal, fully understood. For that moment, however fleeting, that was enough.

OCTOBER 19, 1994

I lay awake much of the night figuring out how to pack out our camp and Jim's elk on only four packhorses. I caught myself hoping for another coyote serenade to facilitate my cogitations. The coyotes did not oblige, and my puzzlement continued. Sometime in the wee hours of the morning the solution popped into my head. But, as was frequently true of my solutions to pressing problems discovered in the midst of twilight sleep, the solution was forgotten—or seemed ridiculous—in the full light of day. Such was the case this morning.

But, not to worry, Bill had figured things out. We departed for the trailhead at midmorning with everything—including Jim's elk—

packed on four packhorses. The packs were a bit heavier than usual, but the horses were supremely fit so late in the packing season and could handle the extra weight. We gave the horses a ten-minute blow every half hour and encountered no trouble. Fortunately, we did not encounter a cow elk along the way that would have compelled me to dismount, pull my rifle out of its scabbard, and shoot to kill.

Bob and Jim followed along on foot, carrying their hunting packs and rifles. After a week of high mountain hunting they were more fit—and likely a little lighter in the poop—than when they started. They arrived at the trailhead only an hour and a half behind us. As we were loading the gear and horses in the horse truck, I noticed a bright green ribbon attached to the windshield wiper of my pickup, bringing my attention to the presence of a letter held in place by the wiper blade.

The letter announced that my travel schedule had been altered and I was expected—"commanded" was a more accurate description—to be in Portland, Oregon, the next day to be deposed by the self-described "ace lawyer" representing the timber industry. Damn, there was nothing I enjoyed less than being badgered by and forced into a battle of wits with lawyers to whom the prescribed processes and rules of the road gave the upper hand. Well, I thought, at least I wouldn't have to travel to Washington to be badgered by lawyers adorned in three-piece suits and sporting fresh haircuts and then go back to Portland. Somehow that seemed small solace.

The trip back to La Grande from the trailhead was without incident. When we pulled into town, I thought to myself, "Welcome back to the real world!" But I could think of no better preparation of mind and spirit for another shootout with sharp legal eagles, who fully intended to kick my ass and the ass of the horse I rode in on, than a week with friends and colleagues elk hunting in the Eagle Cap Wilderness. I had been, once more, to the foremost place in all the world that "restoreth my soul" and cleared my mind. I had no intention of being a pushover on the witness stand.

CHAPTER 10

PURSUING THE WILY CARIBOU IN ALASKA—A NEW WILDERNESS EXPERIENCE

I was in Juneau for meetings with Governor Tony Knowles concerning the management of the national forests in Alaska. After my meetings with the governor ended, I met up with James "Jim" Caplan (Director of Public Affairs, USFS), James Davis (special law enforcement agent, USFS), and my son S. Gregory "Greg" Thomas at a hotel in Juneau. Caplan, Davis, and I declared ourselves to be on annual leave as of the close of business on August 29.

This was my first of three caribou hunts in Alaska. I also took my older son Britt and my stepson Paul Connelly on successful hunts over the next two years. To my lasting regret, I neglected to keep up my journal during those hunts.

AUGUST 30, 1995

Our party of four took a single engine puddle jumper from Juneau to Iliamna arriving in midmorning. The Iliamna airstrip was graveled, and the terminal/warehouse/hanger, along with a few nondescript buildings, appeared to compose most of the town. The "terminal" building was host to some forty men and their gear, which was arrayed in discreet piles on the floor. From the presence of a rifle or several in each pile we presumed them to be fellow caribou hunters waiting for air taxi service to their various hunting camps.

The weather was nasty, with temperatures just above freezing and intermittent rain and snow. Lowering clouds covering the tops of the surrounding mountain peaks. Planes were landing, but none were taking off. More and more hunters and their gear continued to crowd into the terminal. Soon the terminal was filled with hunters patiently waiting for the weather to lift, many of them sleeping on the floor. I picked out three familiar faces in the crowd—wildlife biologists with the U.S. Fish and Wildlife Service and the National Park Service whose paths I had crossed in various places and at various times over the years. That gave me somebody new to visit with as the hours ticked slowly by.

Late in the afternoon, a young Native American man came in through a side door and called, in a loud voice, for the "Thomas party." We gathered up our gear and followed him out to where a battered Chevrolet carryall was waiting. We tossed our gear into the cargo space—except for our rifles, which were more gently treated—and were driven to a nearby lake where two float planes waited to ferry us into our hunting camp at "Lucky Lake"—I liked the sound and the intimation of that.

We had been airborne for just short of an hour when the pilot banked the plane and pointed down to Lucky Lake. He circled the lake and judged the wind direction from waves on the lake's surface. There were no caribou to be seen in any direction, but there were no guarantees in the hunting of caribou that were in the process of migration. They could be here today and miles away tomorrow.

The pilot made a smooth-as-silk landing and taxied up to the shoreline. We set up a line and passed our gear from man to man to make a pile on the beach. Sans the weight of men and equipment, the plane floated free of the lake's gravel bottom. We pushed the plane into the lake and turned it toward the center. The pilot gave us a thumbs-up, cranked the engine to life, and taxied so as to come around into the wind. With a much lessened load, the plane was quickly airborne.

We erected our tents in a drizzling rain that arrived on a chilling north wind just as the float plane became a speck on the horizon. We "guesstimated" the temperature at forty degrees. Jim Caplan, designated as "Chief of Party" in USFS-speak, detailed Greg and me the quite onerous duty of trying to catch enough graylings for supper. The others busied themselves with setting up tents and a cooking area.

The fishing was amazing—it seemed that we had a strike on every second or third cast. It didn't seem to matter what lure we employed. Within a half hour we had our supper, quite literally, "in the bag." And in another forty-five minutes the fish were prepared, crisp-fried, and on our dinner plates. Though eight o'clock seemed a bit early for bed, we considered it preferable to standing around in the drizzling rain. Once we were dry and warm in our sleeping bags and listening to the rain spattering on the taut nylon roofs of our tents, sleep came quickly. The rain continued throughout the night.

AUGUST 31, 1995

It was still raining when we rose to begin our new day on Lucky Lake. Breakfast was prepared and eaten as we stood under a large nylon fly erected to delineate the cook shack and dining room. None of us were familiar with the roadless country, and low-hanging clouds obscured whatever landmarks there might have been rendering our maps but of little use.

We opted to split up and hunt out from camp, relying on our compasses, in the four cardinal compass directions. The plan was for each hunter to locate high ground, wait for the weather to clear, and ambush a group of migrating caribou. About three-quarters of a mile from camp, I came across a half-acre stand of aspen, four feet or so tall, that afforded me some hiding cover and a view of two converging swales that seemed likely to form a pathway between two lakes. Well-beaten trails indicated that this was a likely travel route for migrating caribou.

When the clouds lifted in midmorning, I saw several small bands of caribou moving off in the distance. Off and on during the day, ptarmigan were calling. A pair of bald eagles spent a part of the day perched on the prominence across the valley from where I sat. Once, far off in the distance, I thought I heard a wolf howl—but wasn't quite sure. The low-hanging clouds came and went as the day passed. When the clouds finally lifted, I saw vistas such as I had never before seen stretching out to the horizon—Alaska! The vista, with the bright sunlight leaving shadows of the clouds racing across the tundra, was stunning.

In late evening, as I slowly made my way back to camp, I frequently stopped and sat down to wait and listen and watch. The weather had closed in, and a steady drizzle was setting in. There was much to see and, in some cases, hear—scat of bears and wolves, shed caribou antlers, bones of caribou, snow geese, widgeons, marmots, a gyrfalcon (I thought), and, finally, as I walked into camp, a hunting companion holding out a cup of coffee "with a little something in it." The cold drizzle continued as the skies darkened. The cup—actually several cups—of doctored hot coffee hit the proverbial spot.

After all the hunters returned to camp at the end of the day—days are short this time of year at this latitude—we indulged in a couple of drinks of quite good bourbon, ate a quickly prepared meal of bacon and egg sandwiches, and went promptly to our tents. After twelve hours out in the cold damp, my goose-down-filled sleeping bag felt especially good. I had not slept this much or so soundly for several years—perhaps I just needed to simply free my mind and just feel what I thought of as the rhythms of the earth. I was grateful for the moment and the respite from the fast, increasingly contentious atmosphere of Washington, D.C.

Staring out at the mirrorlike surface of Lucky Lake, I recalled a passage from Psalms—"He maketh me to lie down in green pastures: he leadeth me beside the still waters. He restoreth my soul." This was such a moment. I awoke in the night and, somewhat puzzled as to why, and then realized that the tattoo of rain on the taut nylon of the tent's roof had stopped. The resulting stillness was loud in its own way.

SEPTEMBER 1, 1995

Greg and I were awakened by Jim's calm statement, "Hey guys, the caribou are here." In a very few minutes, we were dressed, outside the tent, and scanning the skyline through our binoculars as caribou appeared: first one after another and then by the dozens. Suddenly, there he was—a magnificent caribou bull that stopped briefly and lifted his head, outlined against the sky, before disappearing behind the rise.

That was enough to set off a scramble of would-be caribou slayers headed off in their variously assigned hunting directions. Each was looking for a spot that they calculated would place them in just the right place to ambush a moving band of caribou. That band, of course, would include such a magnificent beast as we had just seen—and in our dreams! Greg and I set off together at a rapid pace.

It was not long before the younger man left the older farther and farther behind. Soon Greg disappeared from my view over a rise. Only some ten minutes later that I heard two spaced shots from Greg's Winchester .30-06 rifle. From the sounds that followed the shots, I figured that both rounds had struck home. I set out in that direction to see if I could be of help.

Then, as I topped a rise, I could see another bunch of caribou angling away from me at what I estimated to be 300 yards—out of range for me. For the next two hours I played cat and mouse with the small group of caribou as they displayed their typical grazing behavior. They grazed for a minute or two, seemingly taking a bite and taking a step—or several. Then, likely to escape the gnats buzzing about their heads and eyes, they ran forward a few yards and resumed grazing.

I struggled to get within 200 yards. Once within that range, my plan was to assume a prone position, put down the bipod attached to the forearm of my .30-06 Winchester, settle down, and take a steadied shot. My last contact with this group of caribou left me lying prone, sucking for wind, and watching as they moved farther out of range. I had managed to get close enough—within 200 yards—and in proper shooting position. But by then I was breathing too hard to risk a shot. By the time I had collected myself, the caribou I had in mind was too far away for me to shoot with assurance of delivering a killing shot.

Damn! I consoled myself by reasoning that my failure was not from lack of trying or lack of skill. It was time to give up on this bunch of caribou and head for camp. Pooped and drenched with sweat, I had to keep moving simply to ward off the chill. The rains—sometimes a light drizzle and sometimes more—returned. Visibility was dropping rapidly along with the lowering clouds.

As I worked my way back in the direction (I thought) from whence I had come, it occurred to me that I was, just maybe, "a little lost." While I had a good general idea of where I was, the exact location of camp was something of a mystery. I climbed several small hills to get a better view and discovered that I could see at least six lakes that looked more or less alike. Now, just which one was Lucky Lake?

To make things worse, when we rushed out of camp for what we figured would be a quick kill or two, I had left my hunter's pack with extra ammunition, compass, and detailed map behind. Upon reflection, I had only the five rounds of ammunition in my rifle. And as this was quite apt to be grizzly bear country, I had no ammunition to spare firing off signal shots. I convinced myself that the better part of valor was to flop down flat on my ass, suck some serious wind, and chow down on one of my emergency giant Baby Ruth candy bars in the pocket of my rain parka—slowly and methodically—while I puzzled things out.

As I was munching away, the fog and clouds began to lift and I made out a prominent cone-shaped hill that I remembered seeing from camp. Logically enough, I figured that if I could see that hilltop from camp, I could see camp from the hilltop. It took me nearly a half hour of steady, slow travel to get to the top of the small hill.

Another problem arose when I got to the summit though: I couldn't see a half mile in the increasing mist. I remained quite calm. After all, there was no real danger of freezing to death as I had on water-resistant gear. Better yet, I had just eaten a giant Baby Ruth candy bar and—just in case—had another one in my jacket pocket; water was not a problem; and I knew exactly where I was on the top of this hill. The only problem was that I didn't know exactly the way to our camp on Lucky Lake. Truth be told, I didn't even have a general idea.

I had the option of firing the standard three signal shots in rapid succession to solicit an answering shot from camp—which, I reckoned, had a high probability of success. That would leave me only two rounds in reserve for emergencies. Beside that, I was still reluctant to announce to my *compadres* that I was just a tad confused as to the location of camp. They might assume that I needed assistance and come to get me. Patience and reluctance to face embarrassment paid off. After about an hour, just at sundown, the clouds lifted briefly and I made out the white top of the cook tent shining bright in the sun, a mile or maybe a little more away to the north. I thought, "All good things come to those who wait."

The weather held, and I walked into camp within a half hour. It felt really good to be "unlost." There was no one in camp when I arrived. I pumped up and lit the Coleman stove and made myself some stout cowboy coffee and added a dash of spirits to ward off the cold and damp. I was relieved to be in camp, albeit somewhat chagrined about having been a little confused for nearly a half day as to its exact location. Most of all, I was embarrassed about my really rookie stunt of having left camp without my extra ammunition, compass, and survival kit. On a positive note, I was exhilarated by the day's experience.

Comfortably sipping hot coffee and brandy in camp, I told myself that such experiences beat the hell out of living without fear and without testing. And the ultimate failure would, I rationalized, beat dying slowly of the increasingly apparent vicissitudes of old age. At least, that was my rationale at the moment. I wasn't too sure I believed it. Maybe it was my love affair with Ernest Hemingway's *muy macho* stories emerging from the recesses of memory.

While contemplating such weighty matters over my second cup of coffee, I looked up to see Jim and Greg coming over the hill above camp carrying packboards loaded with meat and the cape and head of a nice caribou bull. The two shots I had heard earlier had gone right through the bull's rib cage—not two inches apart—just back of the shoulder. As both a father and a hunting companion, I was most pleased. Greg had his trophy caribou. Well done!

After I helped get the ninety-pound-plus loads off their shoulders, they both slumped to the ground looking a bit drained and disheveled. Greg stretched out his legs, relaxed his shoulders, wobbled his head around, and pronounced, "It just don't get no better than this!" I loved it—intentionally fractured English out of the mouth of an English major and a lawyer to describe a near-perfect experience.

He meant every word, and his audience smiled and nodded in understanding and agreement. I was sure that, come nightfall, when floured medallions of tenderloin of caribou were sizzling in bacon grease, Greg would fill us in on the details. But just now there was one more round trip still ahead to get the rest of the meat into camp and hung from a makeshift meat pole that resembled a hugely oversized sawhorse. The caribou quarters were hung just high enough to clear the ground but not nearly high enough to deny a hungry bear or a wolf access to an easy meal. The man-smells and the noise from our camp a quarter mile away would provide some disincentive to such critters—hopefully, it would be disincentive enough.

After the second loads of meat were hanging from the meat pole, Greg began the tedious task of caping out the bull's head and neck so that a skilled taxidermist would be able to work his magic and the mounted head could come to grace the wall of his den looking adequately lifelike. Hanging there, it would bring back memories of our time together on the Alaskan tundra and enable him to regale friends with enhanced stories—the successful hunter's prerogative—of his adventure in the Alaska wilderness. That was one way, I supposed, to keep the experience more vividly alive in memory while honoring the animal and the hunting experience.

I was not and had never been a "trophy hunter," though I had, in over forty years of big game hunting, taken a number of trophy-class animals. I pondered the reasons for that as I assisted Greg in his task. Certainly, when I first hunted big game in Texas as a boy, I had no money to pay for the services of a taxidermist. In later years, after my economic status had improved markedly, my beloved wife was intolerant of what she referred to as "dead animal parts" being displayed on the walls of "her house." Her decision was, clearly, not open to debate. She had no objection to wild game being her family's primary source of meat. She just didn't grasp the concept of trophies. So trophy hunting was never a driving force for me.

Alternatively, my trophies primarily resided in my memory. They were routinely brought out and perhaps embellished a little in the telling and retelling of stories around campfires in various hunting camps around the world as the years passed. And if the hunts were not as exciting or as arduous and the animals taken not so large and well endowed with horns or antlers as I remembered— and related—there was no one to know for sure but me. That had come to be enough.

Just at dusk, we made out a herd of caribou—likely a hundred or more—moving along the skyline a mile or so to the west of camp. It was a sight to behold and worth the price and effort of the entire trip. I studied Greg's face as he watched the caribou parade through his binoculars. I knew, at least I hoped, that he would always remember this moment—this magic time. The images, I thought, were burning themselves into his brain and heart. The experience was now irrevocably a part of him, and I was proud to be part of that experience. At that moment, my purpose for this journey to Alaska was complete, no matter what transpired on the rest of the trip.

SEPTEMBER 2, 1995

When I stepped outside the tent in the wee hours to answer a call of nature, I was almost startled to be welcomed by a crystal-clear sky and the most brilliant display of stars that I had ever been blessed to see. The Big Dipper was almost directly overhead and it seemed so near that, if I reached out, I could touch the North Star. I thought at first that this was surely a magical night when the stars came nearer to the earth. Then I realized that it was I who had come to this place to be near the stars—after all, they were always there. I felt that I had never before been part of such a glorious night. I stood there in my long johns and moccasins staring up into the sky until I suddenly gave in to being very cold—and shivering. Retreat into the tent and my down sleeping bag suddenly seemed a capital idea. Sleep came slowly as there was much think about and absorb. This was such a different experience and in such a different place than I had ever known before. I had to remind myself that this was very real and not a dream.

I spent my hunting day moving from one elevated vantage point to another, staying several hours in each spot and watching for caribou on the move. My plan, upon spotting caribou, was to position myself ahead of the bunch and ambush a nice bull. But all the caribou I spotted were well over a mile away and only briefly observed when highlighted against the skyline. They seemed to be constantly on the move. Well along toward sundown, I saw a wolf emerge on a little rise and lie down. It seemed to me that she—I didn't know how I knew the wolf was a female; I just knew—was scanning the countryside and perhaps enjoying the passing parade of caribou. She was a magnificent animal with an almost silver-white coat. I lay on my belly and watched the wolf through my binoculars for near on two hours.

I reckoned her to be a little less than a half mile away. She seemed to be enjoying the sunshine, though she periodically and intently watched the western skyline. It dawned on me that perhaps she had a den nearby that contained nearly grown pups and that she and they were waiting for the pack to return from hunting. I thought about trying to stalk closer, but that seemed an unwarranted intrusion that would bring a too rare and precious moment to an end.

As the bottom rim of the sun touched the skyline, I stood up, took my leave, and headed for camp. The wolf sat up and watched me intently. She did not seem alarmed. We stared at one another. It came to me that I was probably the first human she had ever seen. Most certainly, she was one of the very few wolves I had ever encountered. Maybe she was as taken by the sight of a human as I was by the sight of a wolf. It seemed a magic moment that I did not want to end. But there were other sights I wanted to see. Before I turned to go, I raised my arm above my head and waved to the wolf. She took notice, stood up, turned, and disappeared over the rise. I knew that I would remember this moment as long as I lived—a trophy of the mind that would hang always on my wall of memory. Such, I thought, were the trophies that I most treasured. I wondered if she would remember our encounter.

As I headed back to camp, I noted ripening blueberries in nearly every swale. After examining several bear scats, it seemed to me that the bear was eating little else. I supposed that was what I would be doing if I were a bear. The late afternoon was relatively warm and I was sweating. I stuffed my jacket and then later my hunting shirt into my hunting pack. A quickening breeze swept the hillside clean of the constantly pestering gnats. I pulled off the camouflaged head net that had covered my face and ears and stuffed it my pack. I took time to gather a hat half full of berries with the idea of mixing them in with tomorrow's breakfast pancake mix. In the course of my travels back to camp with my hatful of berries, I found that trying to eat just one berry could be likened to trying to eat just one salted peanut. Over the next hour I ate nearly all the blueberries, one delectable morsel at a time.

I felt no guilt in my gluttony by rationalizing that the labor involved was all mine and others in the party might well have had the same opportunity. I did wonder, briefly, if gorging on blueberries might have the same effect on my digestive tract that it obviously had on the bear's. Oh well, if so, it was a small price to pay for such an exquisite banquet in such a well-appointed dining hall.

When I arrived in camp just as the sun set, I came upon Greg fishing in Lucky Lake. I sat on a campstool and watched as he caught and released several one- to two-pound graylings. Every so often, he put down his rod, picked up his binoculars, and scanned the ridgelines for caribou on the move. Now, I thought, that was living—catching graylings while waiting on a trophy caribou bull to appear.

SEPTEMBER 3, 1995

Late in the evening, we sat at the edge of Lucky Lake with our duffel in a pile, basking in the sun and waiting for two float planes from Iliamna Air Taxi to pick us up. I reflected on the previous several days, the last two of which had been clear and warm. Our sightings of caribou had been limited to those we saw as they crossed the ridgelines that surrounded our camp.

I had spent much of my time fly-fishing for graylings with an occasional glance at the nearby ridgelines in case we were in danger of being overrun by a herd of caribou. The fishing was fantastic. In fact, I had never experienced anything quite like it. If too much success did not breed contempt, it did foster a casual acceptance—and expectation—of a strike on every third or fourth cast.

Monotony was relieved by switching back and forth between fly-fishing and spin-casting of hard lures. Such prodigious fishing—of the catch-and-release type, of course—required frequent breaks for me to lie flat out on my back and bask in the sunshine. When queried by my companions as to what I was up to, I replied that I was keeping my ear to the ground listening for thundering herds of caribou that might be just over the next hill. I was the only unsuccessful hunter in the group, and to my surprise I found that I really didn't care.

Just after daylight, I left camp to see if I could locate "my" wolf from yesterday. I saw the wolf emerge from what I guessed was her den and resume her post on the same little hilltop. I had no urge to take up wolf hunting at such an advanced age—I couldn't imagine eating a wolf, and trophies were not my thing.

My wolf trophy was firmly fixed in my memory. That was enough. Then, in the midst of my early-morning wolf watching, I sighted a magnificent grizzly bear as it crossed a bog area a mile or so away from my hillside perch. Through the binoculars I thought I could see the silver-tinged fur ripple with each step.

In the midst of these reflections, from far off in the distance I heard two float planes, that were likely coming for us. Then I made them out, flying low on the horizon. The magic of the solitude of the last five days faded as the planes landed on the mirror-smooth surface of Lucky Lake and taxied up the shoreline. Our gear, the meat, and the antlers were quickly loaded, followed by the passengers.

As the planes lifted off the lake and banked to pick up their heading to Iliamna, the magic of Lucky Lake began to recede into memory. We passed low over where I thought the wolf's den was located. I searched for a last glimpse of "my" wolf and, just maybe, "my" grizzly. I did not see the wolf, but there was the grizzly. Most accommodatingly, I thought, it stood up on its hind legs to watch us pass over. I tapped Greg's shoulder to point out the bear, but it was gone from view before he could catch a glance. The pilots flew us all the way to Iliamna at an altitude of not more than 500 feet or so. I wondered about the low altitude, which was about standard altitude for game survey work, but didn't ask for an explanation. Maybe the pilots were scouting for caribou for clients who would take our place at Lucky Lake.

For the duration of the flight my eyes were glued to the ground as I conducted my own caribou census. My sightings of caribou were few and far between: two lone bulls and seven caribou of undetermined status lying on the bare ground of a dry creek bed that was essentially devoid of vegetation and, maybe, free of gnats.

CHAPTER 11

ALL GOOD THINGS MUST END—BILL BROWN'S LAST WILDERNESS SOJOURN

Every year for the last five years, Bill had proclaimed more frequently and intensely, especially during late-fall elk-hunting trips, that this was his "last wilderness trip." This year, when I called him from Washington just before leaving my office at USFS headquarters, I told him that I was on my way to catch a plane at Washington National Airport and that Bob Nelson and Paul Brouha would meet me there. We would fly to Oregon to join him for an elk hunt in the Eagle Cap Wilderness.

He told me to come ahead—everything was ready—but, in a shocker, said he didn't feel up to hunting himself. Nonetheless, I encouraged him to join the party and assured him that all he had to do was to keep the fire going in the stove and take care of the seven horses when he was alone in camp. And if he didn't feel like being camp tender, I would take over that chore and he could confine his activities to eating, drinking, storytelling, and tending the fire.

I thought about how strange it was that, even at this late date in our long close relationship, it was impossible for us to be straight forward, open, and fully truthful in talking about our horse trips. After all, we both tended to be straight talkers in discussing other matters. Why could he not speak the words that were in his mind? I believed he was thinking that "this hunt will have to last me the rest of my life." It was a sad thing that our shared *macho* culture did not allow grown men conditioned to be taciturn to say such things. But, this day, those feelings lay just barely below the surface—and we both knew it. Our thoughts and feelings on the matter were expressed in code or in other unspoken ways.

OCTOBER 10, 1996

When we arrived at the trailhead at Two Pan on the Lostine River, the place was crowded with horse trucks and trailers and hunters and horses being saddled and packed. As we unloaded and packed our horses, a half-dozen men—all carefully dressed in costume appropriate for the backcountry—recognized me and walked up to say hello and shake hands. They all said, in effect, "Welcome home! We've been worried about you back there in the big city. Thanks for what you're trying to do." You could tell that they couldn't think of a worse fate—not even excluding slow death from leprosy—than living and working in Washington, D.C. A few didn't speak but gave me a "kiss my ass" look. Obviously such were not on the same wavelength relative to the management of the national forests.

With a little help from Bob and Paul, the packing of the horses was quickly accomplished. I was somewhat relieved that I remembered how to pack—especially how to throw diamond hitches—and got the job done under Bill's critical eye with nary a fumble. With that, we mounted and were off up the trail. Bill, of course, was riding in the lead with two packhorses in tow. This may have been his last elk hunt—but, by God, he was still the trail boss!

Bill and I had just celebrated his eighty-second birthday after he had changed his birthday to accommodate my arrival at his place. His some seven decades of hard living—and hard playing—had taken their toll on his body. He no longer had the strength to lift a Decker pack saddle onto a horse's back, and certainly not the heavier panniers and manty packs. He had to struggle to get to his feet and get moving after a night of sleeping on the ground. His hands, with knuckles gnarled from arthritis, simply pained him too much to deal with the ropes, buckles, and straps of the saddles and packs, especially when they were stiffened by cold wet weather.

We were a mile or so up the trail before the horses settled down and lined out. Their packs were riding easy, and that good old much desired feeling of "escape" came over me. As I had frequently done over last decade, I debated in my mind whether I was "escaping from" or "reconnecting with" real life. Maybe, I thought, after due consideration, there was no real difference. This time, however, that old feeling was near to overwhelming. I could feel the weight lifting from my shoulders and the soaring of my soul. I knew my tour of duty as USFS chief was coming to an end—and very soon. While I was far from being totally pleased with what I had been able to accomplish in my short tenure, I was fully content in that I had done the very best I knew how.

My old high school football coach told me once, when I was depressed and crying openly in the locker room over a one-point loss in a championship game, "Get your head up! You left everything on the field. You did your best. That's all any man can do." He was right then and right now—forty-three years later. Good wisdom never goes out of style. "Leave it all on the field! Then, win or lose, get your head up!"

I felt good—really good. I could feel the weight on my soul lifting. I had run my race. I had kept the faith. Debts had been paid and duty fulfilled. Now there was time—God, I hoped there was time— for yet another chapter in my life as the Boone and Crockett Professor of Wildlife Conservation at the University of Montana in Missoula and as a continuing voice for conservation in the twenty-first century. Most important of all was the chance for a new life with a lady of rare quality, intelligence, and grace. Kathleen "Kathy" Connelly would be my bride come January. As I rode up the trail with my mind increasingly free, I contemplated the many blessings that had come to me over my life.

We established our camp at what Bill and I referred to as the "Old Elk Camp"—more commonly known as Frazier Meadows Camp. Bill and I had hunted out of this camp at least a half-dozen times over the past two decades. The camp was located near the juncture of the Minam River Trail and the Frazier Pass Trail. I was ever more certain that this was Bill's and my last elk hunt together, but I had been sure of that more than once before.

Once in camp, we quickly set up the tents, gathered firewood, and cared for the horses. For the first time on one of our trips—and that now spanned something over twenty years—Bill was content to putter around camp, get a campfire going, and then sit close to the fire toasting his shins while nursing a stiff drink of bourbon and branch water and occasionally giving directions. Temperatures dropped precipitously with the setting of the sun, but not enough to drive us away from the fire and into the cook tent. Supper was made up of frankfurters, canned chili, chopped onions, and hot dog buns served on a paper plate—a quick and easy meal without producing many dirty dishes. Obviously the cook was getting too old. Bill gave me something of a disdainful look as he chowed down on what he scathingly referred to as "the cuisine."

OCTOBER 11, 1996

When the alarm clock told me to emerge from my sleeping bag and begin preparations for the day's hunt, dark heavy clouds that seemed to scrape the ridgetops were scudding in from the west. The unseasonably warm weather was attested to by the hunters' dress—no long johns, blue jeans, and a flannel shirt. Of course, just in case there was a change in the weather, each hunting pack contained a wool jacket, wool shirt, rain jacket and pants, a woolen cap, and gloves. Paul, Bob, and I parted company when we left camp at first light, taking different routes up to Minam Lake, where we planned to meet around midday.

As I traveled up the hill, I noticed that if I "hunted too fast" I felt a mild pain in the armpit of my left arm and under my jaw that went away when I stopped for rest. That was both a surprise and, I knew it for what it was—a symptom of coronary distress. After a rest, I found that things seemed to be alright if I climbed slowly and deliberately—and didn't push it too hard. I made up my mind to see a doctor when I got back to Washington. But, by God, for the moment, I had escaped to the wilderness—my wilderness—and I was not going to let a few little chest pains and shortness of breath throw me off my game.

By the time I had Minam Lake in view; the temperature had dropped below freezing and sleet was slanting down from a gray and darkening sky, not so subtlety announcing the arrival of winter. I retrieved my sweater and windbreaker from my hunting pack and built a warming fire. I was donning my wool shirt and windbreaker when I heard a female voice calling out "Hello!" from the trail just above me.

The lady responded to my wave of invitation and walked down to join me. She squatted next to the fire and warmed her hands. What was this very charming, petite lady doing, on foot, pretty much in the middle of nowhere? She was a prim lady with her graying hair pulled back in a bun. I guessed her to be in her late sixties. She apologized for disturbing the silence but confessed that she feared that I might shoot her by accident.

I assured her that, in well over a half century of hunting, I had never shot—or even shot at—anyone. And as an experienced wild-life biologist, I knew the difference between an elk and an attractive petite lady wearing a blaze-orange vest and orange watch cap that seemed to glow in the sunlight. But I assured her that I appreciated her courtesy of sparing me from even the chance of such a mistake. She told me that she was out for a "brisk hike" from Two Pan up to Frazier Pass and, after lunch, back to Two Pan. I reckoned that to be somewhere around eighteen miles. She lamented that this trip, one of her favorites, now took her well over eleven hours to accomplish. She said she was slowing down now that she had just had her seventieth birthday. I felt my *macho* shriveling.

Off and on, when she didn't think I noticed, she had carefully studied my face. Finally, she asked, "Are you Jack Ward Thomas?" I nodded. She said that she would like to have a picture of the two of us with Minam Lake in the background. Being easily charmed by attractive ladies of whatever age, I agreed. She set her fancy camera on a large rock, focused it, set the timer, and hurried to stand beside me. The scene was twice repeated before she picked up her camera and took another picture of me standing alone, after posing me to her satisfaction. She said that her hands trembled a bit as a consequence of having Parkinson's disease and she hoped the picture would turn out. Then she gave me a big hug, a peck on the cheek, and turned and set off down the trail. Just before vanishing out of sight, she turned and waved good-bye and hollered, "God bless you!" I waved back and blew her a kiss.

She was alone in the wilderness—and, I guessed, in life. She was seventy years old and had Parkinson's. But, by God, she was *alive* and wasting no time on self-pity. I felt honored to have been in the presence of such a formidable lady. Life is precious, and she wasn't wasting a single smidge of hers. Maybe this chance encounter deep in the Eagle Cap Wilderness was a message, and she an example. I chose to take it that way.

I moved on up the mountain at my hunter's pace, which didn't set off the twinge in my upper arm and under my jaw. I took three steps and paused, three steps and paused—sometimes with a longer pause when I felt my chest tighten. By early afternoon, the off-and-on spitting of sleet turned to a gentle, steady snowfall. With that turn in the weather, the woods took on a new dimension. Sounds seemed muffled by the silent snowfall, and I saw tracks of animals that are always active but seldom seen. Three steps and a long pause afforded a moment to listen and study my surroundings. I thought back to my Texas days working along the border with Mexico where I learned to move *muy despacio*—very slowly—when hunting.

During the long afternoon, I heard Canada geese talking as they passed over likely headed south for the winter. A bull elk bugled from across the canyon, too far away for me to hear the grunts that I knew followed the bugle. Once I heard two coyotes talking. A red-tailed hawk whistled from somewhere above me, and on two occasions I heard what I thought were elk moving through the trees away toward the ridgeline. The elk had likely heard me or caught my scent and were motivated to leave the basin to me. I encountered tracks of a snowshoe hare, pine squirrels, and several mule deer and elk.

In the late afternoon, on my way back down the mountain to camp, I encountered the tracks of a black bear near the same place I had encountered black bear tracks last year. Maybe it was the same fellow? The bear should have been in hibernation by now. I said aloud, "Well, old friend, I am pleased to see that we both made it through another year. Maybe we will cross paths again—if one of us doesn't winter-kill first." A resurgence of pain under my jaw stifled my smile—at my own joke.

A bit further upslope, I ran across elk tracks quartering uphill. Snow was already accumulating in the tracks, indicating that only quarter hour or so had gone by since the elk passed. Parallel to the elk tracks were tracks that matched the treads on Paul's boots—I reckoned not more than a quarter hour old from the spacing of the elk's tracks and the slide marks, the elk were moving at an unhurried walk and Paul at an accelerated pace in pursuit. If nothing changed—and the elk didn't see, hear, or smell him—Paul might be within rifle range in another fifteen minutes.

Even as I was going through those computations, I was startled—but not surprised—by a rifle shot from not more than a half mile up toward the ridgeline. I heard no almost instantaneous "whomp," and as there were no follow-up shots, I figured that Paul has missed a difficult uphill shot. But maybe I was wrong—I hoped so.

I eased down into the tree line and built a small fire and melted snow in my canteen cup for a badly needed—or at least much desired—cup of coffee. There was no pain under my arm or jaw. The sound of a finishing shot followed by two quick signal shots would have indicated both success and a call for help. After an hour loitering over my fire, I realized that my original assumption was correct—the shot had missed. I kicked snow over the fire and headed downhill toward camp. When I arrived in camp, Paul was cutting firewood. When he heard me, he looked up, and I saw that his nose was red with a trace of blood that had escaped his efforts to wash his face with handfuls of snow. He was not a happy camper—and that was putting it mildly. He had managed to catch up with the band of elk. When the lead cow saw him, he lay down, rested his rifle on his elbows, and took a very steep uphill shot at her as she turned and continued upslope. The recoil from the Remington 7mm Magnum drove the scope down from the bridge of his nose to near the tip, removing some hide in the process. The problem was magnified by having the cartridge case firmly jammed in the rifle's chamber. There was no way to tell if this was the result of a weak extractor spring or some failure in the cartridge case—perhaps an undue expansion or a rupture. Practically, the cause really didn't matter. Stupidly, we didn't have a ramrod. So now we had two serviceable rifles to be divided between three semi-serviceable hunters. Adding to our problems, I had somehow managed to tear a significant three-cornered hole in the side of one of my brand-new rubber-bottomed insulated hunting boots. My left foot was wet, cold, and increasingly uncomfortable.

As Paul was my guest and I really wanted him to kill his first elk, I handed over my Winchester featherweight .30-06 rifle to him. I would help Bill tend camp and care for the horses—a handy excuse for me to spend time with Bill on what we believed to be our last hunt together. We talked about old times while keeping the fire burning and the coffee hot. It was obvious to me that this was what I should have been doing anyway. For the very first time in my long life of hunting big game, I was totally indifferent to whether I killed an animal or not. Suddenly, at least for the here and now, it simply did not matter. And as a bonus, when I loitered in camp, there was no hint of pain under my arm and in my jaw. Maybe those symptoms had been imagined? Really? I knew better.

Bob came strolling into camp just after dark. He had not seen an elk but seemed to have had a great day nonetheless. As this was a night for beef stew, which required considerable time to cook down properly, we had plenty of time to tell our stories of the day and remember the old times, departed friends, days past—and think of days to come. The snow came down thicker and faster as time passed. There was something about sitting on campstools around the Sims stove, with beef stew bubbling, and telling stories of the day that was to be savored in the moment—and stored away in memory for later consumption. Snow was accumulating so rapidly on the tent roof that it was necessary to beat it off occasionally by striking the roof in a methodical pattern with the back of one's hand, starting at the ridgepole and working down.

Bill shared his observation that the only good thing he could say about having an enlarged prostate and drinking copious amounts of doctored lemonade in the evening hours was that one was compelled to get up frequently during the night. After the immediate chore was taken care of, one might as well stick some wood in the stove and beat the snow off the roof. That, I thought, was putting a positive spin on an aggravating circumstance.

OCTOBER 13, 1996

I squirmed out of my sleeping bag well before daylight, poked the fire in the stove, fed in some wood, and began preparing breakfast. Paul and Bob showed up for coffee and, sooner or later, breakfast. They were fully dressed for the day's hunt. Our discussion over breakfast had to do with what new hunting grounds they might explore this day. Bill sagely observed, "The first day of hunting season the elk change pastures. By the third day, the hunters catch on and change pastures, too." It was time for the hunters to change pastures.

Bob and Paul, now well fed and jazzed on boiled coffee, were on their way to new hunting pastures a full half hour before the first inkling of day. Maybe those new pastures would hold a shootable elk or two. In parting, I promised Paul that my Winchester would be two inches high at 100 yards and nearly spot-on at 200 yards. He repeated what I had told him. He would, after all, have to take my word for it.

Bill and I talked away the day, with a work break now and again to feed and water the horses, split wood, drink coffee, eat, take care of other miscellaneous camp chores, and then drink more coffee. We worked in a nap or two just to break the monotony. I patched up my rubber boots with duct tape the best I could. Duct tape was an all-around fix-it solution, along with nylon parachute cord, that had become a necessity in our backcountry camps.

Mostly Bill talked and I listened the day away. He seemed to have a magnified need to talk on the occasion of this, his self-proclaimed last elk hunt in the high Wallowas in his beloved Eagle Cap Wilderness. We both knew that we would not be seeing as much of each other after this hunt. He needed to talk of other hunts, other days, and other adventures—some of which we had shared and some from many decades before we met.

There were hunting stories, stories of manning fire towers, time in the Civilian Conservation Corps in the years of the Great Depression, working his way through college, entry into the U.S. Army in 1939 as an artillery officer, preparing for the equestrian events for the Olympic Games, old army stories, and war stories from the Aleutian and Italian campaigns as well as his early days with the Oregon Department of Fish and Wildlife. He talked mostly about his efforts to establish more Wilderness Areas on the national forests in northeast Oregon. His part in establishing Wilderness Areas was, I thought, the accomplishment of which he was most proud.

I knew then that this really was, at long last, his last elk hunt in the deep wilderness. In his own way, he was trying to come to grips with that reality. He was saying good-bye in this special—so very special—place. I suspected that we would be together again, but our meetings would take place in an apartment in town and then in a retirement home. That sure as hell wouldn't be the same as sharing a camp in the wilderness. We both knew that. Here in this special, even magical place, things finally got said that needed to be said. Those things were spoken, at long last, without fluff, code words, or waffling. These were the things that needed to be said and heard.

The soft, heavy snowfall continued all day. It so muffled sound that, in the moments of reprise from talk, I was aware of the sounds of my breathing and the somewhat erratic pulse in my ears. I didn't believe that I had ever heard and welcomed such silence. Even in those prolonged periods of silence—and the associated quietness of mind and soul—we both knew that our times together in the wilderness were at an end. Bill was saying good-bye in this very special place. Bill and I had ridden and walked many, many hundreds of miles together and shared many campfires. We knew that this was our last time together in the wilderness—or anywhere else relatively wild and free.

But, neither of us acknowledged that, not out loud anyway. We didn't need to. It was simply understood. He told me that he was "ready to move on." I knew he wasn't talking about breaking camp and getting back to town. He was talking about selling his place, our horses, his horse truck, and my horse trailer and moving into an apartment. I thought that, just maybe, he meant more than that.

I wondered how long, and even if, he could live without his horses, without hunting and fishing, and, most of all, without his wilderness sojourns. Maybe, I thought, he could look from La Grande across the Grande Ronde Valley to the Wallowas and travel there in mind and spirit. I doubted that he would find much satisfaction in such journeys of the soul and mind. I hoped I was wrong, but I knew better.

I also knew he would do the best he could. He would bear the cross of a life that goes on and on when the gusto and the joy and the challenges have faded—save for precious memories—to mere existence. I shook off such musings and tried to concentrate on the here and now. For in this precious moment, we were together in a place we treasured—he for much longer than I. We were sharing one last wilderness adventure. It was well to focus on that and let the tomorrows take care of themselves, as they most surely would.

In midafternoon, I shouldered my hunting pack and climbed the gentle slope behind camp, stopping frequently when I felt the first signal of pain in my upper left arm and under my jaw. When I reached the tree line I turned and looked out across the river to the granite wall that towered above our camp. I thought about the first time I rode into this valley two decades earlier. Oddly, I remembered the biblical verse that came to me then. "Where were you, Job, when I laid down the pillars of the earth?" Where indeed? I felt, now as then, very small. When the sun broke through the scudding clouds that grazed the tops of the granite cliffs, darts of sunlight struck the granite walls and mountain peaks allowing each new moment, for the clouds to yield a different composition—a painting on the cliffs with, perhaps, only me for an appreciative audience.

This was a place and a moment to feel very small and equally insignificant. Yet it was a place and an experience that, at the same time, "restoreth the soul." Those realizations combined experience and insight and beauty in a way that was, I thought, much too rare in life—certainly for those who spend their days down below in towns. Those experiences and others akin to them reside here in the wilderness, lying in wait for those who have the capacity to seek, find, appreciate, treasure, and preserve.

I knew, as I looked down at our camp below in the trees, that I would never come here again. It would not be the same without Bill. Already, it had not really been the same since Meg's passing. To come here alone, or even with others I knew less well, would be to diminish the spirit of the place and the treasured memories that reside here. It would be better, I thought, to lock the essence of the place and times in my mind and heart and not return except in reverie.

I saw movement far below and just a way out from the tent. Through my binoculars I could see Bill clearly. He had taken a campstool from the tent and walked out in the open meadow. He sat down stiffly on the campstool and stared up at the granite wall across the river. He sat there for well more than an hour, almost without moving. He was holding a cup, which he never raised to his lips. I wondered, what was he thinking? Were his thoughts and feelings similar to mine?

This last journey to the Eagle Cap Wilderness was, I thought, above all else, a trip of endings. My career in the USFS, after thirty wonderful years, was at an end. Bill's "oneness" with his wilderness was at an end. Bob's career in the USFS would end shortly after mine. But I thought—and trusted—that there were no endings without beginnings. The feelings and emotions that washed over me were ambivalent. The sadness and the sense of loss alternated with the relief of laying down one yoke and the eagerness to pick up another, very different yoke. I hoped, and felt, that what lay ahead had the potential of being even better than what had gone before. While I was saddened by the endings, I was buoyed by the memories and eager for what lay ahead. That, I thought, was what a trip into the wilderness with an open heart and mind could accomplish if given the chance.

There has been a continuous heavy snowfall for the last twenty-four hours. We decided it was time to break camp and get the hell out of Dodge while the "getting was good"—and even if the "getting" was not really good, it was still possible. We were already worried that the pass over into the Lostine River drainage might soon become impassable. And all the old elk biologists in our group were of the unanimous opinion that any elk with an IQ anywhere near spitting distance of average would be, by now, headed downhill and fast toward their winter range.

OCTOBER 18, 1996

On the ride out to the trailhead, through some clever alterations in packing the horses, it was possible for Bob and Paul to ride rather than walk. Walking out to the trailhead through the deepening snow would have been a very tough go. Between the horses eating increasingly generous rations of pelleted feed and our enthusiastic sustained attack on the groceries that we had packed in, there were two more saddle horses available for the trip to the trailhead. On the off chance that this might be the case, we had used two old McClellan cavalry saddles as pack saddles, a very handy feature of the old split-seat saddles that not many people knew about. Enough other riders and their horses had been going down the trail for the previous two days to pretty well pack down a trail. There were elk tracks along with the horse tracks—a seemingly well-broken trail out of the high lonesome attracts all travelers.

The horses were likely thinking of the dry barn where they could get out of the winter winds and enjoy two square meals of hay a day without commensurate effort on their part. I wondered if horses considered who was servant and who was master in their relationships with humans. It was, I thought, a perfect example of "mutualism" in which both men and horses profited. But the horses, free of such philosophical considerations, never slowed down or looked back. They had done their duty, earned their keep, and were on the way home— likely for the last time to the home they had known for so many years. They had been such a significant part of Bill's life—and mine—for so many years.

Riding in the lead, Bill sat tall in the saddle. By God, he was still in charge, if just for this little while longer. I felt certain that I knew what he was thinking and feeling. He rode erect, as befitted an old horse artillery officer, his eyes focused up the trail and toward the horizon. I ducked my head so that he would not see the tears that clouded my eyes and streamed down my cheeks.

After we arrived at Bill's house and unloaded and cared for the horses, Bill and I retreated to his den to do some business—very painful business. It was agreed that Bill would sell all the horses except his mare, Keno. He would also sell my horse trailer and all the horse packing gear. I would buy back my old Ford pickup for the agreed-upon price of one dollar and then retrieve the truck after I got settled in my new job at the University of Montana in Missoula early on in the new year.

We didn't know quite what to say after that. Maybe that was for the best. It was an awkward, painful, poignant moment.

We shook hands and said our good-byes. Bob, Paul, and I left in our rental car for the airport in Pendleton. We made a brief stop in La Grande for lunch. I excused myself for a brief visit to Margaret's resting place on the hillside above town. There was a new life, a new love, and new career waiting for me in Montana that I needed to tell her about. And so my last elk hunt and likely, I thought, my last Wilderness trip was at an end.

OCTOBER 19, 1996

On my flights back to Washington, I still had wilderness on my mind. Then, reluctantly, I focused on making an outline of what I would say at my last meeting at the annual leadership conference of the USFS's line officers and top staff. My remarks would begin with a quote from the Good Book: "To everything there is a season, and a time to every purpose under the heavens." I would continue, "My thirty years in the USFS are at an end. It is time for me to head home to the West. My heart is there. I have been gone too long. I can't—except in my dreams—see the stars nor can I feel the rhythms of the earth and its seasons. And the clock of my life is running out. It is, simply, time for me to go home." My time in the USFS was at an end.

CHAPTER 12

A NEWLY MINTED "GENTLEMAN" DISCOVERS "SHOOTING PRESERVES"

I was invited to participate in a "shoot" at one of the oldest "shooting preserves" in the northeastern United States. A shooting preserve—in this region at least—is a commercial operation where various game birds are raised in captivity and released in various ways to be pursued—in a variety of fashions—by hunters/shooters. Such was a new experience for me, as I had —for most of my life—neither the resources nor opportunities to visit such preserves on my own. In accepting the invitation, I understood that I would be expected to show up in a hunting outfit suitable to a "gentleman hunter." Faded, well-worn Levi's, plaid flannel shirt, frayed shooting vest, and a "gimme" baseball cap were clearly not suitable apparel. I coerced one of my buddies who routinely traveled in such circles to go along with me to the sporting goods store and see to it that I was properly attired. Fortunately, I did own a matched pair of high-end shotguns in fancy leather gun cases that had come to me as gifts over the years.

SEPTEMBER 27, 1997

The first morning's hunts were centered on ring-necked pheasants and chukars, both imports to the New World and therefore referred to as "exotics." The birds, raised to maturity in captivity, were released by employees of the shooting preserve just before daylight in knee-high cover of dwarf maize. The strips of cover were several hundred feet long and fifty feet or so wide. The strips were intersected by mown strips referred to as "stopper strips." Most of the released birds, likely bewildered by the ongoing experience, hunkered down and remained close to where they were released.

Then beautifully trained Labrador retrievers, under the control of their handlers, pushed the birds ahead of them down the cover strips. When the birds came to a stopper strip, most instinctively stopped and squatted rather than moving out into the open and becoming more vulnerable to predation. Their instincts told them that venturing out of cover was not really a good idea. The dogs and their handlers walked in the cover strip while the hunters (called "guns" in this environment) walked into the wind and down the mown strips on each side of the cover.

As we set out, I was puzzling about the significance of being routinely referred to as a "gun" as opposed to a "hunter." This was not the sort of game bird "hunting" I had grown up with when I did hard labor for an hour to buy ten shotguns shells at the local hardware at five cents apiece.

As the entourage of dogs and handlers pushed the birds ahead and the guns neared the end of the cover strips, the birds began to flush and rise into the air—the shooting commenced. Some of the attributes of hunting were there—comradeship, excitement, and the display of cherished, keenly honed skills by both dogs and hunters. But, for all of that, the whole experience seemed somehow and somewhat less than "real"—to me at least. The downed birds, quickly and skillfully retrieved by the dogs, were dropped at the feet of the handlers to go into the handler's game bag. When the weight of the loaded game bags became a burden, the birds were deposited in the back of a trailing "game wagon." Later the birds would be cleaned and frozen—all without any muss or fuss for the guns. In only two hours I saw more pheasants flying than I had ever seen in a week, maybe an entire season hunting truly wild birds.

At noon, we gathered at the clubhouse and donned tweed jackets and ties to partake of a "hunter's luncheon" of venison stew and biscuits. After lunch, we gathered in the living room to draw chits that revealed which "shooting butts" (blinds) that we would each occupy in the first round of the afternoon's "flighted duck shoot." The ducks—semi-domesticated mallards—had been raised and routinely fed in a facility built around a five- to six-acre artificial lake. The ducks were free to occupy the lake at their leisure and even to fly wherever they chose.

They routinely came back "home" to the lake to be fed in pens that were enclosed on four sides and the top. This made it possible for the gamekeepers to pick up and crate as many ducks as were needed to supply the shooting for the number of hunters participating in a particular "shoot." The ducks were hauled to where they would be released on cue. Some of the release points were at ground level. Others were located on towers, some thirty feet or more tall, on a wooded hillside several hundred yards away from the lake. The hunters stationed themselves in their assigned shooting butts between the towers and the lake. When the "hunter's horn" was sounded, the handlers began releasing mallards at a set rate. Once released, nearly all of the ducks made a beeline for the lake and the free lunch of cracked corn to which they were conditioned. In the process they flew over or past the shooting butts and the waiting guns. Most of the birds made it to the lake and lived to run the gauntlet another day. Many were not so lucky.

The releases of the mallards and the shooting continued for fifteen minutes. At the sound of the hunt master's horn, the shooting stopped and the guns rotated to their next assigned shooting position. When the horn sounded again, the release of ducks resumed. The pauses between shooting intervals allowed the dog handlers and their retrieving dogs to gather up the birds downed by the guns. That, most conveniently, gave the guns time for coffee or tea.

The ducks downed on land were retrieved by the dogs and their handlers. Wounded ducks that made it to the pond were picked up by gamekeepers in small one-man rowboats. Cripples were dispatched by .22 caliber "shorts" fired from a rifle, which made very little noise. When the shoot ended, the dead birds were taken to the cleaning facility, where they were cleaned, packaged, and frozen by staff. Members and their guests were invited to take as many as they wanted home—a small fraction of the total. Those remaining were routinely distributed to charity.

After the shooting, the conversations over drinks in the clubhouse were unanimous that this was a first-rate opening "shoot" for the season. As I had no previous experience with such, I could only take their word for it. Toward the end of the happy hour, the club's manager arrived. He called for the group's attention and announced the results of the day's shoot. He announced that 611 mallards had been "harvested" by the seventeen "guns,"—about 36 birds per "gun."

I was struck again by the use of the euphemism "gun" instead of "hunter" or "shooter" or "person." That set me to wondering, had the 611 mallards been killed by the "guns"? Or did the mallards die at the hands of the seventeen men who pointed the guns and pulled the triggers? It mattered but little—certainly not to the ducks.

I had been most generously and graciously entertained. I had participated enthusiastically enough. Yet I could not help pondering this totally new experience. There was, without doubt, a ritual of comradeship and competitive—admitted to or not—tests of marksmanship that had evolved from wild-lands hunting traditions and experiences.

Still I had some difficulty thinking of the experience as "hunting." Certainly, it was not to be confused with the "fair chase" mantra of the Boone and Crockett Club—and, to the credit of the participants, there was no attempt to do so. In the long term, there was no escape for these birds from the guns. The birds that escaped death today had only survived to run the gauntlet another day and then another.

For most of my hunting life, certainly in its beginning, I had been what Aldo Leopold—the recognized "father of wildlife management" in the United States—had referred to as a "one-gallus" hunter (a man so poor that he could only afford a single suspender to hold up his pants). In considering this day's experience, an exchange between the famed authors F. Scott Fitzgerald and Ernest Hemingway came to mind. Fitzgerald said, "The rich are different from us." Hemingway replied, "Yes, they have more money."

Obviously, only the more affluent could afford to belong to such a club and routinely participate in such activities. Yet I, as a guest, had participated wholeheartedly in the events of the day. The contrast gave me something to think about and set my mind to spinning.

What would I do if I had the resources and good fortunate to be invited to join such a group? I wasn't sure of my answer. The fine people and distinguished ladies and gentlemen that I shot with this day could afford to hunt wild game anywhere in the world and routinely did so—or had done so in their younger years. How, then, could I snap my one gallus and stick my nose in the air and condemn, or even belittle, what happened here today? After all, each of the seventeen "guns" killed, on average, some thirty-six pen-raised mallards in one hour and fifteen minutes of shooting—more ducks than the average hunter of truly wild ducks would kill in several seasons. Or, put another way, each gun fired off some 250 shotgun shells—more than I would commonly fire in four to six years of hunting for wild waterfowl. And, to some degree, wild populations of waterfowl and pheasants were spared. Certainly, if the old adage "practice makes perfect" is true, this sort of experience could not help but speed one along toward real expertise as a "wing shot."

Perhaps once a "gun" is conditioned to this kind of activity, the "real thing" might seem too time-consuming, wearing, difficult, uncomfortable, or simply just "not enough" to satisfy the cultivated palate. On the other hand, who really knows? Then I asked myself, did it really matter? There was next to no wounding loss. The bagged birds were consumed by humans, most of whom needed the meat. The people who did the shooting had a good time. Ten percent of the costs of the shotgun shells went to the Pittman-Robertson fund to finance wildlife operations by state wildlife agencies. Hunting pressure was shifted away from wild populations. The gamekeepers and the folks who raised the birds and put on the hunt and processed the birds were provided jobs. Other people who provided lodging and meals were compensated for their services. The area was beautifully maintained as open space and managed as habitat for other species. In the end, I found no real harm in the endeavor and much that was positive. But, to me, it was not really hunting, either. And, admittedly, I was not a pen-raised pheasant, chukar, or duck.

Well, I thought, such are individual decisions. Is this not, after all, just another form of farming and, then, marketing the product? And, given my present and future economic status, I really didn't have to worry too much about it. It was not too likely that I would ever have the opportunity to repeat the experience. Fitzgerald and Hemingway said it all. A lot of money makes a lot of impossible experiences possible. Perhaps it is well not to judge what one does not fully comprehend.

CHAPTER 13

HUNTING ON A HIGH-END HUNTING PRESERVE, SOUTH TEXAS STYLE

It had been some thirty years since I hunted big game "Texas style" when I was employed as a wildlife biologist for the Texas Parks and Wildlife Department in the Hill Country.

Big game hunting in Texas, like many things carried out "Texas style," is a bit different from that in most other states. Why? First, most of the land in Texas is in private ownership, and legal hunting only takes place with the permission of landowners. Second, under the auspices of North American Model of Wildlife Conservation, native species of wildlife are deemed the property of the state. Therefore, the state declares open seasons and rules and regulations for hunting. However—a really big however—access to that wildlife for hunting is at the sole discretion of the landowner. In Texas that set of circumstances had led to a highly developed market for that access to hunting—i.e., the selling of rights of trespass.

Beginning from that premise, the market for hunting evolved to the point that game animals, whether strictly legally so or not, are commonly marketed—often "by the head"—to hunters licensed by the state of Texas. When game animals are so marketed, it is not uncommon for that price to differ depending upon sex and, in the case of antlered animals, their trophy quality. Native wildlife, the access to and the harvesting thereof, has evolved into an increasingly significant commodity and a significant source of revenue for landowners. That, in turn, has led to more and more landowners enclosing their properties—and the resident terrestrial wildlife—behind "deer-proof" fences.

The most productive lands in Texas for plains game—bison, elk, antelope, and deer—were, at the time of European discovery, largely grassland savannahs with interspersed woodlands along rivers and streams. Bison migrated routinely north in summer and south in fall, resulting in what might be called today a massive "rest rotation" grazing system. Fires routinely burned over those savannahs, maintaining them primarily in grassland. Trees and shrubs were most commonly found in riparian zones along river and stream bottoms, providing habitat for deer and turkeys. Bison were essentially wiped out before the turn of the twentieth century by market hunters and interruption of their migration routes by human settlement.

Domestic livestock—horses, cattle, sheep, goats, and swine—took over as the primary grazing/foraging animals. Efforts, largely successful, were made to control wildfires. Sustained overgrazing that removed annual growth was helpful in that regard. Periodic drought and other factors resulted in overgrazing and an ecological conversion from perennial grasslands to annuals and the invasion of such woody plant species as mesquite, juniper, live oak, and shrub oak.

As grazing capacity for domestic livestock (especially sheep and cattle) declined, the newly evolved habitats provided excellent habitat for white-tailed deer and domestic goats. Such predators as wolves, cougars, black bears, bobcats, and coyotes were extirpated over most of the state by the late 1940s. In response to both factors—the evolution of habitat and the virtual elimination of predators—populations of wild ungulates (and imported wild ungulates) soared to the point that habitat damage from overuse was ever more obvious. In some regions of the state white-tailed deer numbers ranged from 30 or less to over 200 per square mile. In good habitat in a year of average or above-average precipitation, yearling white-tailed does commonly produced one fawn per year and adult does two fawns per year—most of which survived.

Beginning in the 1930s, a few landowners began leasing hunting rights to capitalize on these changing conditions. By the 1950s, income from hunting had become a primary source of revenue for many landowners and that trend increased over time. More and more ranches were enclosed by high fences to allow more intensive management and utilization of the "landowner's" deer; management of big game wildlife and habitat management intensified. Then a few land-owners imported big game wildlife from other countries, eventually to be marketed to hunters and other ranchers. Those "exotic" species were/are the sole property of the landowners and, therefore not subject to regulation by the state. As private property, such animals could be bought and sold, dead or alive, in the open market. Some of the species involved were sika deer, axis deer, red deer, barasingha, black-buck antelope, Nilgai antelope, aoudad sheep, and Russian boars.

Wildlife management coupled with the sale of hunting privileges—and upscale facilities for hunters—evolved into big business, which provided fiscal salvation for many marginal ranching operations. Some consider those developments to be an aberration of the concepts of the much praised (but more and more "winked at") North American Model of Wildlife Conservation. Wildlife management "Texas style" resulted in some of the most numerous populations of ungulate wildlife and game birds in North America and provided big payoffs for both landowners and hunters who were landowners, guests of landowners, and those who could and would pay fees for hunting. That outside-the-box success caused all concerned to remember, in one form or another, the old frontier adage that "money talks and bullshit walks." The only losers were those hunters who could not afford the tab for hunting and were thereby severely limited in opportunities when it came to hunting what was blithely referred to, more and more euphemistically—as time passed—as "the public's wildlife."

NOVEMBER 20, 1997

I have been a guest on this South Texas ranch since last evening. I met the owners through my recent induction as a Professional Member of the Boone and Crockett Club. A number of the guests for this particular hunt were landowners who themselves owned ranches enclosed by deer-proof fences. Some were recognized in the business of producing large trophy-quality white-tailed deer for hunters who paid significant fees to "harvest" such animals. The gold standard for recognizing big game trophies and those who killed those animals are the records books maintained by the Boone and Crockett Club,

founded by Theodore Roosevelt and associates in 1887 and the oldest organization of hunter-conservationists in the United States. That
august body has consistently refused to recognize and thereby honor
trophies taken from within big game-proof enclosures. Such animals
are considered, whether justly so or not, as not having been taken in
"fair chase."

That "fair chase" standard was a significant sore spot—and way
more than a minor-league resentment—for some who sat around the
campfire that night and owned such properties and/or routinely managed hunting under such conditions. As we talked around the fire,
reactions varied. Some were incensed that anyone ("who in the hell
is the Boone and Crockett Club?") to presume to make such a judgment. Some, I thought, were concerned that there was an increasing
focus on a way of hunting and managing big game that was steadily
departing from long-standing concepts of "fair chase" and the valid-
ity/viability of the North American Model of Wildlife Conservation,
which championed public ownership of and access to wildlife.

The majority of the landowners in the discussion seemed somewhat spiritually wounded by being, in their view, misunderstood and
unappreciated for their efforts in the husbandry of both land and
wildlife. Some viewed their motivations as essentially altruistic and
took more pleasure in deer (or wild turkey or quail or whatever) husbandry than they did in the associated hunting for themselves, family, friends, including those to whom they sold hunting privileges. In
brief, they felt that they were being looked down upon and given less
than their due for their contributions to wildlife conservation and
maintenance of a lifestyle and the traditions that involved and supported hunting.

This ranch was a well-managed "licensed shooting preserve."
The property was surrounded on three sides by deer-proof fences
erected by neighboring ranchers and, therefore, might be most accurately classified as a "semi-high-fenced" shooting preserve. I suspected
that the construction of deer-proof fencing to complete the enclosure
did not lie too far off in the future.

The ranch was dotted with game feeders mounted on ten-foot
stilts and regulated by timers and powered by batteries to distrib-

ute shelled corn in wide circles at preset intervals. A "blind" to hide hunters from the animals—essentially an eight-foot by eight-foot plywood box with a door—was located within fifty to one hundred yards of each feeder. There were two triangular holes cut in each wall to accommodate an occupant shooting in any direction from either a standing or sitting position. "Shooting lanes"—*senderos*—were cleared of brush and radiated out from the blinds for a hundred yards or more.

There were three pickup trucks on this hunting preserve that had been modified to provide what were essentially mobile shooting platforms. A seat was mounted in the bed of the truck just behind the cab so that a hunter sat five feet or so above ground level and was surrounded on three sides by a padded railing, to be used for a hand hold or, when the time came, provided a handy place to rest a rifle to assure a more certain shot. It was also possible for a rifleman to take a rest over the top of the cab. A winch mounted on the front bumper could pull the vehicle out if stuck; while a winch in the back assisted in loading dead animals into the bed of the truck. There were gun racks to hold rifles and shotguns so they would not be damaged—or create a hazard—when the truck was bouncing over rough terrain. Several of the trucks had been modified so that bird dogs could be hauled under the shooter's platform during quail-hunting exercises.

The hunting rigs were equipped with deer-guard bumpers to protect the grill and headlights in case of a collision with deer on backcountry roads—a not uncommon occurrence. There was a large container capable of holding 200 pounds of shelled corn to be distributed down the *senderos* radiating out from the shooting blinds.

The trucks were also equipped with very powerful spotlights to facilitate the nighttime hunting of wild pigs or "Russian boars" (which, as "exotics," were not considered game animals and not subject to state hunting regulations prohibiting hunting at night using a spotlight). Though it was illegal to shoot native deer at night, it was a legal and much-enjoyed pastime to go "spotlighting" to find and observe deer and other wildlife. Wildlife, especially members of the deer family, could be transfixed and rendered temporarily immobile by the blinding ultrabright lights.

NOVEMBER 21, 1997

The day began with a "pigeon shoot" for some twenty guests. The targets were common exotic pigeons ("rock doves') that were considered pests around ranch headquarters and in adjacent urban areas. The rules of the game were as follows. A square, fifteen by fifteen yards, was marked off by a rope suspended ten or so feet off the ground from four corner posts. The "gun" positioned himself or herself along one edge of the "ring" (actually a square) and ten feet inside it. The "thrower," who would launch the pigeon into flight, stood to the left of the shooter. The thrower removed a pigeon from a crate, turned his back to the shooter, and might extract various tail feathers, thereby inducing varying erratic flight patterns by the bird upon release. Skilled throwers were well compensated for their services.

The shooter stepped into the ring and walked up to the "line"—a rope stretched tight on the ground—and loaded two 7½ shot high-brass shotgun shells. All the shooters, save for me, were old hands at the game. They started with their shotguns mounted to their shoulders to facilitate a quicker first shot. The thrower stepped up beside the shooter with a pigeon in hand, looked to the shooter, and asked, "*Listo?*" (Are you ready?) The shooter called for the release by replying, "*Listo!*" (Ready!).

The thrower spun around, much as a discus thrower, and somewhere in the process "loosed" the pigeon into flight. The pigeon had to clear the rope enclosing the square to become a legitimate target. The shooter had two shots to drop the pigeon to the ground within a circle of 200 feet from the center of the square. Each round consisted of five pigeons per shooter. Shooting occurred in two relays—three birds in the first and two birds in the second. In this case, each shooter put twenty dollars per round into a pot. The first-place winner received 60 percent of the pot and the second-place shooter 40 percent.

When I was a guest here last December, I shot well enough not to embarrass myself but not well enough to keep from dropping a hundred bucks, maybe more, over the course of the day. But that was last year. This year I had had a number of opportunities to shoot skeet, trap, and sporting clays, along with hunting pheasants, chukars, and quail. Although it may not be true that "practice makes perfect," at least it trends that direction.

I learned last year that knocking down a pigeon required a much heavier hit on the target than cracking a clay pigeon. I was now using a tighter choke than when shooting sporting clays. I had not brought along a shotgun but was able to borrow a Model 425 Sporting Clays Model Browning—an exact replica of my favorite sporting clays gun. I inserted full chokes—kill clean or miss clean.

We shot four regulation rounds. I shot well enough to tie for first in the first round and win two rounds outright. Then we shot one round of "miss and out" with fourteen shooters in competition—winner take all. I won when my last competitor missed on bird number eleven. My winnings in dollars, oddly, were not really significant. What was significant was that there were four shooters in the field that had well-earned reputations as top-level competitors in the sport at the national level. Being able to even stay in the game with such shooters was a real achievement—and a great learning experience. I watched closely and learned much.

My style of shooting was vastly different from theirs. Every one of them stepped up to the line, mounted their shotguns to their shoulders, and called for the release of the pigeon. Though natural to them, that seemed very awkward to me. Clearly their technique provided a quicker first shot, which, in turn, provided for a faster second shot if needed, with the pigeon still in range. I was the only shooter who started from a "low gun" position with the stock level with my right elbow. To start tracking the target with the gun coming up to my shoulder and then firing as the stock settled into position seemed so much more natural and effective—at least to me.

Likely, that was maybe because that was the way I had been doing it since I was seven years old walking up behind quail dogs down on point. One of the shooters in the final round, who had once been an alternate for the U.S. Olympic Skeet Team, was laughing when he shook my hand and observed, "Big Jack, you do it all wrong—but you did it all wrong very well." Now, was that a compliment or what?

I admit to being competitive no matter what the contest—football, baseball, basketball, boxing, spitting for distance, horseshoes, or shooting. I enjoyed the competitive shooting and the unique challenge presented by the twisting, turning, erratic flight of the pigeons. It was much more challenging than the most difficult sporting clays course. Yet, for me at least, I had some trouble trying to ignore the fact that the targets were sentient living creatures. This was not hunting—nor was it meant to be. This was highly competitive target shooting—nothing more and nothing less—employing live targets.

It was certainly an exercise for those with more spare change in their pockets than I. By the time the thrower was compensated, each target cost between five and six dollars. Today's shoot, which involved 250 pigeons, cost our hosts some $1,250 and $1,500 for the birds alone. That could be rationalized, at least to some degree, by the fact that the folks who provided the pigeons made money by trapping urban pigeons that were considered both a nuisance and a health hazard. They were routinely controlled—trapped or poisoned—by municipalities for aesthetic and health reasons. Trappers, public health, aesthetics, and public coffers all benefited.

That the pigeons could be marketed for three to five dollars each made this form of "vermin control" economically feasible, even providing a minor-league profit center for nearby municipalities. The pigeons died in either case. Likely the manner of their death mattered but little to the pigeons. But still, as I watched the throwers reach into the crate, extract a bird, pull out some tail feathers, cup it in a special grip, spin and throw the bird so it just cleared the rope in a mad dash for freedom that it was doomed to lose much of the time, I had an uneasy twinge. The $600 in winnings in my pocket at the end of the day didn't change that. As we were leaving the pigeon-shooting venue, I noticed that the live oaks and the power and telephone lines that surrounded the area were festooned with pigeons that had survived the gauntlet. If there was some way they could have asked my advice, I would have said "get the hell out of Dodge." I suspected they would be quite easy to trap a second time around.

The pigeon shoot ended by midafternoon. Now the time had arrived for white-tailed deer, Rio Grande turkey, and wild boar hunting—Texas style! The prescribed technique *de jure* was to enter a hunting blind two and a half hours before full dark, waiting to see what animals came to the bait of shelled corn spread out in the *sen-deros* radiating out from the blinds in one or more directions. There was little doubt that "shootable" animals, of one sort or another, would make their appearance with the arrival of the magic "witching hour"—that last hour of daylight when the animals were most active.

It would be a matter, then, of the examining the animals carefully in order to select an appropriate animal to "take," usually as specified by the host. Our instructions were not to shoot either of a pair of mature, well-antlered white-tailed bucks that were commonly seen from the blind to which I was assigned—one buck sported ten-point antlers and the other twelve points. Our host wished to retain those "big boys" in the herd for purposes of breeding. However, if a certain buck known to come to this setup, recognizable by three antler points on one side and a long spike on the other, was to appear, it was my host's preference that he be "culled" as an "inferior deer." And if wild turkeys showed up, I was free to shoot one with "a visible beard." And if all else failed, any and all feral pigs that might appear were fair game. My plate "runneth over" with options.

The first option that came into view was made up of thirty or so Rio Grande turkeys, an unusually large flock consisting of three adult hens and their young of the year. The soft clucks and purrs from the flock were a pleasure to hear and reminded me of many months of trapping turkeys as part of wild turkey research projects in the early 1960s in the western Edwards Plateau when I was a wildlife biologist for the Texas Parks and Wildlife Department. The two trophy bucks declared by my host as off-limits came into view some half hour before sundown. I studied them through borrowed 7×35 Leica binoculars as they walked by as close as twenty steps from my hiding place. Then, just as the sun touched the horizon, the buck with the deformed antlers stepped into view—though partially hidden by brush—at some fifty steps. I carefully poked my Old Reliable—a .250-3000 Savage lever-action rifle, which was my first big game rifle and still my favorite—through the shooting/viewing port of the blind and tracked his movements through the old 4-power Weaver scope as he moved through the brush along the edge of the opening.

Ten minutes passed and shooting light was fast fading. The buck grazed directly toward me with his head down most of the time. When his head was down to graze, I could just see the top of his back. I put my diaphragm turkey call in my mouth and fixed the crosshairs just over the top of his back, where I figured his neck would be if I could entice him to throw his head up and look my way. I took a deep breath, let half out, held it, and gave a loud turkey alarm call. The buck threw up his head to look for danger, and I touched off a round. I lost the buck in the slight recoil and the muzzle flash in the last minutes of legal shooting time. I was certain that the buck was lying dead in his last tracks.

As instructed by my host, I did not leave the blind until he drove up some half hour later. We walked out to where I thought the buck would be found lying. Sure enough, there he was. The bullet had entered dead center at the lower edge of his white throat patch and severed his spine. He was likely senseless and essentially dead before he hit the ground.

My host backed up his tricked-out hunting truck. I attached the cable around the antlers, and the buck was winched up into the truck's bed. When we arrived at the ranch headquarters, the Hispanic ranch hands unloaded the deer and winched the carcass up to be weighed, eviscerated, and skinned before being hung to cool in the walk-in cooler. For the record, the buck—entrails, hide, head, and all—weighed in at 176 pounds. Looking at his teeth, I estimated his age at five and a half years. When we were finished with the deer and washed up for dinner, the ranch foreman handed each of us a very cold Lone Star beer. It hit the spot.

We walked over to where a mesquite wood fire was burning and sat down in the folding chairs that circled the fire and watched as the ranch hands dressed and skinned out the deer that had come in since my arrival. The ranch hands were skilled at their trade and quite obviously well-practiced. I thought to myself that there were definite advantages to Texas-style deer hunting. On the other hand, such hunting was, in a sense, a somewhat "sterile" business in that the hunter was relieved of physical effort, stalking skills, and any association with the "blood and guts" aspects that go along with big game hunting.

I wondered if that absence of any real effort on the hunter's part produced an incomplete *gestalt* for any of the hunters besides me. I was used to taking care of all facets of big game hunting—finding, killing, gutting, skinning, quartering the carcass, packing it out, cutting up the meat, and packaging it for the freezer. Cooking and eating came later. In this case, all I did was follow the guide's instructions to the letter and shoot straight at the moment of truth.

The other hunters and their guides joined us as they came in from the field. The hunting stories around the fire rounded out a fine day.

NOVEMBER 22, 1997

When I got to the cook shack an hour and a half before first light, a breakfast of pork and deer sausage, bacon, flour tortillas, ranch-style eggs, orange juice, and coffee was waiting. There was a Bloody Mary available for those unfortunates whose well-being might be enhanced by a bit of the "hair of the dog."

Thirty minutes before first light, I was driven to and deposited beside a hunting blind in the Rio Frio river bottom. At first light, I heard turkeys talking from their overnight roosts in the giant live oaks several hundred yards down toward the river. Along with full light, I heard turkeys approaching from two directions, seemingly with great caution. Just then, the battery-powered mechanism that powered the automated feeder to scatter shelled corn went off. Obviously, the turkeys knew the sound, appreciated its meaning, and came running to the feeder. There were, so far as I could tell in the very early morning light, six adult hens and their broods—about fifty to sixty birds in total. The young birds were coming into their adult plumage, and the young males were easily identified by their more iridescent plumage and lack of a visible beard.

No matter how I strained my eyes—even through binoculars—I couldn't find a "visible beard" in the bunch. I watched the highly entertaining show of "gotchas" and "I'm bigger and meaner than you" put on by the flock around the feeder for half an hour or so. The young males, likely on a testosterone high, went through dominance displays and chases and what one of my old technicians in the Texas Parks and Wildlife Department called "hopping and flopping" displays.

Then, from behind the blind, I heard wild pigs snuffing and grunting as they approached the feeder. Soon I could make out a sow and eight half-grown piglets. I kept an eye—and both ears—focused on the pigs, thinking that I would take one if no shot at a gobbler or a nice whitetail buck presented itself. An hour or so had gone by when I saw a truly magnificent fourteen-point buck moving through the trees toward the feeder. My host had asked me to refrain from shooting any buck with more than eight points. Of course, I honored his request—which was really a polite but very clear instruction. However, I admit to shouldering my rifle and putting the crosshairs on the big buck's heart and whispering "bang" more than once during the half hour that he was in sight and in range.

Then some 150 yards down the *sendero*, I saw what I thought were three mature turkey gobblers—that is, they had visible beards. A half hour passed, and they came no closer. Finally, I made out through my binoculars, that all three gobblers had visible beards. Texas, unlike many other states, allows turkey hunting with a rifle. At just less than 150 yards down the opening the gobblers were well within range of my .250-3000 Savage. But a very fast bullet from a big game rifle, designed to expand on impact, was not apt to leave much meat for dinner if the bullet went through the bird's big middle. And a turkey's head and neck was a very small target at that distance. After studying things over for a quarter hour, I determined to try for a head shot—and an instant clean kill or a clean miss. By now, the gobblers had closed the distance to just under 100 yards—close enough I reckoned.

I waited patiently, watching through the 4-power scope, locked into a braced shooting position, and breathing deep and easy with a regular heartbeat. I waited until the birds turned to face me and continued their feeding. I settled down, began to breathe deeply, braced my elbows on the rest provided for just that purpose, and picked my target. I put my diaphragm turkey call in the roof of my mouth and after several more breaths, let out a half-breath and gave out a sharp "pert" alarm call. All three gobblers stopped and stretched their necks up in search of the danger. I held the crosshairs just where the neck began on the closest gobbler and squeezed off the shot. I had six inches of leeway up and down and less than two inches side to side.

The old Savage lever-action .250-3000 (which fired a .25-caliber bullet weighing 87 grains at a velocity of 3,000 feet per second) was one of the first generally available high-velocity flat-shooting deer rifles. This model was not blessed with a crisp trigger, but I was used to that. The old rifle was dead-on, and the bullet essentially decapitated the big gobbler. The other two birds ran off a few yards and then, oddly enough, came back to check out the bird that was in his death throes. They alternatively spread their wings and hopped at the downed bird in dominance displays. Their attention flagged as the dead bird's movements gradually ceased. The survivors moved off into the brush and resumed feeding.

At midmorning, a ranch hand picked me up for the midday lunch break at the ranch headquarters. After a lunch of chili con carne, sweet onions, grated rat cheese, and tortillas—with a Lone Star beer as a chaser—there was still time for a brief siesta before the evening hunt.

I was awakened from my nap by a ranch hand who handed me a cold Lone Star beer and delivered me to a hunter's blind on the other side of the ranch from the Rio Frio. I had no more than settled down in my blind and was catching up on my journal entries when seventeen wild pigs came running, sans caution, into the opening that held the feeder. I picked out the biggest of the bunch—a young boar—and poked my rifle out of the shooting port, shouldered and braced, and tracked him in my scope until he was clear of the other pigs and turned sideways. That afforded me a perfect "meat shot," one that would damage as little of the meat as possible. I shot the pig right in the ear hole, and he dropped like a sack of corn. There was no need for a second shot. As instructed, I stayed put in the blind.

Within three-quarters of an hour, my hiding place seemed surrounded by a flock of eleven young turkey males ("jakes") and a couple of hens. Once again, no matter how hard I wished, wanted, and tried, I could not see a "visible beard" in the entire bunch. Their off-and-on fussing and fighting entertained me for the next couple of hours. Then, just at sunset, white-tailed deer began to appear in all four of the *senderos* that I could see from my hiding place. There were four bucks in the bunch within easy rifle range, three of which sported ten-point or better antlers, making them off-limits. One of the bucks sported eight points, which made him, by my host's rules, fair game or, as he put it, "okay to take." He was what the ranch manager classified as an "intermediate buck"—not a real trophy-class buck and not, in his opinion, apt to mature into a desirable breeding buck. When there was only some ten minutes of shooting time left, I decided to take the eight-point buck. He was feeding about 100 to 120 yards away—a little farther than I like to shoot—and showing me his ass to boot. I settled the crosshairs just over the top of his back and waited for him to turn sideways or, next best, raise his head. I waited and waited and waited as the light faded.

With not more than five minutes of shooting time left, the buck raised his head for a look-see. I squeezed off the shot. He dropped on his brisket and did not move. As instructed, I waited in the blind as darkness settled in. Then I heard wild pigs all around the blind as they grunted and fussed at one another while they fed. Now and again, I made out their black shapes in the starlight. The ranch truck came for me—and my pig and my buck—about "zero dark forty-five" and delivered me to La Cantina (the bar) at the ranch headquarters. All the other hunters were already gathered around the fire telling tall tales when we arrived.

To my delight, one of the chairs in that circle was occupied by General David Lee "Tex" Hill, a fellow Texas Aggie and a retired Air Force officer. As an Air Force officer I had heard many "war stories" that involved General Hill.

When I shook his hand, I said, "I am honored to meet you, General." He quickly gave me to understand that he preferred to be addressed as "Tex." Though I tried—and tried hard—I could not bring myself to address General Hill as "Tex." The man was a legend in Texas, certainly at Texas A&M—and in the Air Force. He had been a U.S. Navy pilot when Japan invaded China in 1939. He volunteered and became a squadron commander for the American Volunteer Group (AVG)—the "Flying Tigers"—which fought against the Japanese in China in 1940 and 1941. He became an ace in that role, having downed five or more aircraft in aerial combat and repeated the trick after rejoining the U.S. Army Air Force, shooting down, in total, eighteen Japanese aircraft. It was honor for me, as a reserve Air Force officer, to make his acquaintance and listen to some of his war stories.

General Hill had killed what he described as a "smallish" white-tail buck that sported a spike antler on one side and a short forked antler on the other. When we walked up, the ranch owner was prais-ing the help Tex had provided in removing such an obvious cull from the ranch's herd. Tex just grunted and allowed that he wasn't very fond of "horn soup" anyway. The hunters and hosts stood around and told lies and jokes as the ranch hands dressed out the two deer and the pig. Our kibitzing was enhanced by the delivery of drinks—made to order, of course.

After a bit, we retreated to a circle of chairs outside surround-ing a blazing fire of mesquite logs. I loved—and suddenly realized how much I missed—the smell of burning mesquite. I thought that if there was any better firewood in the world than seasoned mesquite, I had yet to encounter it in my foreign work assignments. It came to mind that I had smelled mesquite cooking fires in Pakistan, where mesquite had been imported many decades before by the British Raj to provide firewood in semi-arid areas. That seemed a bit odd, as I was more familiar with efforts to control mesquite that was invading grasslands in central Texas. Different strokes for different folks.

The smell of burning mesquite triggered memories from both Texas and Pakistan. It brought to mind other campfires and other hunts and other fishing trips. I recalled the campfires of work crews and working wildlife biologists over the thirty-two years I had lived in Texas. There were memories of fishing trips with my father and uncles on the San Saba, Llano, Brazos, and Trinity Rivers. There had been many a good story told around those campfires. There were memo-ries of my Texas Parks and Wildlife Department technicians, Emmitt "Snuffy" Smith, Calvin Van Hoozer, Harold May, and "Bud" Otto—all passed over now. I thought of Jerry Butler, Rod Marburger, James "Jim" Teer—comrades and colleagues now retired from the "family business" of wildlife management and whose images I conjured up from the smoke of the mesquite fire.

The memories that flooded up out of memory were pleasant and refreshing, though sad at the same time. Suddenly I felt very old knowing that my life was entering the "short rows" now. That did not distress me—such was simply so. Memories resided in the mesquite smoke, and visions emerged full-blown from the glowing coals. This was not a night for me to do much of the talking. It was a night to ask questions and listen carefully and respectfully to the answers. General Hill held court until only coals remained and it was time to retire—perchance to dream. So after one more round of hunting stories, we were off to bed.

NOVEMBER 23, 1997

I slept in. The taking of two whitetail bucks, a turkey gobbler, and a wild pig had nearly satiated my hunting lust. Our host drove me around the ranch and drew me out as to my opinions and advice on various aspects of wildlife management, especially as it related to white-tailed deer and wild turkeys. Without discussion or bargaining, it seemed to both of us that a consulting job in exchange for a wonderful hunt and good company was more than a fair exchange.

He had with him a new custom-made 7mm rifle with a Redfield variable-powered scope especially designed to facilitate long-range shooting. The settings on the scope had been recorded, at 100-yard intervals, out to 500 hundred yards. He drove out to a cleared *sendero* with a blind at one end. Circular steel plates—twenty-four inches in diameter and painted Day-Glo orange—were mounted on posts at 100-yard intervals. There was no guessing at distances for a hunter in this blind.

Starting with the target at 100 yards, the ranch owner repeatedly fired and adjusted the scope until the rounds were grouping in the center of the target. That drill was repeated at each of the distances. At the end of the exercise I had complete confidence in his ability to be dead on target at each of those ranges. Now, given that performance, the only problem for the hunter armed with that rifle was accurately accounting for the distance to the target—and the wind—and being steady on the trigger. Accurate estimates of distance were available from another newfangled gadget in his possession: a laser range finder which would determine distances within three meters. I told him that ought to be, as we commonly said in the USFS, "close enough for government work." That would produce a high probability of killing an animal at a distance beyond which the animal would not likely to be distressed enough to bolt even if it saw the hunter.

While all of this was going on, I took my .250-3000 Savage and wandered down to where two *senderos* intersected at a blind. I spotted two javelinas feeding at some 200–250 yards. I walked back and asked the ranch owner if javelinas were "fair game." He told me to "have a go" for one or both of the little pigs. It had been over thirty years since I had last killed and eaten a javelina. If memory served, javelinas were fine eating if properly cared for and prepared. Besides, I thought, a dinner of javelina would seem quite exotic in the Bitterroot Valley in Montana.

When I returned to the spot, the javelinas had moved but little. I sat down cross-legged, raised the rifle, wrapped my left arm in the sling, and locked my elbows inside my knees—my most stable shooting position when a fixed brace was not at hand. The two javelinas were head-on to me. My rifle was sighted in to be two inches high at 100 yards and on target at 200 yards. If I did my part, the bullet should hit dead-on. So I took a deep breath, exhaled half the air, held the crosshairs on the middle of the snout of one of the pigs, and squeezed off the round. The javelina dropped, kicked a couple of times, and moved no more. Its companion bolted into the brush. I remained locked into my shooting position and waited.

Time passed—five minutes, ten minutes, thirty minutes. I waited and waited. Just as an increasing pain in my back and neck was encouraging me to give up my shooting position, the other javelina came back into view and resumed feeding, seemingly oblivious to its dead companion. I knew my rifle was spot-on. I repeated the process with the same result. When I paced off the distance to the two javelinas—210 yards plus or minus 5 yards—I was pleased that my estimate of distance to target was as good as that provided by the laser gadget—this time anyway. My guide arrived in his pickup and delivered me and my two javelinas to headquarters where we dropped off my kills at the dressing station. After a very tall glass of iced sweet tea, it was time for my guide to take me to a blind located along the banks of the Rio Frio for the afternoon hunt.

I had been in the blind—admittedly nodding off from time to time—for a bit over an hour when I looked out a peephole to see some twenty young male turkeys around the feeder. I carefully glassed each and every bird, several times, in hopes of detecting a "visible beard" but was unsuccessful. The flock wandered off after a half hour or so and disappeared into the brush. Then about ten minutes after sundown, I could see, just barely, a half-dozen dark shapes of wild pigs around the feeder. Their grunts verified my visual identification. Once I had the .250-3000 Savage in position out the hole of the blind, I could use the light-gathering capability of the 4-power rifle scope to see more clearly. I could see the pigs, but judging distance was complicated by the gloaming. By regulation, it was too late to take a shot at a game animal, but the pig was an "exotic" not in that category and was therefore not covered by state hunting regulations.

I picked out the pig I wanted and cleared the background. I figured the distance at 40 to 50 yards and held the crosshairs an inch below the ear hole. I had a perfect sight-picture when I touched off the round. I was stunned when the pig jumped straight up, hit the ground, spun around, and took off for elsewhere, squealing loudly and continuously. I was flabbergasted. There was simply no way I could have possibly missed that shot. Flashlight in hand, I paced off the distance—106 steps. At that distance, the bullet would have struck a full two inches above the aiming point. That would have cleared the pig's ear hole and put the bullet through its ear(s). I figured that I would have squealed too—and burned a little rubber "getting the hell out of Dodge" if a bullet from nowhere had punched a hole through my ears. I found the experience a bit humbling. I had been coming around to the belief, for however brief a time, that I could not miss.

I left the blind and lay spread-eagled in the grass and watched the stars emerge while I waited to be picked up. I listened as the night sounds replaced those of the day. I could hear the "peents" of the Texas nighthawks as they hawked insects out of the air. Every region of the world where I had been blessed to work has its own specific night sounds, smells, and "vibrations." The combination that swept over me here, in this place, seemed to be "mine"—the sounds, smells, and vibrations that I had grown up and matured with. They were ingrained in my brain and soul and identified my place of origin. I surmised that they always would.

Texas was no longer home, and most likely never would be again—and I knew it. But Texas would always be the place of my beginnings and growing up—both as a man and a professional conservationist. A quote from T.S. Eliot's "Little Gidding" came to mind:

> We shall not cease from exploration
> And the end of all our exploring
> Will be to arrive where we started
> And know the place for the first time.

Sure enough, these last few days I had returned to my beginnings and, for a brief precious moment, seemed to know the place for the first time. The spell was broken by the bouncing headlights that I saw coming through the live oaks. We greeted each other—the driver and I—with our stories of things seen and not seen, of shots fired true—and a shot missed. I did not speak of smells, sounds, and "vibrations" or of coming back full circle to "beginnings." Some things are best acknowledged and treasured in silence alone or with those of similar mind.

NOVEMBER 24, 1997

When I arrived at the airport in Missoula, in addition to my hunting gear I picked up the eight well-sealed polyurethane boxes that contained the frozen packaged meat from two white-tailed deer, one wild pig, two javelinas, and one Rio Grande turkey. I left the pile of my stuff in the baggage area of the airport under the watchful eye of a friend that ran the airport restaurant. In the long-term parking lot I searched for and finally located my old Ford pickup, which my wife Kathy had left for me when she flew to Maryland to spend Thanksgiving with her parents and children.

When I got home to Florence, Montana—before anything else—I rearranged the contents of the two side-by-side freezers in the garage to make room for the wild game I had brought home from "the old country." It would, I thought, be an interesting contrast with—or perhaps a complement to—the meat from mule deer, elk, antelope, blue and ruffed grouse, and pheasants already residing therein. The only trouble was that I obviously needed another freezer. My return to my "beginnings" had been a deeply satisfying pleasure. But Montana was home now. I had a new life ahead of me as a college professor in a new place—with freezers full of game to boot. I truly hoped I would be able to convince my new bride of the "eatability" of the wild game. Time would tell.

CHAPTER 14

"MY HEART'S IN THE HIGHLANDS"

My Heart's in the Highlands, my heart is not here;
My heart's in the Highlands a-chasing the deer.

—Robert Burns

I was privileged to be able to hunt red deer stags in Scotland for seven years. I also hunted driven grouse and pheasants in England, Scotland, and once in Spain. Those hunts were not only a privilege—and highly enjoyable—but also afforded me, as a wildlife biologist and big game manager, a chance to see how game management and hunting evolved and has been sustained for centuries in Europe. Most of that hunting took place in what passed for "wilderness" in the Scottish Highlands, and I welcomed the chance to compare the differences between hunting in Scotland (typical of the European Model) and the United States (the North American Model). It is through such comparisons that students of hunting can understand, compare, and appreciate different approaches to sport hunting that evolved for different reasons in differing cultures and circumstances while yielding essentially the same result relative to the survival of hunted species. Furthermore, I had spent a considerable portion of my forty-year professional career to date studying various aspects of the ecology of elk in North America. My long-term partner Dale Toweill and I had compiled two widely recognized tomes that were published by the Wildlife Management Institute (*Elk of North America—Ecology and Management* in 1982 and *North American Elk: Ecology and Management* in 2002). I was fascinated with being able to observe red deer in Scotland; elk and red deer being the same species (*Cervus elaphus*) but a different subspecies.

OCTOBER 12, 1998

To our delight, Kathy and I had been invited for a "wee bit of stag stalking" in Scotland. Our host, Robert "Bob" Model, a close personal friend and a prominent Wyoming rancher and conservationist who served as the chairman of the board of the National Forest Foundation—a nonprofit support group for the U.S. Forest Service—was our host.

Bob picked us up at the Glasgow airport in a rented Land Rover. We could not help but note that the steering wheel was on the right as opposed to the left—as vehicles drive on the left side of the road in the British Isles. We piled our gear into the Land Rover and were on the road to Edinburgh, where we were to spend our first night. For the first day or so, driving on the "wrong" side of the road produced heart palpitations and involuntary and numerous contractions of the sphincter muscles—at least in my case.

Having an American of the Wyoming persuasion at the wheel of the Land Rover added considerably to the excitement. We were halfway to Edinburgh before I released my two-handed white-knuckle grip on the grab bar mounted on the dashboard in front of the passenger seat. Actually, our host drove quite well by concentrating intensely on his driving and exhibiting none of his usual garrulous behavior. While at the wheel, he was tight-jawed, thin-lipped, and dead silent except when begging someone—anyone—to figure out where the hell we were and to provide him ample warning of the next turn.

We spent the night at a hotel in downtown Edinburgh that wasn't all that fancy but plenty expensive. We ate supper at a nearby pub recommended by the hotel's concierge. He steered us right—both the meal and the wine were excellent.

We were joined at supper by an old friend of our host who routinely served as his "loader" when he shot driven grouse or pheasants in Scotland or Britain. Evidently, the shooting could get so hot and heavy that each hunter needed a matched pair of shotguns. The loader carries a bag generously loaded with shotgun shells and one of the shotguns. The loader's duty is to follow and stand behind the shooter—the so-called "gun." After the gun fires one or both barrels, he or she holds the shotgun pointed up in the right hand (assuming the gun is right-handed) and stretches out his or her left hand to receive the forearm of a freshly loaded shotgun passed from the loader, who then takes the shotgun with expended shells from the gun's right hand. The gun is now equipped to fire at will while the loader ejects the empty shells, loads the shotgun, points the muzzle up, and puts it on safety for the next exchange. These two were old friends and hunting companions who talked of remembered "grand" grouse hunts of the past—and the hunt to come tomorrow. Theirs was a most interesting conversation about a style of hunting that I had only read about and never dreamed I would have a chance to experience. I was exhausted, but sleep did not come easy. I was both exhausted and, yet, eager for tomorrow.

OCTOBER 13, 1998

The day's first order of business was to visit a "tweed shop" to allow Kathy and me to be suited out in proper "shooting suits"—woolen pants and jacket, knee socks, tattersall shirt, wool tie, and gaiters. I was informed that "gentlemen hunters" simply did not stalk red deer inappropriately attired—after all, such was "simply not done, Old Boy." The pants were what a Yank would call "knickers"—more properly called "plus fours" in Scotland based on the length of the drop the nickers were over the knee. In the field, the long woolen stockings are covered with heavy canvas gaiters to protect against the damp and the cockleburs. Evidently, when one pursues the wily grouse one also wears a tailored shooting jacket of matching tweed with a fresh tattersall or plaid shirt with a plain woolen tie. The outfit is topped off with a "stalker's cap" of matching tweed.

While I thought I looked pretty damned spiffy in my new get-up, I had a hard time visualizing myself crawling around in the wet peat clad in a "shooting suit" that cost twice what I had ever paid for a suit in my life. I had a vision of the main character from the musical *Fiddler on the Roof* who, when puzzled about what was transpiring around him, belted out the song "Tradition!" So I quit puzzling and just thought "Tradition!"

Our next stop was a "stick makers" cottage located on the loch (inland lake) near the laird's (lord's) estate where we would be "a-stalking on the morrow." A gentleman who is "a-stalking" simply does not go out "on the hill" without a "proper stick." We ended up with two such proper sticks—one for me and one for "Memsahib," as our host sometimes called Kathy. Our sticks were matching, with handles carved from a ram's horn into the shape of a thistle, the symbol of Scotland, at the tip. The stick maker also made cutlery with staghorn handles, which proved too much for Kathy to resist; she acquired a full set, to be delivered to our home in Montana.

I was drawn by sounds to the shed behind the workshop. The floor was littered with horns—mostly from sheep but with a few cattle horns thrown in—and many dozens of antlers from red, roe, fallow, and sika deer in a large pile in the corner. Many of the antlers were of trophy quality—some mounted on plaques for display and others awaiting such treatment. The bone cutter bought deer antlers of less than trophy quality from the shooting estates to provide the raw materials from which he fashioned handles for his cutlery.

The countryside was stunningly beautiful, though it had been in continuous use for the grazing of sheep for several hundreds of years. Once we were on rural roads, the scenery was enhanced by the stone walls that bordered the narrow roads. There were frequent stretches where the roads were bordered by beech and maple trees. The huge overhanging trees sometime gave me the feeling of traveling through a tunnel of overhanging branches. Though beautiful, I could not help but ponder upon the consequences of even a slight error in driving or—heaven forbid—a mechanical malfunction.

The houses and barns were of consistent character, built of quarried limestone walls with slate roofs that spoke eloquently of a venerable culture still valued and carefully sustained. The small villages, with their near-identical row houses with slate roofs, were a delight to the eyes. There was essentially no signage along the rural roadways except that required to meet the absolute minimal needs to ensure public safety—speed limits, warnings of potential dangers ahead, and directions. The signs and their shapes were consistent, tastefully done, and not lighted—parsimony in all things. The overall effect was most pleasing. This was the day that Kathy and I fell in love with Scotland.

We returned to our hotel just a bit late for supper. The ladies had experienced an exciting day of shopping and enjoying the sights, sounds, and smells of old Edinburgh. They had toured the old fortifications above the city—and Edinburgh Castle itself. We were a talkative bunch as we visited over a drawn-out supper at a tiny but quite nice restaurant. The owner served us herself and kept up a constant chatter and repartee—especially with our host, who gave as good as he got.

The food and drink—somewhat exotic for Kathy and me—was the perfect end to a wonderful day. Kathy and I chose to walk back to our lodging via the Royal Mile and past the castle where Mary Queen of Scots had been imprisoned and beheaded in 1587 on charges of plotting the assassination of Queen Elizabeth I of England. Such places really did exist!

The buildings bordering the street were built of quarried cut stone and jammed tightly together. The cobblestone streets were narrow, and the sidewalks could only accommodate our walking in single file. The farther we went, the fewer people we encountered and the streets were less and less well lighted. By the time we reached the castle, we were becoming a bit uncomfortable, as we had not seen a cab for some time. Finally, a cab came by, responded to our hail, and whisked us away to the hotel.

After we were in bed, I got up to close the window in order to shut out, or tone down, the noise from the street below. Edinburgh is a university town, and a prime source of entertainment for the students seemed to involve getting a tad inebriated, wandering the streets in small groups, singing and shouting at other students—or maybe just shouting for the hell of it. As we were still suffering from jet lag, the street noises did not interfere with a sound sleep that came quickly.

OCTOBER 14, 1998

After breakfast at the hotel, we departed Edinburgh. Our next stop would be the estate upon which we would be hunting. The farther north we drove, the fewer trees we saw, and low-growing heather began to dominate the landscape. There were cultivated plantations here and there of Scots pine, larch, Norway spruce—and, to my surprise—lodgepole pine from North America. The dark green patches of trees, planted in geometric patterns, seemed intrusive on the landscape, as the foresters had taken no care to camouflage the fact that these were tree farms. The trees were planted at precise distances apart and in obvious uphill and downhill rows designed to drain water from seasonally saturated soils. The large blocks of trees were surrounded by what had been at one time deer-proof fences.

Most of the fences, having done their duty to protect young seedlings, were now in a poor state of repair. Roe and red deer routinely used the plantations, likely I thought to ameliorate severe winter weather conditions. Evidently, after the plantations were firmly established and the trees were several meters tall, the deer were considered less of a problem. The plantations were originally intended to provide raw materials for pulp mills.

During the latter part of our day's journey, the two-lane "highway" ran along the east coast of the North Sea, adding just one more visual delight to our already overflowing senses. The beautiful straight rock fences that separated paddocks stretched from the roadway to the sea. The paddocks were small—some as small as three or four acres. We were told that this was the result of the ownership being divided among heirs numerous times over the centuries. Finally, we turned off the highway and entered the 40,000-acre highland estate where we would be "stalking" red deer on the morrow.

Our host had hunted on this estate every year for at least the past decade and was well familiar with the territory. He drove past the laird's house on up the dirt road to the Gardener's Cottage, so named because once, in the estate's grander times, it quartered the estate's gardener and family who tended the gardens and grounds. Now the cottage was used during the fishing season to accommodate salmon fishermen who own (or rent) "beats"—i.e., fishing rights along clearly delineated sections of the streams and rivers on the estate. Then when the "stag stalking season" came around, it was used to accommodate hunters. Hunting and fishing provided a significant, steady source of income for owners of the highland estates; in many cases, the additional revenue was enough to make estates economically—often only marginally—viable.

We were early to bed in anticipation of tomorrow's new experience—"stalking" red deer on the moors of northern Scotland. Since I was a boy, I had read of such hunting and the associated traditions and was quite eager to experience the real thing. I went to bed wondering about what differences I would see between North American elk and red deer in terms of appearance and behavior.

OCTOBER 15, 1998

I was up, dressed, and ready to go "a-stalking" well before daylight. No one had bothered to tell us that stag stalking in Scotland was totally different from elk hunting in North America. When hunting elk, I was accustomed to being in the woods—in full hunting mode—well before daylight. Therefore, I had downed way too much quite stout coffee waiting in the Gardener's Cottage when I heard clattering outside emanating from a rather strange-appearing piece of machinery approaching.

It was our "hunting vehicle," manned by two hunting guides ("stalkers" in the Scottish vernacular)—Charlie, the head stalker, and his understalker, "Young" Graeme. Their transport of the moment—referred to affectionately by them as "the machine"—was a tracked vehicle originally designed for use by North Atlantic Treaty Organization (NATO) troops. After being declared surplus, some were sold to the highest bidders. What a machine it was! It was made up of two articulated parts. The driver sat in the front cabin, which contained the engine, had two large driving tracks, and accommodated the driver and three passengers. The back half, which also had driving tracks, was designed to accommodate a squad of eight soldiers and their gear.

Though the machine was designed to travel over snow and ice, it traveled just as well over heather, grasses, and peat leaving but little trace in the process due to its very wide tracks.

Our first stop was the firing range. The ostensible purpose was to make sure that our rifles were spot-on. Though not said, it also served to give the stalkers some idea of our competence as marksmen. As was customary for hunters on this estate, I attached a bipod to the forearm of my Winchester featherweight .30-06, which was fitted with an adjustable 2-6 power scope. I was asked to fire three rounds at the target. The shots formed a half-inch group two inches high of the mark at 100 yards. That meant the rifle—and the marksman—should be near dead-on at 200 yards and some four inches low at 300 yards.

The landscape was characterized by rolling hills essentially devoid of trees except for the conifer plantations that covered 8 to 10 percent of the landscape. The hunting technique was to scout out the terrain—largely from the machine traveling on established roads, which, in general, followed the main streams (called "burns"). Once deer were located, a stalker and a hunter ("gun") might "stalk" them on foot—i.e., try to get within reasonable shooting distance defined at the discretion of the stalker. Groups of hinds (females) and calves of the year, accompanied by one to a dozen rutting stags, could be encountered in groups ranging from a half dozen to a hundred or more.

The younger stags—yearlings (approximately eighteen months old) and two-year-olds (some thirty months old)—hung around the periphery of the herds of hinds and calves, and sometimes they tried to sneak in for a bit of the breeding action. They were routinely challenged by the more mature stags and usually chased away. Mature stags were clearly discernible by their larger body size, much larger antlers, ruffed "mane," and darker coats. The longer hair on their necks and shoulders were stained with urine and peat from the wallows where they urinated and rolled around to assure that they gave off an alluring scent. The more mature males were referred to as "royal" stags because the last three tines of their antlers formed a "crown," which looked more like a basket or cup to me. I had to admit that the term "royal stag" had more of a ring to it than "basket head."

It was common for some younger males and a few hinds to distribute themselves around the periphery of the group—perhaps, I thought, to take a break from the ongoing turmoil of the ongoing "social interactions." It was these "outliers" that added to making stalking within rifle range of the bigger and older stags much more of a problem. Being a wildlife biologist for a lot of years—and a hunter for even longer—I surmised that those behaviors had an evolutionary function. Maybe the deer on the periphery of the group were less critical to successful reproduction and most susceptible to predation. If so, their location might direct predators away from the mature hinds, their calves, and the stags that had survived to full maturity.

Charlie examined each group of deer that we encountered through a 10-power telescope that the stalkers routinely used in lieu of binoculars. The stalkers would commonly lie on a hillside, cross their left leg at the ankle over their other knee, and then brace their telescope at full extension across the left leg. Trying to use such a high-powered telescope offhand proved quite difficult for me. Every trade has its tricks. The purpose of this frequent glassing by the stalkers was to locate a "shootable stag."

Initially I had trouble pining down the exact meaning of the term "shootable" and, finally, came to understand that the term lacked definition beyond being "a stag that suits the stalker's purposes at the moment." If the stalker was after a royal stag for a client, that became the definition of "shootable." If the client had already taken a royal stag, the next "shootable" stag might be one with small or malformed antlers—sometimes referred to as a "cull." "Knobbers" (males of the year) were never "shootable." Males with "whip antlers" (spikes) were usually yearlings and not ordinarily considered "shootable." Males with one spike and one branched antler were sometimes referred to as "culls" and therefore ranked high on the "shootable" list. A gun was compelled to honor the stalker's judgment as to what was "shootable" and "no shootable."

I commented to Charlie that though red deer and the elk of North America were considered the same species, these red deer were decidedly smaller in size than elk—I guessed a bit more than half—and more lightly framed. Charlie surmised that this difference was the result of living "out in the open" with very little cover, forcing an evolutionary trade-off between size and increased chances of survival. He said that red deer farther south in the British Isles—in more forgiving habitats and climates—were considerably larger than those in the more northern parts of Scotland. And those that lived in forested habitats in mainland Europe—say, Germany or France—were larger yet. He attributed this to both nutrition and the fact that red deer protected from the elements, especially winter winds, have an advantage. All that seemed logical enough to me.

My host afforded me the honor of making the first stalk. I remembered the definition of "stalk" (actually I had looked it up)—"to stealthily pursue a quarry or prey." A stalk was on when the stalker and the hunter took off on foot in pursuit of a shootable stag. As this was my first hunt in Scotland, Charlie announced that he would try to get me in position to take a royal stag on my first stalk. I was grateful for Charlie's generosity, though I fully understood that my host had "put a bug" in Charlie's ear. So it was likely the host who—to some degree—defined "shootable" with his pocketbook—at least some of the time. As the day went on, I remarked to Charlie that hunting red deer on the open hillsides of Scotland reminded me more of hunting pronghorn antelope in treeless West Texas than it did of hunting elk in the conifer forests of North America.

In midafternoon, Charlie spotted a royal stag, taking a break from the rutting game and lying at the base of a hill watching the hinds and calves on the opposite slope. We walked what I guessed was about a half mile directly away from the stags in order to get onto the back slope of the hillside where he was lying. I finally comprehended that Charlie wanted to get the wind in our faces before closing in for a potential shot. While the ground appeared to be smooth going from a distance, I quickly discovered that walking over the hummocks and the heather, which hid holes and crevices, was difficult and slow going. Now I fully understood why my host had made a stop at the stick shop. A stick not only helped with balance but served to probe for soft spots and holes. Such was an essential piece of equipment for the conditions. Besides it was "traditional" for hunters to sport "a stick."

Once we were in position to peek over the hilltop, we immediately saw the royal stag Charlie had in mind lying some 600 yards
away. Following Charlie's lead, I began to crawl—knee-crawling at
first and then belly-crawling toward the end. Charlie carried my rifle
in a case—he called it a "slip"—over his back.

Before we started out, he asked me for a box of cartridges. Now
he pulled the box from his pocket and signaled for me to watch. He
loaded four rounds in the magazine and closed the bolt over the top of
the cartridges so that the chamber was empty. At first blush, I thought
it a bit strange that he would carry and load my rifle. Then I surmised
it was a service. Finally, I understood that for the safety of all concerned
and most especially himself, Charlie was controlling the rifle and the use
to which it would be put. The stalker was in charge. Not a bad idea as he
had no knowledge of the hunting skills or "safety smarts" of his client.

In spite of the hilly terrain and the crystal clear skies, the ground
was spongy wet, and small pools of water were common. Our long
crawl into shooting position resulted in a soaking of the elbows, belly,
and knees of our clothing. On this, my very first stalk in Scotland,
Charlie worked me into a position to shoot at what I figured was a bit
over 200 yards and steeply downhill. The targeted "shootable stag"
was basking in the sun and seemed to be nodding in and out of sleep.
Charlie pulled my rifle out of its slip, opened the bipod attached to the
front sling swivel, sat the rifle down on the bipod, worked the bolt,
seated a cartridge in the chamber, put on the safety, and indicated that
I should get ready to shoot.

I crawled into position and snuggled into the rifle. Charlie
asked if I wanted him to make "the beast" stand up. After studying
the situation, I thought it best to take the stag where he lay. I could
see his vitals clearly. The stag seemed to be asleep and there was no
hurry. When it came time to shoot, as was usually true after killing
hundreds of white-tailed and mule deer in the course of my work in
the United States, I was as cold as ice. I let a few minutes go by to
allow my breathing and heart rates to come to their resting rates. As
was my style, I took three deep breaths, slowly let out half of the last
breath, steadied down, and squeezed the rifle's very smooth trigger.
Everything seemed perfect.

To my amazement, I saw the bullet strike several inches over the big stag's back. The stag didn't move. I was perfectly calm and I knew—or thought I knew—that the rifle was spot-on. I steadied down and fired again—and missed again in exactly the same fashion. Now the stag—still confused—stood up and looked around. I settled down and squeezed off another round—and with the same result. The stag trotted away. I held the crosshairs in the middle of his neck, squeezed off another round, and missed again. I was flat-dabbed flabbergasted. The sight pictures were perfect. Every round was methodically squeezed off. And this sure as hell wasn't my first rodeo.

I had missed clean (thank goodness) four times—from a prone position shooting off a bipod. My only conclusion was that my scope was somehow seriously jiggered out of kilter. Charlie, I didn't think, was just being polite when he agreed. He had watched me shoot earlier in the day. And he knew and saw that I was controlled and methodical while shooting. We were both glad that I missed clean instead of botching things up with a wounded stag—a royal stag at that.

The next stalk belonged to my host. I rode in the cab of the machine with Graeme. After my host and Charlie left us, Graeme and I visited away the time. In the course of the postmortem of my botched stalk, Graeme made an observation that was worth pondering. He said, "It is well to remember that the stalk, well executed, is everything—the shot is only the climax." I pondered his statement and decided that it could be taken two ways. Maybe he meant that the skills that brought the hunt and the hunter to the moment of the shot—the fabled "moment of truth"—were primarily those of the stalker. The hunter, "the gun," had merely followed directions. The stalker had done his job. Now the hunter had to complete the *gestalt*—at worst, a clean miss only resulted in an incomplete *gestalt*. The game could go on another day. That would be true enough in this case.

Or maybe he meant that the stalk required skill, patience, knowledge of the prey, the terrain, and execution. Properly executed under difficult circumstances, the stalk was a thing of beauty. The shot, in this case at 200 yards shooting from a prone position, was—or should have been—nothing but the completion of the exercise. My mental exercise didn't make me feel any less incompetent and even embarrassed. In fact, I felt that I had dishonored the gift of a shot at a truly magnificent royal stag. Yet I was grateful that I had not wounded the magnificent beast. After a coffee break back at the machine, Charlie and my host were off on a stalk, walking into the wind.

The sun was out, the breeze steady and mild, and the afternoon relatively warm. I climbed down out of the cab of the machine, found a dry spot in the heather, and stretched out for a "wee kip" (a brief nap) in the sun. I chuckled to myself that I was learning the Scot's language. I was awakened by the sound of three evenly spaced shots off in the direction that Charlie and my host had taken. Soon Charlie and Graeme were talking on the radio. My host had downed a running royal stag at nearly 300 yards.

When we arrived at the spot of the kill, Charlie had already removed the offal, leaving the lungs, liver, heart, and kidneys in place. The rest would be removed when the "beast"—another word the stalkers used in referring to red deer—reached the "larder" (large cooler) at the estate's headquarters to be skinned out and prepared for sale. In the Scottish model of hunting, deer are the property of the landowner. A successful hunter pays for the privilege of stalking and slaying the deer and owns only the antlers and "ivories" (the rounded first teeth in the upper row). The hide and the meat belong to the landowner and can be sold separately, either to the hunter or in the open market. In the North American way the entire animal belongs to the hunter.

When Graeme and I got to where the stag was lying, the six-pointer had been winched into the back of the machine. We loaded up and were off for the Gardener's Cottage. Charlie and I paid a return visit to the shooting range. I fired three rounds from a prone position off the bipod. The three shots made a three-quarter inch group—very good—eighteen inches high on the target—not so good. I readjusted the scope and put three shots spot-on—two inches high of the mark. The scope had indeed, somehow, some way, been knocked out of adjustment—jigged as Charlie described it. I was somewhat baffled, as I had never had that happen before. Charlie just looked at me and shrugged. But tomorrow was another day, and I was ready and eager. My host had contracted for ten stags to be taken in five days of hunting. With one day gone and only one stag hanging in the larder, it could be anticipated that the next four days of hunting would be a bit more intense.

OCTOBER 16, 1998

At dinner last night the ladies announced that they were going "out on the hill" with us today. As I had stalked first yesterday, my host was the first up today. We mounted the trusty machine and were off. We had not gone a mile when Charlie rapped his knuckles on the top of the driver's compartment as a signal for Graeme to bring the machine to a halt. He had spotted two six-point stags crossing over the crest of a hill a mile or so off to the north.

Without conversation, Charlie and our host dismounted our trusty mechanical steed and set off on foot in pursuit. Graeme found a place to park the machine on relatively flat ground. The ladies and I crowded into the cab with Graeme, which was out of the wind and a bit warmer, and accepted his kind invitation for a "spot of tea."

A bit over an hour passed when we heard two shots separated by some half minute. The radio crackled to life and Charlie simply said, "Bring up the machine." When we crossed the top of the hill, we could see Charlie and our host field-dressing two six-point stags that were lying not more than fifty yards apart. When we arrived at the scene, our host was beaming, high on life, thriving on every minute. He was eager to describe his "luck." Upon listening to his hunter's tale, I wouldn't say he was "lucky." Rather, I would say that he was a highly skilled and experienced big game hunter and a well-practiced marksman. And, of course, he had the services of a top stalker. He accepted my praise modestly and blushed, which, in its spontaneous sincerity, the ladies and I found charming.

After lunch, it was again my turn to pursue the wily stag. I trailed behind Charlie as we headed off toward the top of a hill with the wind blowing gently into our faces. Earlier, Charlie had taken a wee spy from the road with his telescope and had spotted some deer—including at least one shootable stag—on the back side of the hill we were now climbing. When we neared the crest, Charlie went down on his belly and signaled me to crawl along behind him as he eased up to the crest where he could look down on the flat on the other side. To make the pressure a little more intense, Graeme—with our host and the ladies on board—had moved the machine to where they could watch the action through binoculars from a distance of near a mile.

It seemed to me that there were simply too many deer lying down in the heather to give me a decent shot at the stag Charlie had selected. Now Charlie showed me how a really good professional stalker makes his living. Carefully judging the wind and using it as a tool, he led me off on a track that angled away from the stag he had selected. His course took us out of the sight of the stag while putting the wind—and our scent—to the deer that were lying down between us and the stag. The six deer that were lying "in our way" scented but could not see us. They got to their feet and slowly moved away and over a hill. That, as Charlie had intended, cleared a path for our stalk.

Charlie took advantage of a slight depression in the terrain that hid us from the stag and allowed us, walking crouched over, to close the distance by a little over a quarter mile. When we came to the top of the hill, Charlie pointed out the tips of the antlers of the lying stag sticking up above the heather. We crawled and rested, crawled and rested, until we closed the distance to some 200 yards. The stag was facing away from us, looking downhill and seemed completely unaware of our presence.

Charlie put down the bi-pod and set up the rifle. When I was in shooting position and breathing regularly, he asked, "Do you want me to make the staggie stand?" Remembering yesterday's embarrassing experience, I nodded yes. He took his telescope out of its leather case and "roared" (the red deer's version of bugling in North American elk) into the echo chamber that the empty case provided.

The stag, which appeared to have been dozing, lifted his head and looked in our direction but did not stand. Charlie repeated the roaring exercise twice more. Still the stag did not oblige us by standing. I was absolutely intent on the lying stag when Charlie tapped me on the shoulder and said, rather calmly, "Perhaps you had better shoot that fellow there." He pointed off to my right.

I turned my head slowly and saw a six-point stag not more than fifty yards away and walking, slowly and steadily, directly toward us with his head up in the slight breeze. I rolled up into a sitting position, fired offhand, and dropped the beast stone dead at thirty yards with a high neck shot. Before I could think, Charlie said calmly, "Now, shoot the other one." The first stag was up and walking away. I sat down cross-legged, wrapped the sling around by left forearm, locked my elbows inside my knees, and shot for the heart. The stag dropped but was trying to get up using only his front feet. His back was broken.

We hurried to the second stag. Charlie stood on one antler and delivered the coup de grace with the point of a thin-bladed knife that severed the spine at its juncture with the skull. I had never seen that done before and was impressed: it was not only more merciful but much less dangerous than severing the jugular vein at the base of the throat—the common practice in North America.

The ladies, our host, and Graeme showed up in short order in the machine. They had been able to watch the entire stalk through their binoculars. My host seemed even more excited about my success than he had been with his own. When I examined the second stag, I noted that the bullet had entered a foot above my aiming point; another inch or two higher and it would have been a clean miss. I was convinced that my miserable performance of the previous day might be explained by scope being seriously off the mark. I told Charlie that I needed a session at the target range before my next stalk. I had, I thought, been very lucky this day.

As we mounted the machine's squad cab—i.e., the trailer—we had to step over and around the three dead stags in the bed. They were covered by a tarp, but Kathy was a bit overcome with the delicate admixture of smells of diesel exhaust, blood, and essence of rutting stags. She was coming alive to my passion for the outdoors, wild lands, and hunting. But for this brief moment, being part of the quick transition from vibrant life to the stillness of death was close to overpowering. She rode the rest of the way standing at the front of the trailer, clutching the grab rail, and looking far away at the loch far below and the surrounding hills above. The progress of the machine blew the smells to the rear. I admired her. She loved me, and she was gamely trying, bless her Irish heart, to understand and even participate in the hunting experience.

Maybe, I thought, unless one is raised as a hunter, it is difficult if not impossible to understand hunting or hunters.

A most kind and feeling woman, she had never been exposed to the realities of the sometimes elaborate dances of life and death upon which nature operates. Why should she? She sometimes referred to herself as "Subway Girl." She and many others—maybe most—with her life experiences do not dwell on the connection between the death of an animal and the appearance of meat in a neat cellophane package at the market or the medium-rare steak that arrives browned just so at the table in a fine restaurant. Hunters at least know where their meat comes from—either from their skill or courtesy of a surrogate hunter who works at the abattoir. Subterfuge and pretending spares many in today's world of the realities of life when it comes to the origin of the meat on the table. There is death and blood in either case. At least the hunter is more honest and aware of the realities of human predation—there are no surrogates.

After delivering the stags to the larder, we headed for the Gardener's Cottage. I suddenly became acutely aware of being chilled and very tired. The aches and pains and chill quickly dissipated as I sat neck deep in a steaming bath, sipping most excellent single-malt Scotch whiskey and chewing a small handful of aspirin. I relived the day, step by step, and enjoyed it all over again—almost as much in memory as in reality. I always thought that the best of all hunting trophies reside in the mind and do not hang on a wall. A supper of lamb stew and fresh-baked bread with good red wine served as the capstone to a most marvelous day.

OCTOBER 17, 1998

After a full day of hunting, we were guests of the estate's owners for dinner. The evening was to be a highlight of our trip. We were "properly attired," in that the "gentlemen" wore tattersall shirts and knit ties under our brushed tweed stalking outfits. The ladies, of course, wore the outfits that they had purchased for just this purpose in Glasgow. The evening was beautifully done and marked by good company, stimulating and wide-ranging conversation, good drink, and wonderful and beautifully served food.

The laird and I visited at length about the biology and management of *Cervus elaphus*—the scientific name of both the North American elk and European red deer. He had a copy of my elk book, which he referred to as the "elk bible." And I had read his books—*Stag at Bay: the Scottish Red Deer Crisis* and *The Scottish Highland Estate: Preserving an Environment*, in which he described the role of commercialized stag hunting and salmon fishing as essential aspects of maintaining the economic viability—and the open space—of the large highland estates.

We began our conversation knowing that we shared a love for both *Cervus elaphus* and wild and open landscapes—and hunting in compliance with the rules of the society in question. He told me that, more so in Scotland than in North America, there was a significant and growing opposition to hunting, exacerbated by a growing hostility to gun ownership, including hunting rifles and shotguns. Those resentments were fueled to some extent, he thought, by class envy and growing resentment of large land ownerships. And because stalking was, to a very large extent, a pursuit of the wealthy. Furthermore, hunting in Scotland was becoming more and more the province of "wealthy foreigners," primarily from France, Germany, Spain, and North America. I could see a distinct correlation with trends in the United States as the vaunted North American Model of Wildlife Conservation rapidly evolved toward commercialization of wildlife and hunting. But if these estates, much like the large land ownerships in North America, were to remain economically viable and intact, their wildlife resources would likely have to provide significant income.

OCTOBER 18, 1998

After a hearty Scottish breakfast, we began our "business day" with a visit to the estate's shooting range to allow me to check the sighting of my rifle on the 100-yard range. Lying prone and shooting off a bipod, I squeezed off three rounds. The three shots were tightly grouped but fully twelve inches high on the target. No wonder that I had shot high yesterday. I had no idea of how the scope had, in Charlie's words, "gotten jiggered" again. After appropriate adjustment, I fired two additional sets of three shots. There were grouped within one-half inch on the target and two inches high, which would put the bullet spot-on at 200 yards. While I remained a trifle upset at my performance in missing the royal stag—four damned times no less—now I knew for damned sure now that the sighting mechanism was off. I had no idea how that had happened—or whether the adjustments just made would hold this time around.

It was my turn to stalk first. After we had gone less than a half mile from the cottage in the machine, Charlie put me on a cull stag after a "walk-up stalk" and a crawl of less than 50 yards. The shot was at just a tad over 100 yards. I took a heart shot just behind the front elbow, and the death of the stag was as nearly instantaneous as it gets. Everything worked correctly and the bullet was dead-on. I was relieved and could feel my confidence returning.

Just before midday, Charlie spotted a cull stag a bit less than a mile away down a long swale and quickly declared the beast "shoot-able." He and our host climbed down from the machine and were away on foot. I was able to watch, through my binoculars, the ensuing stalk from beginning to end. The stag was one of a group of some twenty-five hinds and calves with at least a half-dozen rutting stags in attendance. The stags could not be approached directly without their being aware of the stalkers. So Charlie resorted to the same technique that he had used earlier in the week and angled away from the stags, using the terrain to hide from their view while letting the hunter's scent on the wind entice the deer to move over the ridge and out of sight.

The stalk was on in earnest. Our host and Charlie made their approach up the bottom of a burn out of the sight of the deer. They were able to walk upright for a quarter mile or so and then left the burn and commenced crawling as they reached the upper slope. As they were not completely hidden, it seemed certain—to me at least—that the stag would likely see them approaching in their stooped-over walk. The stag—fortunately for the hunters—spent most of his time looking the other way, and Charlie made the most of its mistake. When the hunters got to some cover in the form of high-growing heather, they dropped down and crawled to within what looked to me to be 200 or maybe 220 yards. Charlie set up the rifle, and our host crawled into position to shoot.

I could clearly see both the stag and the hunters. It was difficult for me to believe that the stag, which was lying down, had not sensed the approaching deadly danger. Lying prone, our host could only see the stag's antlers above the heather. So the stag would have to stand to make a shot possible. However, our host was a purist—at least most of the time—and lived by the code that said a gentleman hunter should wait until "the staggie" stands of his own volition. And so the long wait began and lasted well over an hour. Charlie and our host, I thought, had to be concerned that if the wait continued much longer there would not be enough daylight left for another stalk. We were running behind schedule to take the number of stags that had been contracted for. Finally, I watched as Charlie picked up his case for the telescope, removed the telescope, and "roared" into the empty case.

The stag stood immediately, looked around for a challenger that he could hear but not see, and dropped dead not three seconds later. Then, in an almost exact replica of my earlier experience, another stag got up from his bed and came running to challenge the stag he thought he had heard roaring—i.e. Charlie. Our host got into a sitting position and dropped the stag that was trotting straight toward him at fifty yards. It was quite a show—and I had a front-row seat.

After Charlie and Graeme dressed out and loaded the two beasts into the machine, we ate our lunches seated on the edge of an old pony path paved with small stones. Many decades in the past, these paths had been constructed across the low-lying wetlands when ponies were used to pack out dead stags. That, I thought, must have been something of a challenge—and a show to watch. Wet peat meadows sure as hell ain't horse country—hence the stone-paved pony paths.

The last stalk of the day was mine and turned out to be my best yet. Two hills off in the distance, we could see the group of deer that Charlie had moved off as a prelude to the last stalk. Charlie surmised that we just might get close enough for a reasonable shot by following the burn that ran almost to within what he computed to be acceptable shooting range. For the three-quarters of a mile or so that we were able to walk upright, traveling upstream along the burn, the going was relatively fast and easy.

Charlie pointed out the remnants of large tree stumps that had been buried in the peat—relics of the Caledonian forest that had covered much of Scotland centuries in the past. The red deer had evolved to thrive in a mixed-species complex of forests and openings. They were able, over many generations, to adjust as the forests steadily disappeared, due, for the most part, to make charcoal to smelt metal and, at the same time, clear the forest to produce grazing space for sheep.

As we walked up the burn, a group of deer crossed over the ridge that lay just ahead. When we crawled up the top of the bank to take a "wee spy," we could still see deer moving ahead of us. When we came to a place where we could belly-crawl up to the lip of the burn, we could see what Charlie figured was at least 150 red deer. He thought there were likely many more that we could not see. He gestured to me to sit down while he crept around a bend in the burn. He quickly dropped on his belly. He wormed his way back to me and whispered that there was a shootable stag lying close to the lip of the burn. Careful to make no noise, Charlie eased the rifle out of its slip and slowly and quietly worked the bolt to get a round "up the spout," closed the bolt, and put on the safety. Charlie motioned me to leave my stick and slither up to his side.

He handed me the rifle. We carefully, and as quietly as possible, wormed up the twenty-five-foot bank. When we neared the top, the big stag bolted. We had come within twenty or so feet of where he was lying. I stood up to see if I had a shot. The footing was slippery and I slid back into the burn—nice try, but no cigar. When we crawled out of the burn, we could make out at least 200 red deer, at least 50 of which were stags, moving over a rise off to the west.

What a sight, what a moment! It was every bit as exciting and fulfilling to me as dropping the big stag we were after would have been. I thought of Graeme's earlier observation—"The stalk, well executed, is everything; the shot is nothing." This had been one magnificent stalk—tricky, exhausting, unlikely to succeed, and incredibly lucky. I was exhilarated. I didn't think I would ever forget the experience. Charlie was grinning ear to ear.

As we turned to head back down the hill, I was pleased that this particular stag was still up there, somewhere, on the hill. It was getting dark, and it was a long way down the burn to where the machine was waiting. There would be wonderful stories to tell around the fire this night.

As I lay abed and waited for the magic combination of aspirin and single-malt Scotch whiskey to dampen my aches and pains so that I might sleep, my mind replayed the memory of the royal stag turning himself wrong side out when he turned and saw me eye-to-eye less than twenty yards away. I remembered his eyes going from sleepy to wide open and his preorbital glands flaring open. I wondered if he noted the almost-certain, equally wide-eyed looks on our faces. Probably not—but it was an interesting thought.

Tomorrow will be our last day of stalking. I took Charlie aside and enlisted him in a conspiracy to make sure that our host took the first stalk. I had my reasons. First, killing three stags had satiated my hunting passions. Second, our host was still eager and, quite realistically, was more apt to be successful than I. And he had, most generously, picked up the tab for ten stags. This would be the last day of our hunt, and there were two stags to go. In truth, I had another good reason to defer to my host. My bum football knee was so badly swollen that I could bend it only halfway back. And it hurt—a bunch. I was chewing aspirin—about one tablet per hour. Crawling on hands and knees was becoming ever more painful.

OCTOBER 19, 1998

Charlie, with our host in tow, was off in pursuit of the last three stags for this year's hunt. The laird's oldest son and a classmate from the University at Edinburgh sat around the Gardener's Cottage with me shooting the bull as the morning passed. They were both majoring in another one of my passions, history, which was our topic of conversation. For some reason, they were fascinated with Texas history, primarily the revolution for Texas independence from Mexico culminating with the battle of San Jacinto in 1836. I was in my element, having been saturated—maybe even brainwashed—in my youth with oft-repeated stories of the Texas Revolution. Some of the stories were true, some likely mythical, and the rest lying somewhere in between. The battles of Goliad, the Alamo, and San Jacinto seemed to be of special interest.

As soon as it was convenient, I turned the conversation to the history of Scotland, which my friends seemed to know backward and forward—even sideways. I was especially interested in the ancient broch—a circular stone fort—that we had encountered while hunting. They told me that there were ten such brochs in northern Scotland that were built by the Picts—many hundreds of years earlier—to defend themselves and their livestock from recurrent raids by the Norsemen. The Picts also developed an early warning system of lighting bonfires on the mountaintops when the Norsemen were detected or raiding had commenced. Once warned, the Picts responded by scattering their livestock and gathering people and as many sheep as possible into the brochs.

We set off to visit the broch I had seen earlier in our hunt. The circular stone structure was some forty feet tall with only one small, low entrance that would accommodate one sheep or one crawling person at a time. When the defenders were inside, a large stone was rolled into a depression inside the wall to plug the hole. There were stairs and ladders inside the fort that allowed the defenders to climb to a platform. From that vantage point they could throw down stones and spears and shoot arrows at the raiders. Even in its decayed state, the ancient engineering feat was most impressive. I sat quietly in the broch and let my imagination run rampant—I could smell the sheep and the warming fires and sense the fear of the defenders.

Then they took me to see circular rock-walled pens for sheep that were scattered around the landscape. Those pens, some 200 to 300 years old, had been used for centuries by shepherds to pen up their sheep at night so they could be protected from wolves and bears. They were still sometimes used to pen sheep for various purposes. Most were made from quarried stone and had been maintained in functional condition. When I marveled at the costs in human labor to quarry the stone, haul it to the site in wagons, and construct the walls (which were a marvel of craftsmanship in that they had stood for so many years without mortar), the young laird explained that the laborers—mostly imported from Ireland—had worked for next to nothing during the awful decades of the potato famine. His comment was, "They worked for a quid a day and brought their own stone." The stone fences reminded me of those constructed by the German colonists in the Texas Hill Country in the late nineteenth and early twentieth centuries that still stand today, many of them still functional.

Just as the young laird finished his stories about the broch, we heard two shots off in the distance. An hour later, we heard Charlie's voice crackle over the radio summoning Graeme and the machine. Charlie never mentioned the outcome of the stalk, as stalkers on other nearby estates might be listening. Why he would care about that I didn't now—but he did care. By now, I could detect from the tenor of his voice whether a stalk had been successful or not. In this case, I heard success in his voice. When we arrived at the designated spot, we saw our host bedded down in the heather, sound asleep in the warming sun. Charlie was off looking for his stick that he had left behind somewhere in the excitement of the stalk. Our lucky host—who was not "lucky" at all but rather an expert hunter in the Scotland style—had once again taken two stags in a single stalk. The two stags were quickly loaded into the machine.

We broke out and hungrily consumed our lunches. The still-warm coffee, heavy with whole cream and sugar, provided an energy boost. We were very hungry as fewer than three hours of shooting time remained and we had not eaten since breakfast. We were still one stag short of the contracted number. There was time, just maybe, for one last stalk. As Charlie said, we had no time for him "to be picky" as to "shootable or no."

We scouted hillsides, using the machine, for a bit over an hour. Charlie discerned no opportunities that were apt to pay off with the last stag of the hunt. Finally, he spotted two stags—an odd couple of a royal stag and a cull "whip" with one branched and one spike antler. Charlie looked at me hobbling around and opined that, given my condition, the chances of pulling off a successful stalk on such flat ground were essentially nil. But, he continued, this was almost surely our last chance for the day. It was a thinly veiled challenge—ever so politely and challengingly delivered. I nodded—let's go for it! I knew a challenge when I heard one. I only wished that I was as confident as I sounded.

He smiled and nodded. Charlie had punched my "*macho* but-ton" and, I thought later on purpose. We both laughed. With a jerk of his head he said, "Let's go." We were able to approach the targeted stags within a quarter mile due to a slight swell in the terrain that hid us from the stags. The wind was "squirrely" and quartering away. We would only be able to approach within some unknown distance be-fore the stags picked up our scent. All the cover that existed between us and the stags was one large clump of heather, some four feet wide and three feet tall. That was it.

I thought to myself that there was no way this stalk going to work out. I could tell at a glance that Charlie likely shared my opin-ion. Yet it was so late in the day that there was no tomorrow for us. Our allotted time on the hill for this year was down to less than an hour. Charlie computed the angles and laid out an approach so that the stags were lying with one directly behind the other, with the single clump of heather between us and the stags. You could have drawn a straight line through the two stags and on through the heather clump to the tip of my nose.

Charlie commenced to crawl. My god, the man could crawl faster than I could walk over the rough ground. I put my head down and crawled along behind him. I didn't dare look up. If I did, I just knew I would call it quits. I was bone-tired and hurting. We didn't have any real chance of pulling off this stalk, and we both knew it. But neither of us was willing to be the one who first cried, "Hold, enough." I quit trying to think or feel and just kept crawling with my eyes on Charlie's boots. When he knee-crawled, I knee-crawled. When he belly-crawled, I belly-crawled. When he figured I needed to rest, he lay down flat. I followed suit, keeping my nose to the ground. I had become convinced that stalkers never needed to rest. At least they would never let a client know it if they did.

After what was likely a half hour—but seemed twice that—we actually arrived at the clump of heather. I had thought there was no way in hell we could ever pull this off, but here we were. Now Charlie figured that the stags were lying some 250 yards away. One had his chin resting on the ground, apparently asleep. The other had his head up but was away from us. The bottom edge of the sun was touching the horizon. Charlie looked at me quizzically. His eyes told me that we weren't getting any closer. I nodded my agreement.

He slid my rifle out of its slip, opened the bipod, pushed a cartridge up the spout, flipped on the safety, and wiggled off to the side. I wormed into position, waited patiently until my breathing was slow and even, and gave Charlie the nod to see if he could make one or both stags stand. The sun slipped below the horizon. He grunted into his empty telescope case—with vigor. The whip was the closest by thirty yards. Charlie had declared him the most shootable of the pair. The young stag ignored Charlie's imitation of a mature rutting stag. The royal stag—which Charlie had also deemed "shootable"—stood up, looked in our direction without much interest, and lay back down before I could be sure of my shot. This same scenario was repeated twice more over the next twenty minutes. Now there was less than fifteen minutes of shooting time left.

I had been in position to shoot—and ready to shoot—for so long that my neck was cramping and I could feel the threat of a muscle spasm in my back. Damn. Something needed to happen— sooner rather than later. Charlie called Graeme on the radio and whispered to him to drive the machine toward us. A great idea, but it didn't work. The two stags stretched their necks and laid their chins on the ground, clearly hiding. Charlie whispered to me that, in all his years on the hill, he had never witnessed such behavior. He called Graeme and whispered to him to drive the machine directly toward our position. When the machine was a quarter mile away, both stags took note and stood—first the royal stag and then the cull. The stags turned to face the machine, which was coming up right behind our position.

When the cull reached his feet, I eased down on the trigger. He dropped down dead on the spot. The hunt—for today and the season—was over, with less than ten minutes of shooting light to spare. I rolled over on my back, stretched out flat, breathed deep, and waited for cramped muscles to relax. Charlie did the same. By the time we met Graeme and the machine at the stag, it was full dark.

Our host and the ladies were expecting us to join them for cocktails at the laird's home, and we were late. Then, to make things worse, the machine suffered a broken wheel that drove one of the tracks. The stalkers took off on foot for headquarters to get the Land Rover. My host and I headed straight off the hill for the main road through the estate. We figured the road was a half mile away—it turned out to be over a mile. My bum knee was getting even "bummer" by the time we reached the road and encountered the laird's son and his friend in the estate's Land Rover.

By the time we arrived at the Gardener's Cottage, the ladies were there to greet us, having, in consideration for the laird's family, graciously taken their leave. Our host was leaving very early in the morning for Glasgow to catch a plane to London. Kathy and I were to "take coffee" with the laird and family before we left for the airport. That was okay with me. I was tired, sore, and ready for two shots of good single-malt Scotch whiskey, some aspirin, a hot soak, and bed—not necessarily in that order. What a long, glorious day!

OCTOBER 20, 1998

Our cook/housekeeper's husband had contracted with our host for him to drive Kathy and me to the Glasgow airport. His wife arrived first at the Gardener's Cottage along with their son, who was dressed in kilts, the proper attire for a bagpiper—to "pipe us up the road." Included in his somewhat limited repertoire was "Amazing Grace"— my favorite hymn. He played it well and with gusto. It brought tears to my eyes.

We and our kit were piled into the Land Rover, and we were off for the airport, where I would catch my flight back to Missoula, Montana. Kathy would catch the train to London to visit her daughter Erin—now my daughter as well. She was spending a semester attending the University of London. Our hunt had been a wonderful, almost magical experience, due primarily to the generosity of our hosts, the warmth of the laird and his lady, and the comradeship and the amazing skills of Charlie and Graeme. We hoped to return some day. I truly did.

CHAPTER 15

DOVE SHOOTING IN ARGENTINA

I am my way home after four days of dove shooting near Cordoba, Argentina, as the guest of an old friend. I had heard and read stories about hunting for doves in Argentina for many years and wondered if the reality could possibly match the stories. The descriptions of the populations of doves seemed to me to mirror the described populations of passenger pigeons in the eastern United States in the early 1800s. I was part of a hunting party that included an odd set of *compadres*—a retired sheriff, a retired New York police detective, a Wyoming rancher, a retired Green Beret, a retired Navy Seal, a general contractor, and the CEO of a large chain of grocery stores.

JUNE 10, 1999

The hacienda in which we were lodged sat in the center of a large estate, Estancia La Paz, the summer home of Julio A. Roca, Argentina's president several decades ago. The buildings had been recently refurbished and were, most certainly, fit for a president's country home. Our meals were served in the estate's formal dining room on a table appointed with silver, crystal, and china. The lunches and dinners were accompanied by the finest of Argentinian wines. Admittedly, I had to take my host's word for the quality of the wines as I usually bought wine by the jug. He declared them *excepcional*. I wasn't sure what that meant, but assuming it meant pretty damn good, I agreed wholeheartedly.

Each day of shooting commenced with a leisurely breakfast of eggs, ham, sausage, fruits, and fresh-baked breads. Then we were driven to hedgerows between harvested fields of grain. I had never seen so many doves at one time as they literally swarmed from one grain field to another. In addition, there was a constant passage of doves overhead in singles, pairs, small groups, and in only what could be described as "clouds" or "swarms." Our guides referred, most respectfully, to us as "guns." Each gun was accompanied by two attendants. One picked up downed birds. The other kept a tally of the birds downed and the shotgun shells fired; he also packed boxes of shotgun shells in two bags slung over his shoulders. When the shooting was fast and furious, it was not unusual to go through a box of shotgun shells (twenty-five per box) in well less than five minutes.

It was essential that the guns wore shooting gloves, as the shotguns sometimes got hot enough to raise a blister on a bare hand that came in contact with a barrel. Heat expansion of the rapidly fired shotguns—plus the residue of burned powder—sometimes rendered a shotgun inoperable when it could not be snapped shut after reloading. When such a failure occurred, the attendant who was providing shotgun shells would hand the shooter a backup shotgun. During breaks in the shooting for refreshments and dealing with other necessities, the shotguns were quickly sponged off and the barrels and actions swabbed out with carburetor cleaner and then oiled and reassembled.

Clouds of doves could be seen in all directions, rising from and descending to the hedgerows and the ground. I was reminded of newsreel pictures of plagues of locusts in Africa. We were told that the doves raised two or, more rarely, three broods per year with two and sometimes three squabs per brood. Doves were, understandably, considered a first-class agricultural pest. I could certainly see why. Therefore, there were no constraints on the number of doves shot— the more, the better. Dead and downed birds were picked up during breaks in the shooting for refreshments. We were told that any doves we did not eat were given to charity. Clearly, the dove shooting over several decades had no detectable impact on their incredible numbers. We shot for two half days and two full days.

Lunch was served during a two-hour break under shade trees where lawn chairs had been arranged around the cooking fire. The luncheon fare started with charbroiled dove breasts wrapped in bacon for an appetizer, followed by charbroiled beef loin steaks, chilled salad, and baked potatoes. Various wines were served in crystal glasses. There were various beers for those *norte americanos* who preferred such plebian fare—a description that fit most of the guns in our party. In midafternoon the shooting resumed and continued until almost full dark.

Our suppers were of the gourmet variety, accompanied by what I was told were the finest of wines. I suspected the wine *aficionados* knew what they were talking about, though I would have been hardpressed to tell the difference between "fine wines" and the wines I usually bought at my local supermarket. I tried to keep up a good front relative to being a genuine lover of fine wine. I doubted that I fooled anybody. I finally broke down on the third day and asked for a beer.

At the end of the shooting day we were each handed a "score card" that detailed, by the gun, the number of boxes of shotgun shells fired and the number of birds downed. The scorecard emphasized that this was a "shoot" and not even related to "hunting" as understood in North America. The birds were considered more targets (and pests) than prey, and the guns were shooting as opposed to hunting. In total, the eight guns in our party fired 26,550 rounds and downed some 12,245 doves—2.17 rounds expended per bird downed. The individual "scores" ranged from 7.86 to 14.12 doves per box of shells fired (25 rounds). The 14.12 score was mine. These rather remarkable "scores" could be attributed to the fact that the birds were so thick that a single shot occasionally brought down multiple doves. In my mind, the experience was only remotely a shooting sport, if at all, related to hunting. No one pretended otherwise.

Significantly, this shooting sport is likely the salvation of the habitats that are so productive of both doves and pheasants. That is especially true of the hedgerows that were established in the 1920s and 1930s to alleviate wind erosion over the immense stretches of fields devoted to the production of grains of various sorts. The doves, justifiably, were considered agricultural pests and tolerated in such high numbers only because of the increasingly lucrative business of commercial dove shooting. Put another way, doves had become another agricultural crop that brings increasing revenues into Argentina—largely from other countries—and helps the nation's balance of trade problems. As a result, landowners maintain the habitat conditions conducive to that activity. So the shooting of doves is the salvation of the inadvertently created habitat so productive of doves—and associated species and the people who profit therefrom. It seemed to me that there was a lesson in there somewhere for wildlife managers—and even environmentalists.

Hawks (both buteos and accipters) had learned what gunfire meant and began to gather shortly after the shooting started to feed on downed doves. Several times I saw accipters snatch wounded birds out of the air as the doves fluttered toward the ground. As a result, shooters had to be careful not to accidentally shoot a bird of prey.

The very long flight home to North America from Buenos Aires afforded me time to ponder the experience. The stay at Estancia La Paz was, in itself, an experience to be remembered. The grounds were magnificent and featured a lake of ten to twelve acres surrounded by lush, mowed lawns adorned by wide-spreading oaks sixty to eighty feet tall. Our host spoke flawless English—in addition to being fluent in Spanish, German, and French.

When we departed the hacienda for our trip home, I picked up several brochures that contained testimonials from satisfied clients. Every testimonial contained some reference to hunting, such as: "The success of our hunt," "the hunting trip," "Dove hunting was fabulous," "the best-organized hunt," "superb bird hunt," "the best dove hunt," "best hunting experience," and so on.

To me, the term "hunt" means to search out or stalk or pursue a quarry. Implicit in my definition is that skill, persistence, and knowledge of the prey are not only required but make up the essential attributes of "hunting." To stand in place and fire 2,250 shotgun shells in a four-day period while killing 1,151 doves was not, to my mind, "hunting." Such was, instead, an exercise in wing shooting or perhaps "sport shooting." No wonder the guests are referred to by the hosts and guides as "guns" rather than "hunters."

This was a new—and most educational—experience for one who considers himself a professional wildlife biologist and a game manager. That implies attention to and skills in the management of both wildlife and the hunting thereof. I could not help but think back to many hours of sitting beside farm ponds in Texas waiting for mourning doves to come to water in the late evening. And, when things went well, killing a bag limit of ten or twelve doves. What was the difference between the two experiences except, obviously, the number of birds taken? The experience left me with much to ponder on the long flight home.

CHAPTER 16

RETURN TO THE SCOTTISH HIGHLANDS

Kathy and I arrived at Culloden House on the outskirts of Glasgow, Scotland, in the late afternoon at the culmination of a long drawn-out set of flights from Missoula, Montana. Somewhere toward the end of the trip Kathy marveled that it was at all possible to get from our home in Florence, Montana, to Glasgow, Scotland, in one long day. It was, indeed, a long day.

Culloden House was a sixteenth-century mansion that had been fully restored and converted into a first-class small hotel. The house sits at the edge of the famed Culloden battlefield, where, on April 15, 1746, the victorious English army brought an end to the dominance of the Clans in Scotland. In that crucial battle the British crushed Bonnie Prince Charlie's efforts to establish a Scotland independent of British influence with himself as king. During the course of the battle, the most severely wounded Scots were hidden away in the basement of Culloden House. When the victorious English troops swept the battlefield, the vanquished Scots were forced, reluctantly, to abandon most of the severely wounded to their fates. When the victors discovered them in their hiding place, they dragged them outside, and summarily executed the lot.

OCTOBER 9, 1999

When an attendant showed us to our quarters, he told us of the ghosts that had occupied the basement of Culloden House since that terrible day. He told us that the hotel's employees did not relish their visits to the basement because of "the presence" they sometimes felt there. Then, he laughed—rather weakly, we thought—and assured us that the specters were well behaved and never, so far as he knew, left the basement. That made us feel ever so much better. I smiled—a little. Kathy didn't. By any measure, the story surely added to the "charm" of the place.

The hotel was beautifully restored and, certainly, most charming—as it should have been given the prices. The living room was ornate and furnished with overstuffed couches and chairs. A magnificent huge fireplace dominated one end of the room and contained a vigorously burning fire of large logs six to eight feet in length. There was ample time before dinner for us to sip exquisite single-malt Scotch, stare into the blazing fire, and wonder about "the presence" in the basement. We were too jet-lagged to do much else—or, frankly, give a damn about "the presence."

The four-course meal was most wonderfully presented—and delicious. It seemed *de rigueur* in Scotland for the main dish—at least for foreigners—to be mutton or lamb. After dinner we retreated to our suite to be greeted by a glowing coal fire on the grate in the fireplace. We poured ourselves a nightcap of sherry from the beautifully cut-crystal decanter that we found on the table next to the fireplace.

The warmth provided by the combination of the fire and sherry gave us the time, and reason, to fully grasp that we were really in Scotland and another of our fairy tale adventures was well underway. As we sipped our sherry and stared into the glowing coals, we took time to begin to fully appreciate our adventure—though it was only just beginning and there was so much more to come.

OCTOBER 10, 1999

The owner ("laird") of the highland estate where we would be "stalking" red deer stags picked us up at Culloden House for the drive up the east coast of the North Sea to his estate. The countryside was every bit as starkly beautiful as Kathy and I remembered it from previous visits. We were pleased to see the laird again, as he had been most kind and gracious to us on our previous visits. When we arrived at the estate, we were, once again, quartered in the Gardener's Cottage.

During the afternoon our two hunting guides ("stalkers")—Charlie and Graeme—stopped by to welcome us back to Scotland.

Kathy and I both had a feeling of homecoming, as we had affection for both of these highly skilled and gracious young gentlemen. The smiles on Charlie's and Graeme's faces—plus their animated voices—gave us to believe that they were equally glad to see us again. Though we were not scheduled to "go a-stalking out on the hill" until the next day, Charlie and Graeme offered us a ride in a Land Rover for a "wee spy" around the estate. This particular highland estate, typical of the region, was essentially treeless, except where there were plantations of conifers of several species planted in rows inside more or less deer-proof fences and dominated by heather, forbs, and grasses.

This region of northern Scotland had once been dominated by coniferous forests. Over centuries, the forests were cut down for timber or the making of charcoal to smelt metal and conversion to pasturage for sheep. The red deer that were native to the forest habitats adapted to the open heather-covered hillsides. Initially, the hunting of the red deer—especially the stags—had been reserved for the nobility.

Gamekeepers were employed to see after the wildlife on the estates, protect the red deer and grouse from poaching, and supervise hunting activities. When the lairds were increasingly hard-pressed to produce enough revenues from their estates to sustain them, the commercialization of red deer and grouse hunting—coupled with leasing or sale of fishing rights for salmon in the streams—became a significant contributor to economic salvation of the highland estates.

The Scot's (typically European) relationship with hunted wildlife is, in many ways, almost the exact opposite of the situation in North America. In North America jurisdiction over native wildlife rests with the states, except for those species that migrate across state lines and species declared to be "threatened or endangered." Such species are the responsibility of the federal government. Access to private lands, for whatever purpose, is at the discretion of the landowner. Trespassing upon private property is punishable by law. Many landowners—more and more as time passes—charge "trespass fees" for hunters to enter their properties for purposes of hunting.

Conversely, in Scotland, the people have the "right to roam" over private estates. And wildlife, especially various species of deer and grouse, are the sole property of the landowners and hunting and the harvested game is routinely marketed. The stalking and killing of a stag is sold to the hunter and usually carried out under the direction of the landowner—or stalkers in the landowner's employ. Hunters may kill as many stags as they care to pay for and the landowner will allow.

Upon killing a stag, the hunter is entitled to the head and antlers. The remainder of the dead animal belongs to the landowner and is usually butchered and sold to buyers—including the hides. Excess females (hinds) are commonly "cropped" by the stalkers after the close of the stalking season and the meat sold to markets in mainland Europe as well as the British Isles. Well-run wildlife management and cropping arrangements are commonly an essential aspect of maintaining such large estates in a viable economic state.

After our "wee spy about" we returned to what a Texican would call the estate's "headquarters." We encountered the laird in the hay yard, dressed in rough work clothes and working on some mechanized equipment. While our rapport with the stalkers and the housekeeper and cook was keen, we had also established what I considered a genuine friendship with the laird and his lady. In spite of their titles and a vast estate (by European standards), they had to struggle and use considerable ingenuity to make the estate a paying proposition—and thereby maintaining it intact. The laird was a well-recognized expert and author on the subject of fish and wildlife management in Scotland.

We were not scheduled to "go a-stalking out on the hill" until the following day. That afforded us the pleasure of having time to leisurely recover from jet lag and reacquaint ourselves with the rolling heather-covered hills. It was a pleasure to renew acquaintances with the laird and his lady, the stalkers, housekeeper and cook, and their families. When night came and supper was done, we felt strangely at home as we sat in front of the glowing coal fire—I writing in my journal and Kathy studying the flames and pretending, off and on, to read. It was so very good to be back in Scotland. We felt at home with old friends.

"Young" Graeme glassing stags near Glasgow, Scotland, 1999. Stalkers use telescopes—not binoculars or spotting scopes, as in North America—to assess the whether a stag is "shootable."

OCTOBER 11, 1999

One of the things I most appreciated about stalking in Scotland—as compared to elk hunting in the northwestern United States—was the leisurely start in the mornings. Our cook, Jean, routinely served us what might be called a "hearty Scot's breakfast" of fried eggs, bacon, oatmeal, toast and jam, orange juice, and coffee. Just as we finished breakfast and Jean handed us our lunches, Charlie and Graeme showed up in the "machine," a wide-tracked vehicle acquired as surplus from the military. It was handy for driving cross-country over the heather-covered hills and left little trace in the process.

Our first stop was the rifle range—a stop with two purposes. The first, though not openly stated or even implied, was to allow the stalkers to get some idea of their client's ability as a marksman. The second was to assure that rifles were sighted in and functioning properly. I had just installed a new 3-9x variable Leupold scope on my Winchester featherweight .30-06 but had not yet sighted it in, though it had been bore-sighted by the gunsmith who did the work. That proved to be a good start, as it took me only six shots and adjustments at 100 yards to be "spot-on the target." I let the barrel cool and fired three additional shots just to be sure. The rifle was, indeed, spot-on at the range. We mounted the machine and drove away in a light drizzling rain with temperatures that seemed to us to be only several degrees above freezing—all in all, quite miserable weather. But a day spent hunting with good friends and skilled hunters in such wonderful country beat nearly any other kind of day that I could think of.

We had not gone quite a mile when I saw what I thought were antlers protruding out of the heather just over the bank of a gravel pit that abutted the road. My first thought was that, as a joke on their Yank friends, the stalkers had placed a couple of skulls with antlers in the heather to create this impression. As a result, I wasn't too keen or spry about dismounting from the machine and beginning a lengthy twenty-five-yard stalk. Surely they didn't think I would fall for their "wee joke." But I went along with their prank with a dubious smile on my face. I was stunned when I poked my head up over the lip of the gravel pit and saw two stags lying not five yards away and looking the other way. I ducked back before the stags saw me. Charlie, in the process of checking out whether either of the two stags was deemed to be "shootable," spooked them—I suspected purposely. The two young staggies wasted no time getting over the low ridge in the background and out of sight.

Just after midday Charlie spotted a stag and tapped on the cab of the machine as a signal to Graeme to stop. He looked the stag over through his telescope (the stalkers used telescopes with 10-power magnification as opposed to binoculars) and deemed "the beast" to be shootable. The stag was lying in a swale in the midst of two smaller stags and a dozen or so hinds and calves. Charlie beckoned to me, as if to say, "You're up!" We dismounted and began our stalk by walking in a crouched-over position and out of sight of the herd of deer around an intervening low hill. When the cover provided by the terrain played out, we gained another 300 yards or so by alternating between crawling and walking stooped over through the high grass in the swale. It was well over a half hour before we reached a position from which we again spotted the stag we were after. The calves and hinds were, here and there, getting up and feeding for a while and then lying back down. All of that activity made our final approach to a reasonable shooting position something of a "sticky wicket."

I crawled, stopped, and hugged the ground following Charlie's example. Charlie instructed me to keep my face pointed at the ground and not to look up until he gave the okay. Evidently, a very white face was quite obvious to the deer when contrasted with the heather. The grass and heather were beaded with water, and our woolen hunting outfits were becoming soaked in spite of their advertised propensity to shed water. Finally, after two hours of off-and-on crawling/walking, we arrived at a place from where I could clearly see the antlers of the stag sticking up above the heather—but that was all I could see. There were fourteen or more red deer of both sexes and various ages arrayed in front of us in a rough semicircle. Several stags were adorned with both larger and lesser antlers than the "shootable beast" Charlie had selected.

Charlie whispered in my ear that he could not risk "roaring the stag to his feet" (imitating the stag's territorial vocalization), as it would likely spook the entire bunch. So we would simply lie ready and "wait for the staggie to stand." Charlie took the gun slip off his back and pulled out my rifle, mounted the bipod on the forearm swivel, slowly and quietly worked the bolt to put a round "up the spout," and put on the safety—all while making certain that I was watching each step carefully.

When I squirmed up to where I could see the stag we were after and shouldered the .30-06 Winchester, I was in a perfect prone shooting position—a sign of the stalker's skill. Now all I had to do was wait for the "staggie" to stand and then shoot quickly and accurately. The drizzle turned into a steady rain. I could feel very cold water seeping into my hunting pants and trickling down my neck. Our breaths "smoked" in the still, cold, damp air as we waited and waited and waited.

Time crept by seemingly evermore as I became wetter and wetter and more and more chilled. Here and there a deer stood up—ass end first, stretched, shook off the water, and lay back down, front end first. I held my head up with the deer's antlers in the crosshairs of my scope until my neck ached; I put my head down and rested it on a hummock of grass, Soon Charlie and I alternated holding our heads up and watching the antlers sticking up above the grass—waiting, waiting, and then waiting some more for the selected "shootable staggie" to stand.

After what I thought was surely two hours—or maybe a bit more—my urge to urinate was near to overpowering. Lying belly down on the cold, wet grass and ground with my clothing soaking up water in a most sensitive place was not aiding me to ignore that reality. The sun was now low in the western sky, and the drizzling rain had turned to intermittent sleet. Ice was forming on the grass. I had my head down, resting my neck, and concentrating on not pissing my pants when Charlie nudged me gently and whispered, "The staggie is moving."

All went just as I had choreographed it, over and over, in my mind. The stag's hindquarters came up first, followed by his forelegs. He shook the water off his coat and took two steps forward and lowered his head to graze. I didn't remember thinking—or even squeezing the trigger. I had done that over and over and over in my mind. The roar and the sharp recoil from the rifle seemed to me to originate from somewhere else. The stag collapsed in a heap from a neck shot.

That done, I staggered to my feet with the intent of finally answering nature's urgent call. But due to cold, stiff muscles, I was no more than standing when I lost my balance and fell over backward and landed on the seat of my pants. I tried to get back to my feet but couldn't. So I rolled up onto my knees and did the necessary business from that awkward position. Charlie was only a tad better off. It took some minutes of what he called "limbering up" before we could move freely and take staggering steps without stumbling. Charlie extended his hand and allowed that this was "a stag well earned and well taken!" I considered that high praise from a master stalker. My admiration for Charlie's skills and knowledge was growing steadily. Charlie called Graeme on his two-way radio and instructed him as to our location and to bring up the machine to fetch us.

As we rode back down "off the hill," Charlie and I stood upright in the bed of the machine and held on to the grab bar on the back of the cab so as to absorb shocks and sways with our arms and knees. The tracked vehicle was not overly endowed with either functional springs and/or shock absorbers. I watched the stars emerging as the clouds cleared away. It quickly became colder as the open sky sucked away the day's remaining heat. I was thoroughly chilled but internally warmed by the experience. I relished Charlie's compliment; he was not a generous man with compliments nor long on bullshit. I pondered, what was there about hunting that made such a physically miserable experience—in totality—so satisfying, fulfilling, and exciting?

Somehow the difficulty and the discomfort added to rather than detracted from the overall experience. Are things that are hard-earned more appreciated than those that come too easy? Such was my philosophical insight—question, perhaps—for the day. When Charlie and Graeme dropped me off at the Gardner's Cottage, I could see and smell the peat smoke rising from the chimney and visualized the burning peat glowing on the grate in the fireplace. I knew Kathy was back from her independent adventures of the day, and I was eager to see her—as always—and regale her with my newly acquired hunting tales. The anticipation of getting out of my wet, heavy wool hunting outfit and into a hot soaking bath provided an incredible pleasure. I knew that some excellent brandy was waiting inside, likely already in a snifter. The hot bath and the brandy would be followed by a steaming bowl of mutton stew. All that and a warm soft bed in waiting seemed a most delightful prospect.

OCTOBER 12, 1999

My fellow hunters took the day off from stalking to do some sightseeing. To my delight I was left alone with Graeme and Charlie—just the three of us professionals. The first stalk of the day involved an approach of over a mile across a wide valley to get within rifle range of a group of red deer that Charlie had spotted from the road earlier that morning.

When we neared the crest of the hill that overlooked the valley, Charlie signaled me to "take a knee" and wait as he crawled up to "take a wee spy" over the lip of the valley and down into the swale. He slowly stuck his head up to see into the swale when he dropped

back down and slid backward a couple of yards and vigorously signaled, with a single finger—if that's even possible—for me to crawl
up beside him. When I got within twenty yards, he signaled me to go
down on my belly and slither up to where he was lying. He whispered
that there were two stags grazing together just on the other side of the
crest. The stag that Charlie deemed "shootable" was a "cull" with one
forked antler and one spike antler.

He pulled my rifle from the slip that he had carried over his
shoulder, rolled over onto his belly, and worked his way a couple of
yards to the crest of the hill. He rolled over on his side, snapped the
bipod onto the forearm of the rifle, signaled me to watch as he worked
the bolt and put a round in the chamber, put on the safety, and put
the rifle down on the bipod. He signaled for me to worm my way up
beside him.

I peeped over the rise and immediately saw the stag Charlie
had in mind. I whispered, "200 yards?" Charlie nodded. Perfect. My
rifle should be spot-on at that distance. I settled into the rifle, got the
sight picture, breathed deeply in and out three times, and let out half
of my last breath. I held the crosshairs dead on the heart, just behind
the "elbow" of the front leg, timed my heart beat, and squeezed off the
shot. The stag folded up and rolled limply thirty or forty yards down
the steep slope—and never moved again.

Charlie called Graeme on the two-way radio to tell him to bring
up the machine and help take care of the dead stag. After the stalkers
field-dressed the beast, we lay on our backs in the heather in the sun,
out of the wind and ate our lunch. The stalkers patiently answered my
many questions about red deer management and hunting in Scotland.
They seemed equally interested in my description of elk management
and hunting in North America.

I hoped they enjoyed my company—and my knowledge—as
much as I enjoyed theirs. In my six decades as a hunter, I had hunted
with many fine hunters, many of them highly skilled wildlife biologists as well as superb hunters. But Charlie was more attuned to the
animals we pursued than anyone I had ever worked or hunted with.
Graeme was already highly-skilled and learning fast. I thought any
big game biologist in North America, including me, could profit from

spending some time with the likes of Charlie and Graeme. After a "wee kip" lying on our backs in the sun, Charlie and I commenced a walk cross-country into the wind toward the crests of some rolling hills. When we neared the crest of a hill, I sat down, as instructed, and waited as Charlie knee-crawled and then belly-crawled to the crest to see what just might lie on the other side. We had encountered several groups of red deer, but after Charlie looked them over through his "glass," he found no "shootable staggies" in the lot and we moved on just beneath the crest of hill.

The fourth group of deer that we encountered contained twenty-five animals or so—including three young stags and one very large stag with perfectly matched "royal" antlers (six points on a side). Charlie referred to the big stag as a "truly grand staggie." The stags were moving away from us in a leisurely fashion, stopping periodically to sample the cuisine. We followed. Periodically we had to wait for the group of deer to cross over the next ridge ahead before we could hustle across the swale and climb the hill with the intent, and hope, of getting within rifle range. After pursuing the deer across three such swales, we dropped down on all fours and crawled to the top of the hill and looked over. Charlie immediately crawled back and dropped flat. I followed suit. We were both breathing hard—especially me. We squirmed back to where we could see the group of deer we had been pursuing spread out in front of us and grazing calmly. Charlie looked over the stags in the group through his telescope. He focused on a single stag on the extreme left of the group. He whispered in my ear that this was the stag he wanted me to take. He handed me his telescope to look over the "beast" as he readied my rifle.

My first impression was that I was looking at the wrong stag. The stag was, by far, the biggest, with the most spectacular antlers that I had seen in several years of stalking on this estate—even bigger and more beautiful than the huge stag I had missed several years before. After I settled into the rifle, I checked the stags out through the scope and noted two much smaller stags at much closer range.

I whispered, "Charlie, I don't really need to take that big boy. Either of the two smaller stags will do just fine." Charlie's eyes and facial expression told me a story I should have figured out for myself.

Charlie had saved this magnificent stag for me. It came to me that for the last several months—and certainly for this day—he had this approaching "moment of truth" in mind. It was a gift from one professional to another. Our eyes locked—I nodded my understanding and appreciation. He smiled, winked, and turned back to business. Now it was up to me to shoot well and kill clean and quick.

There was a significant crosswind that further complicated things by blowing in gusts. I estimated the distance to the stag at 250 yards and slightly downhill. I confirmed the distance with Charlie, who estimated 230 yards. That was close enough—not enough difference to worry about. It was a significantly longer shot than I would ordinarily take. Charlie wanted me to have this trophy, and this was as good a shot as I was likely to get. In the process of assuring myself, I reasoned: I am lying prone, shooting off a bipod and breathing normally; the scope is cranked up to 9×; and I can see my normal heartbeat in the crosshairs.

I wanted to be certain of a kill, so I whispered to Charlie, "Clean kill or clean miss—I'm taking a neck shot."

To my surprise—and satisfaction, I was totally calm, cool, methodical, and collected in the situation. I took three deep breaths, partially let out the last breath, steadied the crosshairs, timed my heartbeat, and squeezed off the shot. I was so focused that the report and the recoil actually startled me. The big stag collapsed on the spot, fell over on his side, and lay still. Charlie quietly commented, "Spot-on. Nicely done."

Charlie picked up the rifle and made a beeline for the big stag, carefully pacing off the distance as he went. My football knee was protesting its ongoing and continued mistreatment, and I was suddenly aware of being very close to physically used up for the day. When I caught up, Charlie announced that the distance covered by the shot was 234 yards—four yards off his estimate. I had not paced the distance but—just to be ornery—I declared the distance to be exactly 251 yards. Charlie shook his head and suggested that I took short steps, likely attributable to "my increasing age and short legs." Clearly we had become friends as well as professional colleagues.

He extended his hand and I took it; he smiled a broad smile with eyes sparkling. There was no need to say more. Charlie had accorded

Charlie, the head stalker, took this photograph of Jack and Graeme with Jack's spectacular stag, October 12, 1999.

me the highest honor he could bestow as a stalker. I understood, and he knew that I understood his gesture and was appreciative. He had helped provide an experience—a "trophy of the mind"—that I had already mounted on my trophy wall of memory to be revisited, privately, from time to time for as long as I might live.

Back at the cottage, I had no more than cleaned up, put on fresh clothes, and sipped some single-malt Scotch whiskey that Kathy had poured me when another hunter showed up. It was Arthur, who had been my host for the dove hunt in Argentina the past spring—a most generous, gracious, and genial man. As our host was away tending to other things, I took over—justified or not—the role of "host" based on my newly acquired two year's worth of experience with stalking stags in Scotland. At least I had a keenly developed line of bullshit and hunting tales that I could employ to match the circumstances.

OCTOBER 13, 1999

We left the Gardener's Cottage at the civilized hour of nine o'clock and made a stop at the shooting range. As they did with each newly arrived hunter, the stalkers wanted to know if their new hunter could shoot and to make sure that his rifle and scope were sighted in "spot on." First Charlie, firing from a prone position off a bipod, put three rounds spot-on in a half-inch group two inches high on the target at 100 yards.

Then Arthur, our "newbie" hunter, with only a little coaching, came close to replicating Charlie's performance. Either Arthur was a natural or he had more shooting experience with large-caliber hunting rifles than he was letting on. After that, we took a ride in the Land Rover to the back side of the estate to meet up with Graeme and the machine.

The stalkers put the standard operating procedure into play. Using the machine to travel to vantage points, Charlie and Graeme looked over several groups of deer on distant hillsides in search of shootable stags in a location and situation that would yield a significant probability of a successful stalk. Arthur's keenness for the experience became more and more obvious as the day wore on. He seemed increasingly "raring to go." Just after noon, Charlie found the essential combination of a shootable stag in a situation that seemed promising for a successful stalk. Charlie and Arthur were off, leaving Graeme and me to guard the machine, drink tea from a thermos, and trade "war stories"—hunting tales.

I took advantage of the opportunity to engage Graeme in conversation about what went into becoming a certified stalker. It was our first real chance to visit privately. He was open and enthusiastic in his detailed responses to my questions. Our conversation was ended by a rifle's report off in the direction that Charlie and Arthur had gone. Ten minutes later the two-way radio crackled to life as Charlie gave Graeme directions to his position. We were off by a round-about route that took us to where Charlie had indicated there was a dead stag awaiting our attention. It took us the better part of an hour to locate the dead stag. Charlie and Arthur were nowhere to be seen. They were off in a search for another stag. The dead stag had four antler points on one side and a single "switch" on the other—a "cull" and therefore declared "shootable."

Just as we were winching the dressed-out stag into the back of the machine, Charlie and Arthur appeared over the brow of the hill opposite the one where we were standing. When they reached us, Arthur was all smiles and his story tumbled out. After he had dropped his first stag with a clean, one-shot kill, Charlie noted that a group of deer that had scattered at the sound of the shot had slowed to a walk before they crossed over the top of the rise off to the north. Charlie thought he knew the route they would take, and he led Arthur through a cutoff that he thought might provide opportunity for an ambush.

Charlie told Arthur that getting into position for a potentially successful ambush would require that they move hard and fast—uphill most of the way. Charlie, of course, knew he could do it but he didn't know about Arthur. Arthur, who turned out to be a dedicated recreational runner, just nodded. They were off. Sometimes such a play pays off. This was one of those times. Charlie and Arthur managed to get into position and well hidden in the heather by the time the deer came around the contour of the hill and paraded past their hiding place. The three stags were tagging along behind the hinds and calves. Arthur dropped the shootable stag pointed out to him by Charlie with one shot at some seventy-five yards.

Arthur was now two for two one-shot kills as a neophyte stag hunter. Quite deservedly, he was pretty damn proud of himself and as high as the proverbial kite. On the ride back to the Gardner's Cottage, he gave me a blow-by-blow account of the second kill. Charlie listened with a big smile on his face. He was happy that he had done his job and his client so obviously appreciated the experience and acknowledged the key role played by his stalker's skills. When we arrived at the cottage, Arthur once again recounted his exploits in vivid detail—much to the delight of our host. It was obviously important to him that Arthur had a memorable, first-time big game hunting experience. I was pleased to have served satisfactorily as surrogate host and to have been part of the adventure. After the entire party—hunters and nonhunters—showed up at the cottage, a somewhat raucous party broke out.

The ladies retired shortly after dinner, but our host, Arthur, and I stayed up late in front of the peat fire in the cottage to talk of "manly" things—mostly one hunting story after another. Somewhat lubricated by exquisite single-malt Scotch whiskies, we began to applaud the storytellers with excellent (mine) and not so accurate (Arthur and our host) imitations of roaring stags. Kathy remarked the next morning that she assumed, from the raucous racket, that both good Scotch whiskey and testosterone were flowing in copious amounts. The "roaring," loud talk, and boisterous laughter continued until the wee hours. It was fair to say that a good time was had by all—at least by those who were not trying to sleep.

OCTOBER 14, 1999

As we talked over breakfast, our host tallied up our kills and computed how many stags remained to be taken of the twenty he had contracted for. He declared, "Two to go." I was more than satisfied with the three stags I had taken. A certain amount of polite debate followed with the conclusion that Arthur, who had gotten off to a slow start, was just the man to complete the contract.

Our host quietly discussed with Charlie the plan that, if things went well, Arthur would take one stag today and one tomorrow. Beyond that, it was agreed that the stalkers would make every effort to put Arthur in position to take a royal stag. Arthur was not in on the discussion. Again, to my delight, I was to play the role of Arthur's surrogate host.

By midafternoon, Charlie had taken Arthur on two unsuccessful stalks. In the first case, after a two-hour stalk and ending with a 300-yard creep and crawl, Charlie finally ascertained that the bunch of stags they were stalking did not contain a royal stag of adequate stature. In the second case, a shift in the wind betrayed Charlie and Arthur to their intended quarry, a big beautiful royal stag that had disappeared over the hill in a dead run. It was late afternoon before Graeme and I picked up the two hunters. There was, just maybe, time for one more stalk before the sun disappeared. Carrying out a successful stalk is clearly much more difficult when the definition of "shootable" is limited to a truly trophy-class royal stag. Such "big boys" weren't born yesterday and had not lived so long by sheer accident or even at the discretion of the stalkers.

Earlier, Charlie had spied a group of deer containing a suitable royal stag on the back side of the estate (i.e., about as far north from the main road on the estate as was possible). Charlie and Arthur took off on foot with the intent of "ringing round" the hill on the "front side" (closest to the road) to give them a chance to intercept the group of deer and get within shooting range all the while moving into the wind. The stalk played out just the way Charlie had choreographed it in his mind when he spied the royal stag's antlers sticking up above the heather at an estimated distance of some 200 yards.

Charlie dropped down below the crest of the hill and worked Arthur into a position from which he would be able, if things worked out, to shoot from a prone position off a bipod. Once in position, Arthur nestled into the rifle's sling. Charlie put his hand on Arthur's shoulder and delayed things, though discreetly, until Arthur had time to catch his breath and was breathing slow, deep, and steady. By now, the sun had dropped below the brow of the hill and darkness, and the end of shooting time, was coming fast.

Charlie whispered to Arthur to take off the safety on the rifle and be ready to shoot quickly—and straight. Then Charlie grunted loudly into the empty leather case in which he had carried his telescope—a remarkable imitation of a challenging stag. The royal stag came immediately to his feet and, looking for a rival that dared challenge him for his harem of hinds, turned directly toward the sound. Within fifteen seconds of Charlie's grunt, Arthur fired. The bullet entered just under the stag's chin and severed the spinal cord. The stag dropped out of sight in the heather.

Arthur, a first-time big game hunter, was now three stags for three well-placed shots—which now included a real honest-to-god trophy-class royal stag. When Graeme and I arrived on the scene with the machine, I crawled down from the cab, looked over the beast lying dead in the heather, and extended my hand and congratulated Arthur. "As my old granddaddy used to say, 'You can't hardly do no better than that!'"

I could tell that Arthur agreed, though he just grinned and said nothing. After Charlie field-dressed the stag, he winched him into the bed of the machine. We loaded up and banged on the top of the cabin, the signal to take us "home from the hill." There was very little conversation; Charlie and Arthur were fading rapidly in vigor as their adrenaline charge dissipated and weariness took over. With good reason, we were all early to bed this night.

OCTOBER 15, 1999

This was my last day of stalking stags in Scotland—for this year at least. There was one stag yet to be taken. Once again I insisted that my lust for hunting was satiated for this trip. Our host declared that he was likewise done for the year. Arthur, gentleman that he is, put up a mild protest. Then continuing to feign reluctance, he gave in and agreed to make the sacrifice and do his best to take the last stag for the year. Smiling, he observed, "After all, somebody has to do it." I figured this would be a comparatively easy day. After all, we had all day and there was only one hunter and only one "shootable" stag yet to take. The pressure was off.

By noon, we had ridden the machine to the top of a hill three times, only to see no stags that Charlie deemed "shootable" on the surrounding hillsides and swales. The fourth time, Charlie spotted a group of deer in a burn containing several stags that he considered, for whatever reason, "shootable." Graeme was the designated stalker. To make things a bit more challenging for Graeme, our host's daughter and Kathy wanted to go along on the stalk. Arthur agreed—insisted might be a better word. It made for quite a sight as young Graeme set out with the rifle in a slip over his shoulder, trailed—in order of march—by Arthur, Kathy, and our host's daughter Faith. I remarked to Charlie that Graeme had a regular entourage. And, to add a bit more pressure, Graeme had a gallery made up of our host, Charlie, and me watching every move through our binoculars. Just to add to the moment, I called out to Graeme. When he turned around, I encouraged him by giving him a double thumbs-up and calling out, "Hey, no pressure!" Graeme smiled and waved. I thought the smile a bit wan and, perhaps, more polite than genuine.

Fortunately for young Graeme, things couldn't have gone off better. He and his entourage quickly encountered a group of deer. Graeme left the observers where they could see what was going on and set off with Arthur in tow. The stalk was a bit tricky, as the prevailing winds and the lay of the land dictated that the only feasible approach was to move directly toward the deer, in spite of the fact that there were no obvious features of either topography or vegetation that could be used for cover. Graeme and Arthur crawled from one low-growing patch of heather to another freezing in position from time to time when a deer lifted its head.

Over the course of the next hour and a half, Graeme and Arthur closed to within what I figured was about 200 yards of the selected stag. Even then, the shot would be difficult—long, steeply down-hill, with a strong gusting crosswind. But Graeme probably thought, "Hey, what the hell?" Arthur was three for three—all spot-on, clean, one-shot kills. Given the circumstances in this case—the rifle had to be at least three feet above ground level to enable a braced shot—there was no way Arthur could shoot using the bipod. Furthermore, the potential shot was too long to risk off-hand. So Graeme sat up straight and instructed Arthur to use his shoulder as a rest. Graeme poked his fingers in his ears and opened his mouth wide. That bracer gave Arthur a better chance than shooting off-hand but not nearly so steady a chance as shooting from a prone position off the bipod. Both Graeme and Arthur breathed deep three times. Graeme held his breath. Arthur let out half of his last breath and squeezed off his shot. The stag sat back on his haunches, wavered for a couple of seconds, and fell over dead from a heart shot. Arthur had put on one fine performance for a first-time big game hunter who had never before fired a big-bore rifle. After Graeme field-dressed the stag, he and Arthur dragged it through the heather and down the hill and got it into the bed of the machine. We broke out the thermos of celebratory coffee and flask of brandy.

As our hunt was now over, Charlie deemed it appropriate that the flask be passed and we each "took a wee dram"—well, maybe two—to "honor the staggie" and the hunter. We ate our lunch sitting in the sun and shielded from the cold wind by the machine. As we rode down the mountainside toward the loch, I felt a creeping sadness at the ending of a very special time in a very special place in the company of very special people.

CHAPTER 17

A TROPHY FOR KATHY

Kathy and I were once again privileged to travel to Scotland as guests of our good friend Robert "Bob" Model. This, regrettably, was to be my last hunt in Scotland.

OCTOBER 2004

The weather turned especially foul the day we arrived on our hunting grounds. Winds gusted in from the North Sea, and dark clouds scudded across the sky, bringing intermittent cold rain with temperatures hovering just above freezing. Patches of heather glowed orange on the dark hillsides when and where shafts of sunlight cut through gaps in the gloaming. Despite the conditions, Kathy wanted to accompany me "out" on the hill.

A tracked surplus military vehicle, referred to by the stalkers as "the machine," carried us across the hillsides. We stopped from time to time to allow the new lead stalker, John "Johnny" McDonald, to employ his telescope for a "wee spy" of the surrounding hillsides. Many stalkers and experienced hunters prefer a telescope to binoculars. There is something to be said for "tradition!"

Johnny is who I think of when I think of a Scotsman: tall and lean, red-haired, and with a notable Scottish burr in his speech and a keen, if quite subtle, sense of humor. As a hunter, stalker, naturalist, gamekeeper, guide, and pleasant companion, he was the personification of professional hunting competence.

The red deer were in full rut and gathered into groups that ranged in size from a half dozen to near a hundred. Groups of hinds and calves were often surrounded by several rutting stags vying for

Kathy with Jack's stalker, Johnny, Scotland, October 2004.

breeding rights as evidenced by their seemingly incessant "roaring" and the chasing of lesser stags away from the harem. As the afternoon became evening, Johnny had not yet identified a "shootable" stag in any of the bunches of red deer we encountered. Making things difficult, the winds were especially "squirrelly" frequently changing direction and velocity. Finally Johnny announced that we would abandon the machine and walk the moors, heading into the wind and taking full advantage of the rolling topography to reduce the chances of the deer hearing or even scenting us as we approached.

The heather was a foot or two tall with tussocks of bunchgrasses interspersed between the heathered clumps. Walking was difficult for both Kathy and me, as the heather hid holes, some small and some knee-deep. To help maintain an upright posture and probe ahead for solid ground, all hands carried a walking stick with a crook on the end carved from a red deer antler or a domestic ram's horn.

The *modus operandi* involved walking into the wind and stopping near the crest of each hill for Johnny to move ahead to the crest. As he neared the crest, he dropped down and crept forward—first on his hands and knees and then on his belly—to avoid exposing himself to whatever red deer might be on the other side. Then he extracted his telescope out of its tubular leather case and took a "wee spy about." If he saw no deer, Johnny signaled to Kathy and me to stand up and walk up to join him.

Near midday we stopped for lunch just shy of an especially sharp ridge. After he finished his lunch, Johnny belly-crawled up to the crest of the hill to take a "wee spy." He popped his head up and ducked down just as quickly. He hand-signaled that there was a group of red deer just on the other side and motioned for us to crawl up beside him.

When we were lying beside him, hidden from the deer by the topography, he whispered that there were over forty hinds and calves just over the rise. Using my binoculars, I eased up to the crest and verified his estimate.

There, less than a quarter mile away, several dozen deer were grazing and others lay in the heather sleeping or chewing their cuds. One royal stag, with magnificent antlers, was running about, keeping a dozen younger "staggies" away from the hinds—his hinds. Johnny declared the royal stag "shootable." Now all that remained was to get me—"the gun"—close enough for a more or less certain killing shot. Game on!

Johnny whispered that we would retreat to the last burn we had crossed and follow it a half mile or so around the flank of the group of deer. At that point Johnny would try for another look. For the next half hour we picked our way carefully along the sheep trails that flanked the burn. The old stumps and roots of the trees that had covered this land several hundred years ago were preserved in the peat soils. Every few minutes, each time a bit closer, we could hear a big stag roaring.

Johnny signaled for us to sit down and take a breather. He never seemed to need a break—and most likely wouldn't admit if he did. He belly-crawled to the top of the burn's bank and slowly raised his head to take a look—and immediately ducked down. He held his finger up to his lips—"shhhh!"—and signaled for us to belly-crawl up to join him. He pointed out two young stags lying some 90 to 100 yards apart and around 150 yards ahead. The intermittent roaring was coming from just over the next ridge and directly behind the young stags. Johnny whispered that we would have to crawl between the two young stags, undetected, to get into a position that might afford me a shot at the royal stag he had in mind for my trophy.

For nearly an hour, we crawled, sometimes on hands and knees and sometimes worming along on our bellies. We never looked up for fear of exposing our very white faces. Our noses took in the smells of the heather, the sheep and deer shit, and other plants crushed in our passing, along with those of the peat soil and urine of sheep and red deer.

I kept my eyes focused on tiny plants and insects that would have passed notice had we been walking. From time to time we rested; crawling was quickly evolving into hard tiring work. There was no sound save for the intermittent roaring of the big stag somewhere just over the ridge, the sound of the breeze, and our sometimes labored breathing. Finally, we had successfully crawled, undetected, right between the two resting stags. I was incredulous.

Johnny signaled us to lie still as he wormed his was up to the hilltop. Once there, he cautiously rose up on his knees for a look and instantly dropped flat with his face buried in the heather. He slithered back down the slope a few yards to where Kathy and I were lying. He removed the .243 caliber Remington rifle from its slip, extended the attached bipod, and placed the rifle carefully on the ground. He worked the bolt very slowly and pushed a cartridge "up the spout" and put on the safety.

To me everything seemed to move in slow motion. Johnny held one hand open with five fingers and the other with thumb and forefinger indicating a zero—the royal stag was lying only some 50 yards over the rise. I gingerly raised my head for my own wee spy—and ducked down quickly when I saw the stag's antlers above the heather. The hinds and calves were another 75 to 100 yards downslope. By God, Johnny had done it—no, we had actually done it!

I squirmed up and snuggled into the rifle's stock, concentrated on bringing my breathing under control, and centered the crosshairs on the base of the stag's neck. If I fired now, there was no way I could miss. But the code of the hunt—at least for Johnny McDonald— mandated that "the gun stays his shot until the staggie stands."

Cold mist and rain came and went over the next two hours as we lay still and silent—and waited. Several younger stags chased each other—once within 30 yards of where we lay—but did not detect our presence. Shivers came and went as we lay motionless, watching the rain drip from the visors of our caps and feeling it trickle down our necks.

Then, with no warning, the big stag heaved to his feet and stood broadside to us. I squeezed the trigger. The big stag dropped and never even twitched. I was so cold and stiff that when I lurched to my feet, I staggered and performed an outstanding pratfall.

The stag was, as Johnny put it, "a truly magnificent beast." Kathy sat down next to the stag and stroked its wet coat. She looked up at Johnny and said quietly, "Johnny, I want these antlers mounted to remind me always of this wonderful day." She was radiant—and so very alive. Her Irish red hair blended with the reddish cast of the heather, and her Irish green eyes sparkled. Johnny winked at me and smiled—just a little smile—so that Kathy would not see. He was clearly very pleased with her heartfelt compliment, and he had noticed the sincere emotion and appreciation in her voice.

The antlers from that stag are the only "animal part" that adorns the walls of our house—well, admittedly, the wall in question is in my workshop across the driveway from our house. They are not the largest antlers from a red deer that I was to take over the years, but they conjure up the best memories. To me, they simply personify what a trophy should be. And somehow I will always think of it as "Kathy's trophy."

In the course of seven stalking seasons in Scotland, Kathy never wanted to be "the gun." But she was a constant companion and thrilled by the most fair-chase hunting I have ever done or seen. She insisted on "going up on the hill" with the hunters rather than hanging out around the lodge. In the process, she developed an understanding of what hunting should be and could be—and why I loved it so.

I have been fortunate to have been totally blessed and lucky in love—twice.

EPILOGUE

Much has been written, both pro and con, about what motivates hunters—and most surely motivations do differ from one hunter to another. For me, hunting—especially hunting in the high lonesome—is, at its heart, an individual enterprise but one best savored in the company of other motivated, skilled, and kindred spirits. After all, every hunter can only be but a temporary denizen of the high lonesome who feels, sees and hears, learns, remembers, and savors the experiences in distinctly personal ways. For me, the entirety of the very experience of hunting alone in the high lonesome was significant—it was everything. Killing an elk or a mule deer or grouse or chukars, or feasting on trout from a high mountain cirque lake, was just a part of the experience, but it was the cord that lashed it all together. There is a reason the experience is called "hunting" rather than "killing." One can seek after and hunt for much more than prey.

Hunting skills, when coupled with a little luck, can—more often than not—bring an animal to bag. But that, the killing, is significant but it is only the beginning. Dressing out and skinning the beast, quartering the carcass, rolling and tying the quarters into manty packs, boosting and lashing them onto packhorses, packing the loads to the trailhead, butchering the meat, and preparing meals for family and friends are but a few of the integral parts of the overall experience. Even for hunters in the high lonesome, all these things could have been accomplished more easily, quickly, and cheaply by hunting lower slopes and relatively gentle ground closer to roads. Or by just making a visit to the corner butcher's shop.

Yet my hunting partners—especially my *compadre* Will H. "Bill" Brown—and I, when at all possible, hunted the high lonesome, pursuing more the place and the experience than prey. We had the mountains to ourselves as much as is possible in an ever more crowded world. We put our well-trained and experienced saddle and packhorses to their highest and best use. We practiced the increasingly archaic skills of horse-packing, stalking, killing, and packing out big game, relying totally on our own skills and heart. We could, for a precious few days, live the old-fashioned way in the outback, as in times stretching back into antiquity when skills such as ours routinely made the difference between life and death.

Hunting the high lonesome is riskier than hunting down below, requiring an ever more deft practice of an arcane set of skills that makes the experience—at least to some—all the more enticing and exciting. Along with the use of our accumulated skills, along with the increased risks, came feelings of being more intensely alive, cautious, aware, careful, and attentive to the nuances of time, place, and circumstance.

The hunting experience itself—including coping with unusual and unexpected developments—emerges as paramount. All else was put aside for a few precious days. And if the gods of the hunt chose to smile, there was a well-earned encounter every now and then with a bull elk or a mule deer buck.

Hunters are increasingly under attack by a portion of the American public that looks upon hunting as a cruel affair for the animals and a dehumanizing experience for hunters. Others write about the role of hunting in human evolution and extol its virtues. I don't worry and never have all that much about why I hunt—it simply suits me and has as long as I can remember. My extensive hunting as a youth probably played a significant role in bringing me to my profession of natural resource management via my first job out of college dealing with big game and hunting management. Big game management morphed into education and research into wildlife ecology that slowly evolved to include the new emerging fields of "ecosystem management" and "conservation biology."

It pains me to see people who really care about wildlife—and there aren't that many true *aficionados*—fight among themselves over the legitimacy of sport hunting while the real threats to wildlife such as habitat degradation and loss continue essentially unabated. But the attack on hunting is simple—and too-often simple-minded while being charged with real emotion. And in the end hunting is subject to control through legislation and rules and regulations. If I were a consultant to those who prefer that consideration of wildlife in land-use decisions be given less attention, I would encourage such fratricidal carnage on the part of wildlife *aficionados* coming from different points of view. Debates over sport hunting diverts minds, efforts, and money from the much more important basic issues related to conservation and management of wildlife habitats.

In my early years as a wildlife biologist, I conducted annual public meetings in a county courthouse in West Texas about the number of antlerless deer permits to be issued in that county for the upcoming deer season. An attractive older woman badgered me—sometimes quite aggressively—off and on throughout my presentation. She demanded that I explain to the crowd why anyone, in the middle of the twentieth century in a nation as affluent as the United States of America, would participate in what she called "the bestial archaic pastime" of hunting.

I put forth every explanation that came to my mind. She, most clearly, did not agree with me and continued to make her heartfelt points. In the process, she severely agitated most of the audience—which was composed mostly of hunters and landowners of the male persuasion. Finally, somewhat exasperated, I came to my bottom line: "Well, madam," I said, "in the final analysis, I guess that's just the kind of son-of-a-bitch I am. And for that I make no apologies!"

I received a standing ovation from an audience. That room was evidently filled with the same kind of sons-of-bitches. My adversary was quiet for a moment, and then her frown morphed into a charming smile. She nodded and sweetly replied, "That's honest enough. I can respect that." Sometimes the simplest explanation is the best—Occam's razor.

At that point in my career—and in my evolving life as a hunter—I had, and still have, some difficulty with fancy words and artful explanations. When I examine my own motivations for a lifetime of hunting, they do not seem to me to be especially sophisticated nor deeply seated in philosophical introspection. I was a hunter simply because I enjoyed hunting in all of its aspects, including—in addition to the camaraderie—the development, exercise, and teaching the requisite skill sets. As time passed and experiences accumulated, I became ever more expert and successful in the application of those skills and teaching them to others.

I enjoy anticipating and planning the hunt. I enjoy being with valued friends and family in the field. I love fine firearms. I appreciate the horses and the pack mules and the development and utilization of the skills required in their use. I love the camping, cooking, and camaraderie involved. I enjoy the pursuit and the thrills, even the agonizing fatigue and deep disappointments—and especially—the treasured trophies of memories. I rejoice in the kill ethically and well done and inevitably suffer short-lived pangs of conscience in the process. I love preparing and eating the meat. I believe that those I hunted with and came to respect over many decades in many places—in North America and other countries—I believe, felt more or less the same.

I don't recall any of my hunting companions spending much time sitting cross-legged on the ground around the campfire humming and examining their belly buttons while contemplating the deeper meanings of the hunting experience. Most of them, like me, hunted simply because it was part of their culture and because they relished the experience from start to finish. They appreciated the entire hunting experience: thinking about it, developing requisite skills, hunting, sometimes killing, caring for the meat, preparing meals from that meat, and remembering and relating hunting stories.

I loved hunting with my father, uncles, and grandfather—my highly treasured "Big Dad." What I wouldn't give to hunt with them again and sit around the campfire spinning yarns—just one last time.

They did not fill my head with fancy reasons to love hunting and the comradeship. They didn't need to. It simply was.

I don't recall ever killing an animal because I was doing my duty of "reducing the size of the herd for its own good." I participated because it provided me opportunity to hunt within the mores of my culture. And, as a bonus, my family ate the meat that I cared for put on the table. I sought out, pursued, killed, dressed, butchered, cooked, and ate my prey. Most of the meat my family ate as the boys were growing up came from animals that the three of us had "harvested" from nature's bounty: white-tailed deer, mule deer, antelope, elk, turkeys, quail of several species, ruffed and blue grouse, doves, ducks, geese, and fish. Especially in my early years of employment as a wildlife biologist in Texas, our killing of wild game was a significant part of feeding our family. Even in the United States, so-called "subsistence hunting" does not lie as far in the past as some might think—in fact, it still exists in some regions.

When I began hunting in Texas during World War II, we hunters were praised by our families for our skills and the meat we put on the table. I knew little of the laws and regulations governing the taking of game and fish. Looking back, it seems likely that they made little sense to those from whom I learned hunting, trapping, and fishing skills as, under the circumstances of the time and place—the wildlife species that provided our sustenance were not being depleted through our actions. But when the war ended, financial problems eased, and meat rationing ceased, my grandfather and father and uncles made me aware that the hunting and trapping situation had changed. From that point forward, we would all scrupulously obey the laws and regulations relative to hunting and fishing. And, furthermore, we would comply with the standards of what passed for "fair chase" in our society. In the winter of 1946, I encountered my first game warden in the woods who was to become my mentor and guided me toward becoming a wildlife biologist.

Today, more than ever, some concept of "fair chase" is essential in sport hunting for two related reasons. First, the general public— most of whom do not hunt—collectively "owns" the wildlife under the vaunted North American Model of Wildlife Conservation. That model prescribes that there are standards of hunter behavior—e.g., "fairness" in hunting. After all, in a democracy, the citizenry must be, at the very least, accepting of sport hunting if it is to continue over the long run. Second, hunters need the assurance and reinforcement of their views of themselves as a principled group deeply concerned, at the very core, with the conservation and welfare of legally hunted wildlife. In turn, hunters as a group need to feel—and sincerely believe—that they pursue their passion for hunting under an ethical code that elevates, and sustains, hunting on a plane far above the simple act of killing. For me, "fair chase" simply means that there are rules—governmental, peer group, and personal—that should/ must be adhered to if hunting is to legitimately continue in modern societies. This is especially true in circumstances where wild lands and wildlife decline as human populations inexorably increase and wildlife habitats diminish.

In my later years, I have done my best to wear out several rifles and shotguns just carrying them around—in a scabbard on a horse or slung over my shoulder. I don't believe my hunting prowess has declined all that dramatically with age. But most certainly my discrimination has increased. My need, or desire, to demonstrate success by making a kill—and thereby attaining the trophy that validates a hunter's prowess—has withered significantly. Yet my appreciation and need for shared adventure with valued friends—while attaining the quiet times in primitive surroundings—became ever stronger.

Young hunters should appreciate—and tolerate—the development of such "discrimination" in their older mentors and companions. They too, if fortunate enough, will come to appreciate this higher order of the hunting-fishing mystique. In speaking of such things, the Spanish philosopher Ortega y Gasset observed, in his classic *Meditations on Hunting*, "To sum up, one does not hunt in order to kill; on the contrary, one kills in order to have hunted." A psychologist might call that a complete *gestalt*.

Now that I am older, much older, I have come to believe that most fully mature hunters hunt—and kill and eat what they kill—in order to continue to play a role in the ongoing play that has spanned hundreds of generations of hunters who crouched around their fires and talked of the hunt—past, present, and those yet to come. I pondered the Native American's reference to "heaven" as the "happy hunting grounds." But, I suspect, it is mostly the young males who most need to hunt and kill in order to acquire and demonstrate ancient essential skills and thereby prove their worth to themselves—and to others whose opinions they respect. Older, more seasoned hunters, most with nothing left to prove having gained an understanding of their roles in the on-going and ages-old play, become content to leave the cast of the play and become part of the audience—all the while cherishing the memories gathered along the way.

Seven hunting trips on the moors of northern Scotland, plus a driven grouse shoot in Spain, finished my hunting career. By the end of the last day of my last hunt, I had reached a long-delayed decision—perhaps one too long delayed. The time had come for me to cease my pursuit of big game. Though my spirit still soared on the hunt, I was in constant significant physical distress. My mind and spirit were willing, even eager, but my body increasingly begged to differ. The consequences of too many football injuries, accidents with horses, vehicular mishaps, airplane and helicopter wrecks, and wrestling deer and elk in the course of my professional activities had so accumulated and interacted as to make them impossible to ignore or wish away. Now, I fight pancreatic cancer and will likely, inevitably lose. But, not just yet—not yet. I will not go easily into the dark still night—not today. Maybe tomorrow—but not today. Now the time has finally come to set aside what the ignorant might call "childish things."

I sealed my decision by saddle-soaping and oiling my two old McClellan cavalry saddles and saddlebags and my two Decker pack saddles. The saddles went to old companions who still had their horses.

My rifles and shotguns reside in their cabinet in my library/ office across the driveway from my house in Florence, Montana. I frequently and carefully clean them. Some came to me as gifts from my dad and Big Dad. Four of the rifles are fancy, engraved commemorative rifles presented to me as gifts over the years. Two were specially engraved 1895 Browning lever-action rifles made to commemorate the 100th anniversary of the establishment of the Forest Reserves in

1879. Two others, Winchester .45-70 lever-action rifles, were engraved to celebrate the establishment of the USFS in 1905. Each piece has a tag that designates who will receive it upon my death. Sometimes I think that perhaps they shouldn't wait for my passing to find a new home. Maybe I ought to distribute them—or at least most of them—to sons, a stepson, and grandsons. But I can't seem to bring myself to do that—not just yet. As long as they are safe and ready in the gun cabinet, I can somehow bring myself to believe that there is just one more hunt—one more adventure—left in me. I know better but I choose to think otherwise.

I trust that the guns will represent, over the years and maybe for generations to come, and produce equally cherished memories for their new owners. It seems sad that I can't pass along my memories that are attached to the rifles, shotguns, and pistols. But that's as it should be. Guns and their owners should create their own memories together.

PUBLISHER'S NOTE

The Boone and Crockett Club would like to recognize several individuals whose hard work, diligence, and support—both financially and professionally—made this book project possible. As with most publishing projects, this was indeed a group effort.

First and foremost we must thank the author, Jack Ward Thomas. He is a true conservationist, biologist, and hunter beyond reproach. His contributions to our natural world will be felt for generations to come. Jack's choice of the Boone and Crockett Club as the recipient of his journals and manuscripts is an honor for which our publishing program is deeply indebted. This generosity was facilitated by two Boone and Crockett Club Honorary Life Members, John P. Poston, and Daniel H. Pletscher. These two gentlemen initially met with Jack and through several conversations approached the Club's publications program with the idea that we should publish this trilogy of Jack's journals and memoirs. Who better to publish this great conservationist's work than Boone and Crockett—founded in 1887 by Theodore Roosevelt and George Bird Grinnell, with over 120 years of publishing experience. We are indebted to John and Dan for their foresight and their tenacity.

A special acknowledgment and debt of gratitude needs to be extended to John Poston for his financial support that made this project happen. It would not have been possible otherwise to move this project from an idea in the fall of 2014 to three finished books by the summer of 2015. John's support, reflecting his friendship and respect for Jack Ward Thomas, allowed us to get the ball rolling on a much faster schedule than anyone could have hoped for. We can only hope to have a faithful friend like John Poston in our lifetime!

The Boone and Crockett Club has a long history with publishing books about outdoor adventure, conservation, and hunting. The Club's publishing program is overseen by myself and Jeffrey A. Watkins (Cartersville, Georgia). Jeff's enthusiasm, suggestions, and oversight were instrumental in developing the publishing concept. Most importantly we are fortunate to have the assistance of Julie Tripp, B&C's director of publication. Julie is the foundation helping Jeff and me develop a working plan to get the project underway and see it through to completion. Julie especially enjoyed her trips down the Bitterroot Valley from B&C headquarters in Missoula to visit with Jack and his wife Kathy throughout the publishing process. Time was spent pulling photographs, going through edits, selecting authors to write the forewords, but more importantly, just "shooting the breeze" with Jack. If only we had had a stand-around fire to set the stage for those conversations!

There are a few others whose hard work made these books happen, and we'd be remiss not to mention them here. Fellow Texican Alison Tartt did an exemplary job editing and arranging the three manuscripts into their final form. B&C Lifetime Associate Hanspeter Giger (Charlotte, North Carolina) volunteered countless hours of his time providing a final read-through of the books before they went to the printer.

Thank you to everyone who helped us in the creation of this worthwhile project. It is our hope that these books will entertain, inform, teach, and induce reflection in the readers about the natural world we all have the privilege to enjoy.

Howard P. Monsour Jr., M.D.
CHAIRMAN, B&C PUBLICATIONS COMMITTEE
HOUSTON, TEXAS

AUTHOR'S ACKNOWLEDGMENTS

This book project has been decades in the making. Along the way, I was blessed with two strong women in my life who need to be acknowledged for their part in this great process.

Farrar Margaret ("Meg") Thomas and I were married in June of 1957, the week after I graduated from Texas A&M. We were full partners for the next thirty-six years—including, in the beginning, some very lean years when she taught piano lessons and I worked on weekends and holidays at part-time jobs to make ends meet. She never, not even once, complained. She also taught music in the public schools, and privately, to enhance our meager income.

Though she was no hunter, she seemed to relish going hunting with me. She seemed, especially, to enjoy my hunting bob-white and blue quail. I think she was partial to the bird dogs. When, in 1977, I asked her what she thought about leaving Texas so I could take a job with the U.S. Forest Service in West Virginia, she said she would go anywhere if she didn't have to cook and eat venison "nearly every damn day." We were off to West Virginia—and she still cooked and ate a lot of venison. But for the first time in our married life she didn't have to. That made all the difference.

She died of cancer in 1993 in Washington, D.C. Though severely ill, she insisted that "we" accept President Clinton's offer for me to be the thirteenth chief of the U.S. Forest Service. The president referred to Meg as the "First Lady of American Conservation."

In 1996, I was married to Kathleen Hurley Connelly, who worked with me in the Washington office of the U.S. Forest Service

as the Deputy Chief for Administration. She was not a "country girl" and even referred to herself as "Subway Girl." Though no hunter herself, she relished accompanying me on hunting trips in the United States and foreign lands. Shortly after we married, we moved to Missoula, Montana, when I accepted an offer to become the Boone and Crockett Professor of Wildlife Conservation in the College of Forestry at the University of Montana. I enjoyed teaching and dealing with graduate students. Kathy served us all as "Mom in Residence." And thoroughly relished the role.

I had a number of bosses over my forty-year professional career. Those bosses—every single one—guided me with a loose rein, which was bound to be, from time to time, a bit nerve-racking. They, in general, gave me the opportunity to "be all that I could be" in both the professional and personal sense. Over a half-century career, my supervisors—in both wildlife research and land management—guided me well and supported me, while "looking the other way" on numerous occasions. There are too many such colleagues to mention by name, but we both know who you are.

My idea of heaven would be to, simply, do it all over again.